THE PSYCHOLOGY
OF WEALTH

THE PSYCHOLOGY
OF WEALTH

The Practical Guide to Enduring Success

NAPOLEON HILL

MACMILLAN
BUSINESS

First published 2024 by St Martin's Essentials

First published in the UK 2024 by Macmillan Business
an imprint of Pan Macmillan
The Smithson, 6 Briset Street, London EC1M 5NR
EU representative: Macmillan Publishers Ireland Ltd, 1st Floor,
The Liffey Trust Centre, 117–126 Sheriff Street Upper,
Dublin 1, D01 YC43
Associated companies throughout the world
www.panmacmillan.com

ISBN 978-1-0350-5974-4

1 3 5 7 9 8 6 4 2

A CIP catalogue record for this book is available from the British Library.

The Master Key to Riches was originally published in 1945
The Magic Ladder to Success was originally published in 1930
'Adversity—A Blessing in Disguise' was originally published in 1915
'Let Ambition Be Your Master' was originally published in 1917
'What I Have Learned from Analyzing Ten Thousand People'
was originally published in 1917

Printed and bound by CPI Group (UK) Ltd, Croydon, CR0 4YY

Visit **www.panmacmillan.com** to read more about all our books
and to buy them. You will also find features, author interviews and
news of any author events, and you can sign up for e-newsletters
so that you're always first to hear about our new releases.

CONTENTS

INTRODUCTION

The title of this collection of books by Napoleon Hill is particularly accurate. While many people believe that Napoleon Hill
wrote books about money and what to do with it, what he actually wrote about was the *mindset* of money. If you increase
your mental attitude about money, and then match your actions
to that increased mental attitude, it makes sense that you will
see an increase in your financial status. More importantly, the
"wealth" that Hill refers to is not just financial wealth—he refers
to a wealth of ideas, a wealth of imagination, a wealth of experience, and a wealth that comes from pursuing your passion. The
question is: How? That's the question that this volume answers.

When I first became acquainted with Hill's material, I was
deeply in debt and didn't foresee a prosperous future. The idea
that there is a mindset I could practice that would help me attain
wealth—or at least get out of debt—became a focus for me. I was
working to pay bills and was using my credit cards to "rob Peter
to pay Paul." I kept falling further and further behind. My biggest
financial goal was to just get to zero, that is, to get out of debt.

At one point I started reading a number of books about what
to do with my (lack of) money, how to get out of debt, where to

invest, and so on. These were all written by wealthy people, but none of those books "sparked" me. They all seemed complicated and unattainable, and they all dealt with money itself. However, I did notice one thing that was common to nearly all of those books on financial wealth: the authors mentioned being originally inspired by the writings of Napoleon Hill. It occurred to me that if those authors were all inspired by Napoleon Hill, maybe I should skip their books and go right to their source. So I did, and everything changed for me.

While those other authors wrote about the effects of money (e.g., what to do with money, specific financial steps to get out of debt, which stocks and bonds the reader should investigate, etc.), Hill's books all dealt with the cause of money. In other words, he wrote about the mindset of money—and why certain mindsets tend to cause less success and other mindsets tend to cause more success. He didn't talk about 401(k) plans and IRA accounts—he wrote about making goals, using your imagination, the power of decisions, and more. These were transformative concepts for me. I did as Hill suggested, and my life improved. The more I used the principles, the more my life opened up.

The book you are reading now contains those very principles. *The Magic Ladder to Success* (originally published in 1930) was published seven years before his most famous book, *Think and Grow Rich*, and many consider it to be his most powerful book. *The Magic Ladder to Success* distills the seventeen factors for a life of success that he originally outlined in his huge multivolume series The Law of Success (later published in one large volume). It's strikingly clear and motivational.

The Master Key to Riches (originally published in 1945) is a wide-ranging book of the many steps and ideas that lead to a richer life. One of the main messages is that "riches" is an outlook, not bank accounts and material items. When you *feel* rich, you *are* rich, and this book shows practical steps toward that outcome.

In addition to those two full and original books, this volume contains several articles Hill wrote that further state some of his ideas succinctly and clearly.

It's worth noting that Hill wrote these books at a time when the world was very different. I suggest reading his book with two things in mind. First, while his language is often of its time, try to get the main idea of what he was saying and translate that into how we would understand it today. Second, while many of his examples and illustrations are outdated, the principles behind them are not. Rather than say "Well, this idea isn't relevant because he wrote about it using correspondence courses," a more useful mindset would be "What is the idea behind this example, and how can I use it today?" In that way, you'll see how timeless the principles are and you can put them into action. The principles go beyond personality or generation; they were true before Hill discovered them, and they are still true to this day.

Hill writes that we are each one hundred percent responsible for our own actions. When we infuse our thoughts and actions in positive ways, we tend to see positive results. While this seems simple and like common sense, if it were easy, everyone would do it. I didn't do it until someone laid out the principles in plain and clear language for me to follow. Once I understood the principles, I was able to enact them.

Now it's your turn.

Read this volume, take notes, use a journal, underline and highlight passages that speak to you. Spend time ruminating the ideas and how they can be applied to your situation. Notice when you resist an idea, and examine if there is an opportunity to grow beyond your limitations. In other words, don't just read this volume, *experience* it. Immerse yourself in the ideas. Live the principles to the best of your ability. Keep doing more of what works, and when something doesn't work for you discard it and move on to the next idea. In this way, you'll not only be making positive changes for your own life, you will also no doubt inspire those around you to do the same. That is a rich life indeed.

—Joel Fotinos

THE MASTER KEY
TO RICHES

CONTENTS

THINK!

Many centuries ago a very wealthy and wise philosopher by the name of Croesus, an adviser to Cyrus, King of the Persians, said:

"I am reminded, O King: and take this lesson to heart; that there is a Wheel on which the affairs of men revolve, and its mechanism is such that it prevents any man from being always fortunate."

There is a Wheel of Life that controls the destiny of men! It operates through the power of thought.

The Master Key to Riches was designed for the purpose of aiding men in the mastery and control of this great Wheel, to the end that it may be made to yield them an abundance of all that they desire, including the Twelve Great Riches of Life described in the second chapter.

Remember, you who are beginning the study of this philosophy, that this same Wheel which "prevents any man from being always fortunate," may provide also that no man shall be always unfortunate, provided he will take possession of his own mind and direct it to the attainment of some Definite Major Purpose in life.

THE PROLOGUE

"I give and bequeath to the American people the greater portion of my vast fortune, which consists in the philosophy of individual achievement, through which all of my riches were accumulated . . ."

Thus began the last will and testament of the richest man that the richest nation on earth ever produced, and it now serves as the beginning of the prologue of a story which may well mark the most important turning point in the lives of all who read it.

The story began in the late Fall of 1908, when Andrew Carnegie called in a man whom he trusted, and whose integrity and judgment he respected, and entrusted to him what Mr. Carnegie said was *"the greater portion"* of his vast fortune, with the understanding that the legacy was to be presented to the American people.

This story has been written to *notify you of your right to share in this huge estate,* and to inform you as to the conditions under which you may do so.

Lest you do the perfectly natural thing that many would do—that of reaching the false conclusion that the conditions under which you may share in this huge estate are too rigid to permit you to comply with them—let us relieve your mind by saying that the conditions are well within the reach of any adult of average intelligence, and *there are no tricks or false hopes,* either in connection with the conditions or in this promise.

So that you may know whether or not this promises anything you need or desire, we hasten now to tell you precisely what it does promise, viz:

A clear description of the formula by which you may have the full benefit of the Master Key to Riches—a key that should unlock the doors to the solution of all of your problems, that will help you convert all of your past failures into priceless assets, and lead you to the attainment of the twelve great riches, including economic security.

An inventory of the vast riches which Andrew Carnegie provided for distribution to those who are qualified to receive them, together with detailed instructions through which you may appropriate and use your full share.

A description of the means by which you may have the full benefit of the education, experience and technical skill of those whose cooperation you may need for the attainment of your major purpose in life, thus providing a practical means by which you may bridge the disadvantages of an inadequate education and attain the highest goals of life as successfully as may those who are blessed with a formal education.

The privilege of using the philosophy of success which was organized from the life experiences, by the trial and error method, of more than five hundred successful men, among whom are Henry Ford, Thomas A. Edison, William Wrigley, Jr., Cyrus H. K. Curtis, J. Ogden Armour, Elbert Hubbard, Charles M. Schwab, F. W. Woolworth, Frank A. Vanderlip, Edward Bok, Dr. Alexander Graham Bell, Clarence Darrow and Luther Burbank. A definite plan by which anyone who works for wages or a salary may promote himself into a higher income, *with the full consent and cooperation of his employer.*

A definite plan through which anyone who works for others may get into a business or a profession of his own, with more than average chances of success.

A definite plan through which any merchant may convert his customers into permanent patrons, and through their willing cooperation add new customers who will likewise become permanent.

A definite plan through which any salesman of life insurance, or of other useful service or merchandise, may convert his buyers into willing workers who will aid him in finding new clients.

A definite plan through which any employer may convert his employees into personal friends, under circumstances which will enable him to make his business more profitable for both himself and his employees.

You have here a clear statement of our promises, and the first condition under which you may benefit by these is that you read this book *twice*, line by line, and *think as you read!*

Nothing ever happens without a definite *cause!*

It was by no mere chance that the United States came to be known as the "richest and the freest" country of the world. This is a land of plenty because of definite, understandable causes, each of which we have clearly defined.

The desire for plenty may be selfish, but we all know that it is a natural desire. Andrew Carnegie understood this when he decided to give away his huge fortune, but guided as he was by the wisdom of a lifetime of practical experience in dealing with people, he safeguarded his gift by attaching to it certain conditions with which all who receive any part of it must comply.

Mr. Carnegie adopted a novel method for the distribution of his riches because he recognized the weakness of mankind in wanting something for nothing. He knew that men in all walks of life, all down through the past, have been looking for a "land flowing with milk and honey."

He also knew that the gift of riches in any form, without some sort of consideration in return, generally harms more than it benefits the one who receives it. Therefore he wisely attached to his gift certain conditions by which those who receive it are protected against this common weakness of desiring something for nothing.

Looking backward into the history of mankind, Mr. Carnegie recognized that this desire for something for nothing was the object of the search of the scouts who were sent out by Moses and Joshua, because the children of Israel, after they had worked in slavery in Egypt for many years, making brick without straw, had escaped the Pharaohs and were waiting, after a long period in the wilderness, for an opportunity to cross over the sea into the land of plenty.

The glowing description of plenty in that land served as the incentive which enabled their leaders, against strong opposition, to hold the solidarity of the people until they reached their objectives.

A counterpart of this same story is found in the migration of subdued people from Old England to the New World. They came not only in search of a land of material plenty, but for a land which afforded plenty of opportunities for the expression of personal initiative, freedom of worship, freedom of speech, and the very purpose of their migration served as an assurance of the success of the most outstanding step ever taken by any group in modern history.

They developed a land of plenty. The plenty came from their efforts simply because their endeavors were based upon a sound philosophy, a constructive objective which Andrew Carnegie recognized centuries later, and he not only converted it into a huge fortune for himself, but he left to the American people of today a simple set of rules—a Master Key—by which they too may acquire riches.

Out of their pioneering toil down through the years the descendants of those pilgrims of progress have built a civilization never before known in the history of the world; a culture which exceeds the greatest culture of all times; standards of living which are higher than ever before known to mankind; conveniences, comforts, luxuries, opportunities available to the humblest person, such as the world had never known. All of these advantages were the result of a sound foundation—the foundation stones of a budding new democracy; something new under the sun; a modified form of perfect state which was destined to prove successful because it was practical.

Such a civilization had never before been known in the entire history of mankind. There have been many periods in history when the advance of civilization was heralded with glowing terms, yet the civilization of the particular age in each instance was confined to a *relatively small percentage* of the people.

The difference between each of these periods of the distant past and the present, which we of the New World enjoy, lies in the fact that the masses of people of the past were under the heels of sovereigns, many of whom were tyrants, while we enjoy a standard of living which was unknown even to the kings of those days.

Thus we represent a difference between the cultural eras of the past and the culture of today. Study if you will the picture of the advantages enjoyed by the American people today, even to the lowliest and the humblest. Free education, free entertainment, the radio, the automobile, the airplane, the network of free highways, advanced modes of communication, free worship— these and thousands of other advantages denied to the peasants of the past are now the common property of all of the people in America today.

This difference, which is due to the fundamental difference in motives and objectives, has been made possible because of practical developments under the American way of life which have never been experienced in Europe or in any other part of the Old World.

In America men and women have been free to follow the dictates of their own consciences; they have had freedom of worship, freedom of speech, freedom of the press, freedom of political convictions, freedom for the fullest exercise of their own personal initiative in any calling of their choice, and they have been protected by a form of government which assured them the fruits of their labors.

This has arisen out of the fact that freedom, life, liberty and the pursuit of happiness constituted the basis of the development of our young republic, with its program of plenty as the goal of every citizen.

As workers began to express their personal initiative as individuals, and later as groups; later still for security and protection as corporations, with the capital financed by workers and nonworkers, the people learned the art of salesmanship, the art of competition, the blessings of individual initiative, and the necessity of honest production to justify the art of advertising.

All of these factors combined have justified greater production at lower cost, that more people may afford to purchase American commodities, that more people may be engaged in manufacturing.

This, briefly stated, is the heart of the American system—a well-expressed faith, thrift, cooperation, confidence in each other, personal initiative, and a sense of fairness in human relationships.

In describing this story of the road to riches under the American way of life, it is necessary that the reader supply a part of the story by *his own thoughts* and by comparing our statements with his own experiences. This in turn makes it necessary for the reader to have a clear picture of the history of the American sources of riches in order that he may be sure of appropriating his share of those riches.

We are face to face with a "New Social Order," and we may well recognize its nature, and anticipate if we can tell where it is leading us.

One thing of which we can be sure—that we wish no such "New Order" as the European dictators have forced upon their people. We have had liberty, freedom and the right to exercise personal initiative for so long that we could not, and we shall not, willingly give up these privileges.

Our feeling toward dictators, who get their power by robbing others of their right to liberty, was expressed eloquently by Colonel Robert G. Ingersoll, in his appraisal of Napoleon, viz:

"A little while ago I stood by the grave of the old Napoleon.

"It is a magnificent sepulcher of gilt and gold, fit almost for a dead deity. I gazed upon the sarcophagus of rare and nameless marble in which rest at last the ashes of the restless man.

"I leaned upon the balustrade and thought of all the career of the greatest soldier of the modern world.

"I saw him upon the banks of the Seine contemplating suicide.

"I saw him quelling the mob in the streets of Paris.

"I saw him at the head of the army of Italy.

"I saw him crossing the bridge of Ladi with the tricolor in his hand.

"I saw him in Egypt in the shadows of the pyramids.

"I saw him conquer the Alps and mingle the eagles of France with the eagles of the crags.

"I saw him in Russia, where the infantry of the snows and the cavalry of the wild beasts scattered his legions like winter's withered leaves.

"I saw him at Leipsic in defeat and disaster, driven by a million bayonets, clutched like a beast, banished to Elba.

"I saw him escape and retake an empire by the magnificent force of his genius.

"I saw him upon the frightful field of Waterloo, where Chance and Fate combined to wreck the fortunes of their former king, and I saw him a prisoner on the rock at St. Helena, with his arms calmly folded behind his back gazing steadfastly out upon the sad and solemn sea.

"And I thought of all the widows and orphans he had made; of all the tears that had been shed for his glory; of the only woman who had ever loved him torn from his heart by the ruthless hand of ambition.

"And I said, I would rather have been a poor French peasant and worn wooden shoes; I would rather have lived in a hut with the vines growing purple in the amorous kisses of the autumn sun, with my loving wife knitting by my side as the day died out of the sky, with my children upon my knees and their arms about my neck; yes, I would rather have been that poor peasant and gone down to the tongueless silence of the dreamless dust, than to have been that imperial impersonation of force and murder known as Napoleon the Great."

In this spirit do we approach the description of the Master Key, from the use of which come all riches known to the American people.

Let it be known at the outset that when we speak of "riches" we have in mind *all riches,* not merely those represented by bank balances and material things.

We have in mind the riches of liberty and freedom, of which we have more than any other nation.

We have in mind the riches of human relationships through which every American citizen may exercise to the fullest the privilege of personal initiative in whatever direction he chooses; and the riches of the System of Free Enterprise which has made

American industry the envy of the whole world; and the riches of a free press, free public schools and free churches.

Thus, when we speak of "riches" we have reference to the abundant life which is everywhere available to the people of the United States, and obtainable with a minimum amount of effort.

Meanwhile, let it be understood that we shall offer no suggestions to anyone as to the nature of the riches for which he should aim, nor the amount he should undertake to acquire.

Fortunately the American way of life offers an abundance of all forms of riches, sufficient in both quality and quantity to satisfy all reasonable human desires, but we sincerely hope that somehow every reader will aim for his share, not only of the things that money can buy, *but of the things that money cannot buy!*

It is with profound grief that we see so many of our fellow-men eating the husks and throwing away the rich grain of their American opportunity to live a full and abundant life, which consists of both the tangible and the intangible riches of a great nation such as ours.

We shall not undertake to tell any man how to live his life, but we know, from having observed both the rich and the poor of America, that material riches alone are no guarantee of happiness.

We have never yet found a truly happy person who was not engaged in some form of service by which others were benefited. And, we do know many who are wealthy in material things, but have not found happiness.

We mention these observations not to preach, but to quicken those who, because of the great abundance of material riches in America, take them for granted, and who have lost sight of the priceless things of life that are to be acquired only through the intangible riches we have mentioned.

Although the American people already enjoy the highest

standard of living existing in the whole world, we are not satisfied with this standard, and we propose to describe how we believe it can be raised still higher. Our belief is not based upon the false hope of something for nothing, but it is founded on a philosophy which has the advantage of having been tested and proved practical by more than five hundred of the most distinguished men of achievement this country has ever known— among them Andrew Carnegie.

The philosophy is inseparably associated with the legacy which Mr. Carnegie left to the American people, and we are prepared to prove its soundness because it has already been tested and is being tested daily by hundreds of thousands of beneficiaries located in practically every town, village and city of the United States and in many foreign countries.

1

THE BEGINNING OF ALL RICHES

*As Revealed by the Masked Rich Man
from Happy Valley*

*The largest audience ever assembled in the history of mankind sat
breathlessly awaiting the message of a mysterious man who was about
to reveal to the world the secret of his riches.*

In that audience were men who had tried and failed so often
that they had all but lost hope!

And there were young men and young women—mere boys
and girls—who were filled with hope and courage and eager-
ness to learn the way to riches.

There were doctors, lawyers, dentists, engineers and school-
teachers, waiting to hear what the speaker might have to say
which would put them on the road to riches.

Clergymen of every religion on earth were there, with the
hope that they might gather from the message of the speaker

some inspirational ideas they could pass on to the members of their congregations.

Newspaper reporters were more numerous than bees; a great battery of cameras trained upon the speaker's platform, and the newsreel men were present with their moving picture cameras and sound equipment.

There were taxicab drivers, mechanics, bricklayers, merchants, barbers, and newsboys, representing every trade and every calling on earth, and many of them had come from distant places.

Slowly the curtain began to rise, the Chairman walking to the speaker's dais raised his hand for silence! The noise died down and a silent hush spread over the great audience.

The introduction of the speaker was brief. The Chairman simply said, "Ladies and Gentlemen, I have the honor to introduce to you the richest man in all the world. He has come to tell you about the MASTER KEY TO RICHES."

The speaker walked briskly to the speaker's dais.

He was dressed in a long black robe and wore a mask over his eyes.

His hair was of a grayish tint, and he appeared to be about sixty years of age.

He stood silently for a few moments, while the cameras flashed. Then, speaking slowly, in a voice soft and pleasing, like music, he began his message:

You have come here to seek the MASTER KEY TO RICHES!

You have come because of that human urge for the better things in life, which is the common desire of all people.

You desire economic security which money alone can provide.

Some of you desire an outlet for your talents in order that you may have the joy of creating your own riches.

Some of you are seeking the easy way to riches, with the

hope that you will find it without giving anything in return; that too is a common desire. But it is a desire I shall hope to modify for your benefit, as from experience I have learned that there is no such thing as something for nothing.

There is but one sure way to riches, and that may be attained only by those who have the MASTER KEY TO RICHES!

This MASTER KEY is an ingenious device with which those who possess it may unlock the door to the solution of all of their problems. Its powers of magic transcend those of the famous Aladdin's Lamp.

It opens the door to sound health.

It opens the door to love and romance.

It opens the door to friendship, by revealing the traits of personality and character which make enduring friends.

It reveals the method by which every adversity, every failure, every disappointment, every mistaken error of judgment, and every past defeat may be transmuted into riches of a priceless value.

It kindles anew the dead hopes of all who possess it, and it reveals the formula by which one may "tune in" and draw upon the great reservoir of Infinite Intelligence, through that state of mind known as Faith.

It lifts humble men to positions of power, fame and fortune.

It turns back the hands of the clock of Time and renews the spirit of youth for those who have grown old too soon.

It provides the method by which one may take full and complete possession of one's own mind, thus giving one unchallengeable control over the emotions of the heart and the power of thinking.

It bridges the deficiencies of those who have inadequate education through formal schooling, and puts them substantially on the same plane of opportunity that is enjoyed by those who have a better education.

And lastly, it opens the doors, one by one, to the Twelve Great Riches of Life, which I shall presently describe for you in detail.

Listen carefully to what I have to say, for I shall not pass this way again. Listen not only with open ears, but with open minds and eager hearts, remembering that no man may hear that for which he has not the preparation for hearing.

The preparation consists of many things, among them sincerity of purpose, humility of heart, a full recognition of the truth that no man knows everything; that the combined knowledge of mankind has not been enough to save men from cutting one another to pieces through warfare, nor to restrain them from cheating and stealing the fruits of labor from their fellowmen.

I shall speak to you of facts and describe to you many principles of which many of you may never have heard, for they are known only to those who have prepared themselves to accept the MASTER KEY—a small but ever-increasing number of people who have attained the Degree of Fellowship.

The Fellowship is made up of men and women from many walks of life, of all nationalities and creeds. Its purpose is to reveal to mankind the benefits which are available through the spirit of the Brotherhood of man.

The Fellowship was born of the necessity of rehabilitating a war worn world into which civilization was brought to the very brink of destruction through World War II. The Fellowship is non-sectarian and non-commercial.

Its members work individually. It has no authorized leaders, but every one who qualifies for the Degree of Fellowship becomes a leader unto himself.

The only condition that is required for membership is that all who qualify for the degree shall share with others the benefits they receive through the MASTER KEY TO RICHES—as many others as they may find who are willing to prepare themselves to receive the benefits.

The Fellowship prepares men and women to relate themselves to one another as brothers and sisters.

It recognizes the great abundance of material riches available for mankind and provides a rational plan by which every person may share in these riches in proportion to his talents, as they are expressed through useful service.

It frowns upon the idea of too much for the few and too little for the many, but it also discourages all who endeavor to get something for nothing. And it discourages the accumulation of riches by individuals whose greed inspires them to seek more than they can use for their own economic security and to provide opportunities through which others may attain such security.

The Fellowship has a stupendous task ahead of it.

Civilization must live and go forward, not backward, for that is the plan of the Creator of all things.

Men must learn to live together as brothers, so that they may walk arm in arm, do the world's work and reap their just reward without poverty, without hardship, without fear or trembling.

The members of the Fellowship have learned to do this without suffering the loss of any of the joys of living or sacrificing any of their rights as individuals. Nay, they have discovered that the Fellowship way is the only path to enduring happiness.

I have come to tell you about the Fellowship and to place in your hands the MASTER KEY to all riches.

My identity will not be revealed, for it would be of no benefit to you. If you wish to speak of me you may call me the "Rich Man from Happy Valley."

Before I describe the Twelve Great Riches let me reveal to you some of the riches you already possess; riches of which most of you may not be conscious.

First, I would have you recognize that each of you is a plural personality, although you may regard yourself as a single personality. You and every other person consist of at least two distinct personalities, and many of you possess more.

There is that self which you recognize when you look into a mirror. That is your physical self. But it is only the house in which your other selves live. In that house there are two individuals at least who are eternally in conflict with each other.

One is a negative sort of person who thinks and moves and lives in an atmosphere of fear and doubt and poverty and ill health. This self expects failure, and seldom is disappointed. It thinks of the circumstances of life which you do not want but which you seem forced to accept—poverty, greed, superstition, fear, doubt, worry and physical sickness.

And one is your "other self," a positive sort of person who thinks in terms of opulence, sound health, love and friendship, personal achievement, creative vision, service to others, and who guides you unerringly to the attainment of all of these blessings. It is this self which alone is capable of recognizing and appropriating the Twelve Great Riches. It is the only self which is capable of receiving the Master Key to Riches.

These are not imaginary personalities of which I speak. They are real, for they have been revealed through scientific investigation of irreproachable authenticity.

Then you have many other priceless assets of which you may not be aware; hidden riches you have neither recognized nor used. Among these is a modern radio broadcasting and receiving station so powerful that it may pick up and send out the vibrations of thought from or to any part of the world, including the potential capacity to reach out into the cosmos and tune in with the power of Infinite Intelligence.

Your radio station operates automatically and continuously, when you are asleep just as when you are awake.

And it is under the control at all times of one or the other of your two major personalities, the negative personality or the positive personality. When your negative personality is in control your radio station picks up only the negative thought vibrations which are being sent out by hundreds of millions of other negative personalities throughout the world. These are accepted, acted upon and translated into their physical equivalent in terms of the circumstances of life which you do not wish.

When your positive personality is in control it picks up only the positive thought vibrations being released by millions of other positive personalities throughout the world, and translates them into their physical equivalent in terms of prosperity, sound health, love, hope, faith, peace of mind and happiness; the values of life for which you and every other normal person are searching.

I have come to reveal to you the Master Key by which you may attain these and many other riches. That mysterious key which unlocks the doors to the solution of all human problems, acquires all riches, and places every individual radio station under the control of one's "other self."

I am known as the Rich Man from Happy Valley because I have come into possession of the Master Key to Riches. The nature of my riches I shall presently reveal to you. But first let me tell you that I was not born to riches.

I was born in poverty and illiteracy.

My formal education has been limited to the knowledge available through a country grade school.

And the entire universe, as far as I was concerned, extended no further than the boundary lines of the backwoods county into which I was born.

Then came a great awakening. Love came into my heart, and with it the influence of the greatest person I shall ever hope to know. She became my wife and guide, for she came from the outer world—that world I had not suspected to exist. She was a woman of culture and education. From her I learned some of the secrets of biology, and chemistry, and astronomy, and physics. She reached deeply into my soul and uncovered that "other self" of which I had no knowledge.

Step by step, patiently and with love, she lifted me into a higher and yet higher plane of understanding, until at long last I was prepared to receive the great Master Key to Riches—the gift which I shall share with you in the hope that you may become as rich as I.

With that blessing came also a responsibility consisting of an obligation to reveal the secrets of the great Master Key to as many of you as may prepare yourselves to receive it. But let me here warn you that the Master Key may be retained only by those who accept the obligation to share it with others. No man may use it selfishly, for his personal aggrandizement alone.

I shall reveal to you the means by which you may share the blessings of the Master Key, but the responsibility of sharing must become your own.

The founders of the Rotary Club movement must have recognized the benefits of sharing, for they adopted as their motto: "He profits most who serves best."

And every close observer must have recognized that all individual successes which endure have had their beginning through the beneficent influence of some other individual, through some form of sharing.

My great opportunity consisted in the willingness of my wife to share with me the knowledge which she had acquired, plus the knowledge I gained from the principles which placed the Master Key within my reach.

Your opportunity may well consist in my willingness to share this knowledge with you. But I have not come to give you material riches alone. I have come to share with you the knowledge by which you may acquire riches—all riches—through the expression of your own *personal* initiative!

That is the greatest of all gifts!

And it is the only kind of gift that anyone who is blessed with the advantages of a great nation like ours should expect. For here we have every potential form of riches available to mankind. We have them in great abundance.

So I assume that you too wish to become rich.

Let us become partners in the attainment of your desire, for I have found the way to all riches. Therefore I am prepared to serve as your guide.

I sought the path to riches the hard way before I learned that there is a short and dependable path I could have followed had I been guided as I hope to guide you.

Before we begin our journey to the land of riches let us take inventory so that we may know the true nature of riches. Yes, let us be prepared to recognize riches when we come within their reach.

Some believe that riches consist in money alone!

But enduring riches, in the broader sense, consist in many other values than those of material things, and may I add that without these other intangible values the possession of money will not bring the happiness which some believe it will provide.

When I speak of "riches" I have in mind the greater riches whose possessors have made life pay off on their own terms— the terms of full and complete happiness. I call these the "Twelve Riches of Life." And I sincerely wish to share them with all of you who are prepared to receive them, in whole or in part.

You may wonder about my willingness to share, so I shall tell you that the MASTER KEY TO RICHES enables its possessors to add to their own store of riches everything of value which they share with others.

This is one of the strangest facts of life, but it is a fact which each of you must recognize and respect if you hope to become as rich as I.

Now let us pass on to the description of the Twelve Riches.

2

THE TWELVE RICHES
OF LIFE

The Greatest of All Riches Is . . .

1. A POSITIVE MENTAL ATTITUDE

All riches, of whatsoever nature, begin as a state of mind; and let us remember that a state of mind is the one and only thing over which any person has complete, unchallenged right of control.

It is highly significant that the Creator provided man with control over nothing except the power to shape his own thoughts and the privilege of fitting them to any pattern of his choice.

Mental attitude is important because it converts the brain into the equivalent of an electromagnet which attracts the counterpart of one's dominating thoughts, aims and purposes. It also attracts the counterpart of one's fears, worries and doubts.

A positive mental attitude is the starting point of all riches, whether they be riches of a material nature or intangible riches.

It attracts the riches of true friendship.

And the riches one finds in the hope of future achievement.

It provides the riches one may find in Nature's handiwork, as it exists in the moonlit nights, in the stars that float out there in the heavens, in the beautiful landscapes and in distant horizons.

And the riches to be found in the labor of one's choice, where expression may be given to the highest plane of man's soul.

And the riches of harmony in home relationships, where all members of the family work together in a spirit of friendly cooperation.

And the riches of sound physical health, which is the treasure of those who have learned to balance work with play, worship with love, and who have learned the wisdom of eating to live rather than of living to eat.

And the riches of freedom from fear.

And the riches of enthusiasm, both active and passive.

And the riches of song and laughter, both of which indicate states of mind.

And the riches of self-discipline, through which one may have the joy of knowing that the mind can and will serve any desired end if one will take possession and command it through definiteness of purpose.

And the riches of play, through which one may lay aside all of the burdens of life and become as a little child again.

And the riches of discovery of one's "other self"—that self which knows no such reality as permanent failure.

And the riches of FAITH IN INFINITE INTELLIGENCE, of which every individual mind is a minute projection.

And the riches of meditation, the connecting link by which any one may draw upon the great universal supply of Infinite Intelligence at will.

Yes, these and all other riches begin with a positive mental attitude. Therefore, it is but little cause for wonder that a positive mental attitude takes the first place in the list of the "Twelve Riches."

2. SOUND PHYSICAL HEALTH

Sound health begins with a "health consciousness" produced by a mind which thinks in terms of health and not in terms of illness, plus temperance of habits in eating and properly balanced physical activities.

3. HARMONY IN HUMAN RELATIONSHIPS

Harmony with others begins with one's self, for it is true, as Shakespeare said, there are benefits available to those who comply with his admonition, "To thine own self be true, and it must follow, as the night the day, thou cans't not then be false to any man."

4. FREEDOM FROM FEAR

No man who fears anything is a free man! Fear is a harbinger of evil, and wherever it appears one may find a cause which must be eliminated before he may become rich in the fuller sense. The seven basic fears which appear most often in the minds of men are (1) the fear of POVERTY, (2) the fear of CRITICISM, (3) the fear of ILL HEALTH, (4) the fear of LOSS OF LOVE, (5) the fear of the LOSS OF LIBERTY, (6) the fear of OLD AGE, (7) the fear of DEATH.

5. THE HOPE ACHIEVEMENT

The greatest of all forms of happiness comes as the result of hope of achievement of some yet unattained desire; and poor beyond description is the person who cannot look to the future with hope that he will become the person he would like to be, or with the belief that he will attain the objective he has failed to reach in the past.

6. THE CAPACITY FOR FAITH

Faith is the connecting link between the conscious mind of man and the great universal reservoir of Infinite Intelligence. It is the fertile soil of the garden of the human mind wherein may be produced all of the riches of life. It is the "eternal elixir" which gives creative power and action to the impulses of thought.

Faith is the basis of all so-called miracles, and of many mysteries which cannot be explained by the rules of logic or science.

Faith is the spiritual "chemical" which, when it is mixed with prayer, gives one direct and immediate connection with Infinite Intelligence.

Faith is the power which transmutes the ordinary energies of thought into their spiritual equivalent. And it is the only power through which the Cosmic Force of Infinite Intelligence may be appropriated to the uses of man.

7. WILLINGNESS TO SHARE ONE'S BLESSINGS

He who has not learned the blessed art of sharing has not learned the true path to happiness, for happiness comes only by sharing. And let it be forever remembered that all riches may be embellished and multiplied by the simple process of sharing them where they may serve others. And let it be also remembered that the space one occupies in the hearts of his fellowmen is determined precisely by the service he renders through some form of sharing his blessings.

Riches which are not shared, whether they be material riches or the intangibles, wither and die like the rose on a severed stem, for it is one of Nature's first laws that inaction and disuse lead to decay and death, and this law applies to the material possessions of men just as it applies to the living cells of every physical body.

8. A LABOR OF LOVE

There can be no richer man than he who has found a labor of love and who is busily engaged in performing it, for labor is the highest form of human expression of desire. Labor is the liaison between the demand and the supply of all human needs, the forerunner of all human progress, the medium by which the imagination of man is given the wings of action. And all labor of love is sanctified because it brings the joy of self-expression to him who performs it.

9. AN OPEN MIND ON ALL SUBJECTS

Tolerance, which is among the higher attributes of culture, is expressed only by the person who holds an open mind on all subjects at all times. And it is only the man with an open mind who becomes truly educated and who is thus prepared to avail himself of the greater riches of life.

10. SELF-DISCIPLINE

The man who is not the master of himself may never become the master of anything. He who is the master of self may become the master of his own earthly destiny, the "master of his fate, the Captain of his soul." And the highest form of self-discipline consists in the expression of humility of the heart when one has attained great riches or has been overtaken by that which is commonly called "success."

11. THE CAPACITY TO UNDERSTAND PEOPLE

The man who is rich in the understanding of people always recognizes that all people are fundamentally alike in that they have evolved from the same stem; that all human activities are inspired by one or more of the nine basic motives of life, viz:

1. The emotion of LOVE
2. The emotion of SEX
3. The desire for MATERIAL GAIN
4. The desire for SELF-PRESERVATION
5. The desire for FREEDOM OF BODY AND MIND
6. The desire for SELF-EXPRESSION
7. The desire for perpetuation of LIFE AFTER
   DEATH
8. The emotion of ANGER
9. The emotion of FEAR

And the man who would understand others must first understand himself.

The capacity to understand others eliminates many of the common causes of friction among men. It is the foundation of all friendship. It is the basis of all harmony and cooperation among men. It is the fundamental of major importance in all leadership which calls for friendly cooperation. And some believe that it is an approach of major importance to the understanding of the Creator of all things.

12. ECONOMIC SECURITY

The last, though not least in importance, is the tangible portion of the "Twelve Riches."

Economic security is not attained by the possession of money alone. It is attained by the service one renders, for useful service may be converted into all forms of human needs, with or without the use of money.

Henry Ford has economic security, not because he controls a vast fortune of money, but for the better reason that he provides profitable employment for millions of men and women, and also dependable transportation by automobile for still greater numbers of people. The service he renders has attracted the money he controls, and it is in this manner that all enduring economic security must be attained.

Presently I shall acquaint you with the principles by which money and all other forms of riches may be obtained, but first you must be prepared to make application of these principles. Your mind must be conditioned for the acceptance of riches just as the soil of the earth must be prepared for the planting of seeds.

When one is ready for a thing it is *sure to appear!*

This does not mean that the things one may need will appear without a cause, for there is a vast difference between one's "needs" and one's readiness to receive. To miss this distinction is to miss the major benefits which I shall endeavor to convey.

So be patient and let me lead you into readiness to receive the riches which you desire. I shall have to lead *my way!*

My way will seem strange to you at first, but you should not become discouraged on this account, for all new ideas seem strange. If you doubt that my way is practical take courage from the fact that it has brought me riches in abundance.

Human progress always has been slow because people are reluctant to accept new ideas.

When Samuel Morse announced his system for communication by telegraph the world scoffed at him. His system was unorthodox. It was new, therefore it was subject to suspicion and doubt.

And the world scoffed at Marconi when he announced the perfection of an improvement over Morse's system; a system of communication by wireless.

Thomas A. Edison came in for ridicule when he announced his perfection of the incandescent electric light bulb, and Henry Ford met with the same experience when he offered the world a self-propelled vehicle to take the place of the horse and buggy.

When Wilbur and Orville Wright announced the perfection of a practical flying machine the world was so little impressed that the newspapermen refused to witness a demonstration of the machine.

Then came the discovery of the modern radio, one of the "miracles" of human ingenuity which was destined to make the whole world akin. The "unprepared" minds accepted it as a toy to amuse children but nothing more.

I mention these facts as a reminder to you, who are seeking riches by a new way, that you be not discouraged because of the newness of the way. Follow through with me, appropriate my philosophy and be assured that it will work for you as it has worked for me.

By serving as your guide to riches I shall receive my compensation for my efforts in exact proportion to the benefits you receive. The eternal law of compensation insures this. My compensation may not come directly from you who appropriate my philosophy, but come it will in one form or another, for it is a part of the great Cosmic Plan that no useful service shall be rendered by anyone without a just compensation. "Do the thing," said Emerson, "and you shall have the power."

Aside from the consideration of what I shall receive for my endeavor to serve you, there is the question of an obligation which I owe the world in return for the blessings it has bestowed upon me. I did not acquire my riches without the aid of many others. I have observed that all who acquire enduring riches have ascended the ladder of opulence with two outstretched hands; one extended upward to receive the help of others who have reached the peak, and the other extended downward to aid those who are still climbing.

And here let me admonish you who are on the path to riches that you too must proceed with outstretched hands, to give and to receive aid, for it is a well-known fact that no man may attain enduring success or acquire enduring riches without aiding others who are seeking these desirable ends. To GET one must first GIVE!

I have brought this message in order that I may GIVE!

And now that we know what are the real riches of life I shall reveal to you the next step which you must take in the process of "conditioning" your mind to receive riches.

I have acknowledged that my riches came through the aid of others.

Some of these have been men well known to all who will hear my story. The men who have served as leaders in preparing the way for the rest of us, under that which we call "The American way of life."

Some have been strangers whose names you will not recognize.

Among these *strangers* are eight of my friends who have done most for me in preparing my mind for the acceptance of riches. I call them the "Eight Princes." They serve me when I am awake and they serve me while I sleep.

Although I have never met the "princes" face to face, as I have met the others who have aided me, they have stood watch over my riches; they have protected me against fear and envy and greed and doubt and indecision and procrastination. They have inspired me to move on my own personal initiative, have kept my imagination active, and have given me definiteness of purpose and the faith to insure its fulfillment.

They have been the real "conditioners" of my mind, the builders of my *positive mental attitude!*

And now may I commend them to you so that they may render you a similar service?

3

THE EIGHT PRINCES

The princes serve me through a technique that is simple and adaptable.

Every night, as the last order of the day's activities, the Princes and I have a round table session, the major purpose of which is to permit me to express my gratitude for the service they have rendered me during the day.

The conference proceeds precisely as it would if the Princes were revealed to me in the flesh, but of course they exist on a higher plane than the physical, and I contact them through the power of thought.

Here you may receive your first test as to your capacity to "condition" your mind for the acceptance of riches. When the shock comes just remember what happened when Morse, and Marconi, and Edison, and Ford and the Wright Brothers first announced their perfection of new and better ways of rendering service. It will help you to stand up under the shock.

And now let us go into a session with the Princes:

GRATITUDE!

"Today has been beautiful.

"It has provided me with health of body and mind.

"It has given me food and clothing.

"It has brought me another day of opportunity to be of service to others.

"It has given me peace of mind and freedom from all fear.

"For these blessings I am grateful to you, my Princes of Guidance. I am grateful to all of you collectively for having unraveled the tangled skein of my past life, thereby freeing my mind, my body and my soul from all causes and effects of both fear and strife.

"PRINCE OF MATERIAL PROSPERITY, I am grateful to you for having kept my mind attuned to the consciousness of opulence and plenty, and free from the fear of poverty and want.

"PRINCE OF SOUND PHYSICAL HEALTH, I am grateful to you for having attuned my mind to the consciousness of sound health, thereby providing the means by which every cell of my body and every physical organ is being adequately supplied with an inflow of cosmic energy sufficient unto its needs, and providing a direct contact with Infinite Intelligence which is sufficient for the distribution and application of this energy where it is required.

"PRINCE OF PEACE OF MIND, I am grateful to you for having kept my mind free from all inhibitions and self-imposed limitations, thereby providing my body and my mind with complete rest.

"PRINCE OF HOPE, I am grateful to you for the fulfillment of today's desires, and for your promise of fulfillment of tomorrow's aims.

"PRINCE OF FAITH, I am grateful to you for the guidance which you have given me; for your having inspired me to do that which has been helpful to me, and for turning me back from doing that which had it been done would have proven harmful to me. You have given power to my thoughts, momentum to my deeds, and the wisdom which has enabled me to understand the laws of Nature, and the judgment to enable me to adapt myself to them in a spirit of harmony.

"PRINCE OF LOVE, I am grateful to you for having inspired me to share my riches with all whom I have contacted this day; for having shown me that only that which I give away can I retain as my own. And I am grateful too for the consciousness of love with which you have endowed me, for it has made life sweet and all my relationships with others pleasant.

"PRINCE OF ROMANCE, I am grateful to you for having inspired me with the spirit of youth despite the passing of the years.

"PRINCE OF OVERALL WISDOM, my eternal gratitude to you for having transmuted into an enduring asset of priceless value, all of my past failures, defeats, errors of judgment and of deed, all fears, mistakes, disappointments and adversities of every nature; the asset consisting of my willingness and ability to inspire others to take possession of their own minds and to use their mind-power for the attainment of the riches of life, thus providing me with the privilege of sharing all of my blessings with those who are ready to receive them, and thereby enriching and multiplying my own blessings by the scope of their benefit to others.

"My gratitude to you also for revealing to me the truth that no human experience need become a liability; that all experiences may he transmuted into useful service; that the power of thought is the only power over which I have complete control; that the power of thought may be translated into happiness at will; that there are no limitations to my power of thought save only those which I set up in my own mind."

My greatest asset consists in my good fortune in having recognized the existence of the Eight Princes, for it is they who conditioned my mind to receive the benefits of the Twelve Riches.

It is the habit of daily communication with the Princes which insures me the endurance of these riches, let the circumstances of life be whatever they may.

The Princes serve as the medium through which I keep my mind fixed upon the things I desire and off of the things I do not desire!

They serve as a dependable fetish, a rosary of power, through which I may draw at will upon the powers of thought, with "each hour a pearl, each pearl a blessing."

They provide me with continuous immunity against all forms of negative mental attitude; thus they destroy both the seed of negative thought and the germination of that seed in the soil of my mind.

They help me to keep my mind fixed upon my major purpose in life, and to give the fullest expression to the attainment of that purpose.

They keep me at peace with myself, at peace with the world, and in harmony with my own conscience.

They aid me in closing the doors of my mind to all unpleasant thoughts of past failures and defeats. Nay, they aid me in converting all of my past liabilities into assets of priceless value.

The Princes have revealed to me the existence of that "other self" which thinks, moves, plans, desires and acts by the impetus of a power which recognizes no such reality as an impossibility.

And they have proved, times without number, that every adversity carries with it the seed of an equivalent benefit. So, when adversity overtakes me, as it overtakes everyone, I am not awed by it, but I begin immediately to search for that "seed of an equivalent benefit" and to germinate it into a full-blown flower of opportunity.

The Princes have given me mastery over my most formidable adversary, myself. They have shown me what is good for my body and soul, and they have led me inevitably to the source and supply of all good.

They have taught me the truth that happiness consists not in the possession of things, but in the privilege of self-expression through the use of material things.

And they have taught me that it is more blessed to render useful service than to accept the service of others.

My daily conference with the Princes is regarded as a profound ceremony, and my expression of gratitude for the service they render me is offered as thanks.

Observe that I ask for nothing from the Princes, but I devote the entire ceremony to an expression of gratitude for the riches they have already bestowed upon me.

The Princes know of my needs and supply them!

Yes, they supply all of my needs in over-abundance.

The Princes have taught me to think in terms of that which I can GIVE and to forget about that which I desire to GET in return. Thus they have taught me the proper approach to the impersonal way of life: that way of life which reveals to one the powers which come from within, and which may be drawn upon at will for the solution of all personal problems and for the attainment of all necessary material things.

They have taught me to be still and to listen from within!

They have given me the FAITH to enable me to override my reason and to accept guidance from within, with full confidence that the small still voice which speaks from within is superior to my own powers of reason.

The Princes have thus bestowed upon me the Master Key which opens the gates to the great Estate of Happy Valley, and it is my desire to share this estate with all who will condition their minds to accept as much of it as they can use beneficially.

My Creed of Life was inspired by the Princes.

Let me share it with you, so that you may adopt it as your Creed.

A Happy Man's Creed

I have found happiness by helping others to find it.

I have sound physical health because I live temperately in all things, and eat only the foods which Nature requires for body maintenance.

I am free from fear in all of its forms.

I hate no man, envy no man, but love all mankind.

I am engaged in a labor of love with which I mix play generously. Therefore I never grow tired.

I give thanks daily, not for more riches, but for wisdom with which to recognize, embrace and properly use the great abundance of riches I now have at my command.

I speak no name save only to honor it.

I ask no favors of anyone except the privilege of sharing my riches with all who will receive them.

I am on good terms with my conscience. Therefore it guides me correctly in all that I do.

I have no enemies because I injure no man for any cause, but I benefit all with whom I come into contact by teaching them the way to enduring riches.

I have more material wealth than I need because I am free from greed and covet only the material things I can use while I live.

I own the Estate of Happy Valley, which is not taxable because it exists mainly in my own mind in intangible riches which cannot be assessed or appropriated except by those who adopt my way of life. I created this vast estate by observing Nature's laws and adapting my habits to conform therewith.

Happy Valley is a large Estate!

It has room for all who will prepare themselves to dwell

there. In fact it is precisely the size of the entire United States of America. And it is rightly called the "richest and the freest nation of the world."

Happy Valley Estate is protected by a form of Government based on a Constitution which the great statesman, William E. Gladstone, described as "the most wonderful work ever struck off at a given time by the brain and purpose of man."

Gladstone was right! The Constitution of the United States guarantees every person the right to live in Happy Valley, and the privilege of acquiring riches in whatever form and quantity one may desire.

It provides everyone with a fitting background for the expression of personal initiative.

It inspires men to acquire riches and protects them in the possession of their riches.

It provides every conceivable opportunity for men to use their riches for the good of themselves and their fellowmen, and this provision has given the people the great American way of life, the major portion of which consists in the American System of Free Enterprise—a system so flexible that it belongs to the people, provides employment at high wages for millions of men and women, and supports every profession, every trade, and provides most of the taxes for the support of the government.

The American System of Free Enterprise is the great medium of exchange through which the people market their talents in return for economic security, and it has been so designed as to inspire men to develop their talents by the fullest and the freest expression of their own personal initiative.

The American System of Free Enterprise has been set to the pattern of the American Constitution. The two parallel one another so nearly that injury to one means injury to both!

The Constitution stipulates the rights of the people.

The System of Free Enterprise provides the major portion of the means by which these rights may be translated into money and transportation and communication and into all of the material things that have made the American standard of living the highest man has yet evolved.

I mention these facts because they are directly related to the service rendered me by the Eight Princes.

Now let us get on with our story by a description of the philosophy one must adopt in order to acquire the Twelve Riches.

I have described a method of preparing the mind to receive riches. But this is only the beginning of the story. I have yet to explain how one may take possession of riches and make the fullest use of them.

The story goes back more than a quarter of a century, and has its beginning in the life of Andrew Carnegie, a great philanthropist who was a typical product of the American System of Free Enterprise.

Mr. Carnegie acquired the Twelve Riches, the financial portion of which was so vast that he did not live long enough to enable him to give it away, so he passed much of it on to men who are still engaged in using it for the benefit of mankind.

Mr. Carnegie was also blessed with the services of the Eight Princes. The Prince of Overall Wisdom served him so well that he was inspired not only to give away all his material riches, but to provide the people with a complete philosophy of life through which they too might acquire riches.

That philosophy consists of seventeen principles which conform in every respect to the pattern of the great Constitution of the United States and the American System of Free Enterprise.

Organization of the philosophy required twenty years of labor, in which Mr. Carnegie and more than five hundred other great American leaders of industry had a part, each of them having contributed the sum *total of all he had learned* from *a lifetime of practical experience under the American System of Free Enterprise.*

Mr. Carnegie explained his reason for having inspired the organization of a philosophy of individual achievement when he said:

"I acquired my money through the efforts of other people, and I shall give it back to the people as fast as I can find ways to do so *without inspiring the desire for something for nothing.* But the major portion of my riches consists in the knowledge with which I acquired both the tangible and the intangible portions of it. Therefore, it is my wish that this knowledge be organized into a philosophy and made available to every person who seeks an opportunity for self-determination under the American form of economics."

It was this philosophy which Mr. Carnegie was inspired to give to the people that provided me with the Twelve Riches and an opportunity to live in Happy Valley. And it is the philosophy which you must adopt and apply if you hope to accept the riches I desire to share with you.

Before I describe the principles of this philosophy I wish to give a brief history of what it has already accomplished for other men throughout more than half the world.

It has been translated into four of the leading Indian dialects and has been made available to more than 2,000,000 people of India.

It has been translated into the Portuguese language for the benefit of the people of Brazil, where it has served more than 1,500,000 people.

It has been published in a special edition for distribution throughout the great British Empire, where it has served more than 2,000,000 people.

It has benefited one or more people in practically every city,

town and village in the United States, numbering in all an estimated 20,000,000 people.

And it may well become the means of bringing about a better spirit of friendly cooperation between all the peoples of the
world, since it is founded on no creed or brand, but consists of
the fundamentals of all enduring success, and all constructive
human achievements in every field of human endeavor.

It supports all religions yet it is a part of none!

It is so universal in its nature that it leads men inevitably to
success in all occupations.

But more important to you than all of this evidence, the philosophy is so simple that you may start, right where you stand,
to put it to work for you.

So, we come now to the description of the secrets of the
MASTER KEY to all riches!

The seventeen principles will serve as a dependable roadmap leading directly to the source of all riches, whether they be
intangible or material riches. Follow the map and you cannot
miss the way, but be prepared to comply with all of the instructions and to assume all of the responsibilities that go with the
possession of great riches. And above all, remember that enduring riches must be shared with others; that there is a price one
must pay for everything he acquires.

The MASTER KEY will not be revealed through any one of
these seventeen principles, for its secret consists in the combination of all of them.

These principles represent seventeen doors through which
one must pass to reach the inner chamber wherein is locked the
source of all riches. The MASTER KEY will unlock the door to
that chamber, and it will be in your hands when you have prepared yourself to accept it. Your preparation shall consist of the
assimilation and the application of the first five of these seventeen principles which I shall now describe at length.

4

DEFINITENESS OF PURPOSE

It is impressive to recognize that all of the great leaders, in all walks of life and during all periods of history, have attained their leadership by the application of their abilities behind a Definite Major Purpose.

It is no less impressive to observe that those who are classified as failures have no such purpose, but they go around and around, like a ship without a rudder, coming back always empty-handed, to their starting point.

Some of these "failures" begin with a Definite Major Purpose but they desert that purpose the moment they are overtaken by temporary defeat or strenuous opposition. They give up and quit, not knowing that there is a philosophy of success which is as dependable and as definite as the rules of mathematics, and never suspecting that temporary defeat is but a testing ground which may prove a blessing in disguise if it is not accepted as final.

It is one of the great tragedies of civilization that ninety-eight out of every one hundred persons go all the way through life without coming within sight of anything that even approximates definiteness of a major purpose! And it was Andrew

Carnegie's recognition of this tragedy that inspired him to influence some five hundred great American leaders of industry to collaborate in the organization of this philosophy of individual achievement.

Mr. Carnegie's first test, which he applied to all of his associate workers who were under consideration for promotion to supervisory positions, was that of determining to what extent they were willing to GO THE EXTRA MILE. His second test was to determine whether or not they had their minds fixed upon a definite goal, including the necessary preparation for the attainment of that goal.

"When I asked Mr. Carnegie for my first promotion," said Charles M. Schwab, "he grinned broadly and replied, 'IF YOU HAVE YOUR HEART FIXED ON WHAT YOU WANT THERE IS NOTHING I CAN DO TO STOP YOU FROM GETTING IT.'"

Mr. Schwab knew what he wanted! It was the biggest job within Carnegie's control.

And Mr. Carnegie helped him to get it.

One of the strange facts concerning men who move with definiteness of purpose is the readiness with which the world steps aside that they may pass; even coming to their aid in carrying out their aims.

The story behind the organization of this philosophy is one with dramatic connotations in connection with the importance that Andrew Carnegie placed upon definiteness of purpose.

He had developed his great steel industry and accumulated a huge fortune in money when he turned his interest to the use and the disposition of his fortune. Having recognized that the better portion of his riches consisted in the knowledge with which he had accumulated material riches and in his understanding of human relationships, his major aim in life became that of inspiring someone to organize a philosophy that would convey this knowledge to all who might desire it.

He was then well along in years and he recognized that the job called for the services of a young man who had the time and the inclination to spend twenty years or more in research into the causes of individual achievement.

After interviewing more than two hundred and fifty men whom he suspected might have such ability, he met by mere chance a young man who had been sent by a magazine to interview him for the story of his achievements. Carnegie's keen insight into the characters of men helped him to recognize that this young man might have the qualities for which he had long been searching, so he set up an ingenious plan by which to make a test.

He began by giving the young man the story of his achievements. Then he began to suggest to him that the world needed a practical philosophy of individual achievement which would permit the humblest worker to accumulate riches in whatever amount and form he might desire.

For three days and nights he elaborated upon his idea, describing how one might go about the organization of such a philosophy. When the story was finished Mr. Carnegie was ready to apply his test, to determine whether or not he had found the man who could be depended upon to carry his idea through to completion.

"You now have my idea of a new philosophy," said he, "and I wish to ask you a question in connection with it which I wish you to answer by a simple 'yes' or 'no.' The question is this:

"If I give you the opportunity to organize the world's first philosophy of individual achievement, and introduce you to men who can and will collaborate with you in the work of organization, do you wish the opportunity, and will you follow through with it to completion if it is given to you?"

The young man cleared his throat, stammered for a few

seconds, then replied in a brief sentence that was destined to provide him with an opportunity to project his influence for good throughout the world.

"Yes," he exclaimed, "I will not only undertake the job, but I will finish it!"

That was definite! It was the one thing Mr. Carnegie was searching for—definiteness of purpose.

Many years later this young man learned that Mr. Carnegie had held a stopwatch in his hand when he asked that question, and had allowed exactly sixty seconds for an answer. If the answer had required more time the opportunity would have been withheld. His answer had actually required twenty-nine seconds.

And the reason for the timing was explained by Mr. Carnegie.

"It has been my experience," said he, "that a man who cannot reach a decision promptly, once he has all of the necessary facts for decision at hand, cannot be depended upon to carry through any decision he may make. I have also discovered that men who reach decisions promptly usually have the capacity to move with definiteness of purpose in other circumstances."

The first hurdle of Mr. Carnegie's test had been covered with flying colors, but there was still another that followed.

"Very well," said Carnegie, "you have one of the two important qualities that will be needed by the man who organizes the philosophy I have described. Now I shall learn whether or not you have the second.

"If I give you the opportunity to organize the philosophy are you willing to devote twenty years of your time to research into the causes of success and failure, without pay, earning your own living as you go along?"

That question was a shock to the man chosen by Mr. Carnegie

for so important a job, for he had naturally suspected that he would be subsidized from Mr. Carnegie's huge fortune.

However he recovered quickly from the shock by asking Mr. Carnegie why he was unwilling to provide the money for so important an assignment.

"It is not unwillingness to supply the money," Mr. Carnegie replied, "but it is my desire to know if you have in you a natural capacity for willingness to GO THE EXTRA MILE by rendering service before trying to collect pay for it."

Then he went on to explain that the more successful men in all walks of life were, and had always been, men who followed the habit of rendering more service than that for which they were paid. He also called attention to the fact that subsidies of money, whether they be made to individuals or to groups of individuals, often do more injury than good.

And he reminded the young man that he had been given an opportunity which had been withheld from more than two hundred and fifty other men, some of whom were much older and more experienced than he, and finished by saying:

"If you make the most of the opportunity I have offered you it is conceivable that you may develop it into riches so fabulous in nature as to dwarf my material wealth by comparison, for that opportunity provides the way for you to penetrate the keenest minds of this nation, to profit by the experiences of our greatest American leaders of industry, and it might well enable you to project your influence for good throughout the civilized world, thereby enriching those who are not yet born."

The opportunity was embraced!

The Carnegie tests had found the man for whom he had been so long searching, and the man had received his first lesson on definiteness of purpose and a willingness to GO THE EXTRA MILE.

Twenty years later, almost to the day, the philosophy, which Mr. Carnegie had designated as being the better portion of his riches, was completed and presented to the world in an eight-volume edition.

"And what of the man who spent twenty years of time without pay?' some ask. "What compensation has been received for this labor?"

A complete answer to this question would be impossible, for the man himself does not know the total value of the benefits received. Moreover, some of these benefits are so flexible in nature that they will continue to aid him the remainder of his life.

But, for the satisfaction of those who measure riches in material values alone, it can be stated that one book written by this man, and the result of the knowledge gained from the application of the principle of GOING THE EXTRA MILE, has already yielded an estimated profit of upward of $3,000,000.00. *The actual time spent* in *writing the book was four weeks.*

Definiteness of purpose and the habit of GOING THE EXTRA MILE constitute a force which staggers the imagination of even the most imaginative of people, although these are but two of the seventeen principles of individual achievement.

These two principles have been here associated for but one purpose. That is to indicate how the principles of this philosophy are blended together like the links of a chain, and how this combination of principles leads to the development of stupendous power which cannot be attained by the application singly of any one of them.

We come now to the analysis of the power of definiteness of purpose and psychological principles from which the power is derived.

First premise:

The starting point of all individual achievement is the adoption of a definite purpose and a definite plan for its attainment.

Second premise:

All achievement is the result of a motive or combination of motives, of which there are nine basic motives which govern all voluntary actions. (These motives have been previously described.)

Third premise:

Any dominating idea, plan or purpose held in the mind, through repetition of thought, and emotionalized with a burning desire for its realization, is taken over by the subconscious section of the mind and acted upon, and it is thus carried through to its logical climax by whatever natural means may be available.

Fourth premise:

Any dominating desire, plan or purpose held in the conscious mind and backed by absolute faith in its realization, is taken over and acted upon immediately by the subconscious section of the mind, *and there is no known record of this kind of a desire having ever been without fulfillment.*

Fifth premise:

The power of thought is the only thing over which any person has complete, unquestionable control—a fact so astounding that it connotes a close relationship between the mind of man and the Universal Mind of Infinite Intelligence, the connecting link between the two being FAITH.

Sixth premise:

The subconscious portion of the mind is the doorway to Infinite Intelligence, and it responds to one's demands in exact proportion to the quality of one's FAITH! The subconscious mind may be reached through faith and given instructions as though it were a person or a complete entity unto itself.

Seventh premise:

A definite purpose, backed by absolute faith, is a form of wisdom and wisdom in action produces positive results.

THE MAJOR ADVANTAGES OF DEFINITENESS OF PURPOSE
Definiteness of purpose develops self-reliance, personal initiative, imagination, enthusiasm, self-discipline and concentration of effort, and all of these are prerequisites for the attainment of material success.

It induces one to budget his time and to plan all his day-to-day endeavors so they lead toward the attainment of his MAJOR PURPOSE in life.

It makes one more alert in the recognition of opportunities related to the object of one's MAJOR PURPOSE, and it inspires the necessary courage to act upon those opportunities when they appear.

It inspires the cooperation of other people.

It prepares the way for the full exercise of that state of mind known as FAITH, by *making* the mind positive and freeing it from the limitations of fear and doubt and indecision.

It provides one with a success consciousness, without which no one may attain enduring success in any calling.

It destroys the destructive habit of procrastination.

Lastly, it leads directly to the development and the continuous maintenance of the first of the Twelve Riches, a positive mental attitude.

These are the major characteristics of DEFINITENESS OF PURPOSE, although it has many other qualities and usages, and it is directly related to each of the Twelve Riches because they are attainable only by singleness of purpose.

Compare the principle of definiteness of purpose with the Twelve Riches, one at a time, and observe how essential it is for the attainment of each.

Then take inventory of the men of outstanding achievement

which this country has produced, and observe how each of them has emphasized some major purpose as the object of his endeavors.

Henry Ford concentrated upon the building of low-priced, dependable automobiles.

Thomas A. Edison devoted his efforts entirely to scientific inventions.

Andrew Carnegie specialized in the manufacture and sale of steel.

F. W. Woolworth centered his attention upon the operation of Five and Ten Cent Stores.

Philip D. Armour's specialty was that of meat-packing and distribution.

James J. Hill concentrated on the building and maintenance of a great Transcontinental Railway System.

Alexander Graham Bell majored in scientific research in connection with the development of the modern telephone.

Marshall Field operated the world's greatest retail store.

Cyrus H. K. Curtis devoted his entire life to the development and publication of the *Saturday Evening Post.*

Jefferson, Washington, Lincoln, Patrick Henry and Thomas Paine devoted the better portion of their lives and their fortunes to a prolonged fight for the freedom of all people.

Men with singleness of purpose, each and every one!

And the list might be multiplied until it contained the name of every great American leader who has contributed to the establishment of the American way of life as we of today know and benefit by it.

HOW TO ACQUIRE A DEFINITE MAJOR PURPOSE
The procedure in the development of a Definite Major Purpose is simple, but important, viz:

a. Write out a complete, clear and definite statement of your MAJOR PURPOSE IN LIFE, sign it and commit it to memory; then repeat it orally at least once every day, more often if practicable. Repeat it over and over, thus placing back of your purpose all of your faith in Infinite Intelligence.

b. Write out a clear, definite plan by which you intend to begin the attainment of the object of your DEFINITE MAJOR PURPOSE. In this plan state the maximum time allowed for the attainment of your purpose, and describe precisely *what* you intend to give in return for the realization of your purpose, remembering that there is no such reality as something for nothing, and that everything has a price which must be paid in advance in one form or another.

c. Make your plan flexible enough to permit changes at any time you are inspired to do so. Remember that Infinite Intelligence, which operates in every atom of matter and in every living or inanimate thing, may present you with a plan far superior to any you can create. Therefore he ready at all times to recognize and adopt any superior plan that may be presented to your mind.

d. Keep your MAJOR PURPOSE and your plans for attaining it strictly to yourself except insofar as you will receive additional instructions for carrying out your plan, in the description of the MASTER MIND PRINCIPLE, which follows.

Do not make the mistake of assuming that because you may not understand these instructions the principles here described are not sound. Follow the instructions to the letter; follow them in good faith, and remember that by so doing you are duplicating the procedure of many of the greatest leaders this nation has ever produced.

The instructions call for no effort that you may not easily put forth.

They make no demands upon time or ability with which the average person may not comply.

And they are completely in harmony with the philosophy of all true religions.

Decide now what you desire from life and what you have to give in return. Decide where you are going and how you are to get there. Then make a start from where you now stand.

Make the start with whatever means of attaining your goal that may be at hand. And you will discover that to the extent you make use of these, other and better means will reveal themselves to you.

That has been the experience of all men whom the world has recognized as successes. Most of them started with humble beginnings with little more to aid them than a passionate desire to attain a definite goal.

There is enduring magic in such a desire!

And lastly, remember:

"The Moving Finger writes; and, having writ,
Moves on: nor all thy Piety nor Wit
Shall lure it back to cancel half a Line,
Nor all thy Tears wash out a Word of it."

Yesterday has gone forever! Tomorrow will never arrive, but Today is yesterday's Tomorrow within your reach. What are you doing with it?

Presently I shall reveal to you a principle which is the keystone to the arch of all great achievements; the principle which has been responsible for our great American way of life; our

System of Free Enterprise; our riches and our freedom. But first let us make sure that *you know what it is that you desire of life.*

IDEAS THAT LEAD TO SUCCESS BEGIN AS DEFINITENESS OF PURPOSE

It is a well-known fact that ideas are the only assets which have no fixed values. It is equally well known that ideas are the beginning of all achievements.

Ideas form the foundation of all fortunes, the starting point of all inventions. They have mastered the air above us and the waters of the oceans around us; they have enabled us to harness and use the energy known as the ether, through which one brain may communicate with another brain through telepathy.

All ideas begin as the result of Definiteness of Purpose.

The talking machine was nothing but an abstract idea until Edison organized it through definiteness of purpose, and submitted it to the subconscious portion of his brain where it was projected into the great reservoir of Infinite Intelligence, from which a workable plan was flashed back to him. And this workable plan he translated into a machine which worked.

The philosophy of individual achievement began as an idea in the mind of Andrew Carnegie. He backed his idea with definiteness of purpose, and now the philosophy is available for the benefit of millions of people throughout the civilized world.

Moreover, his idea has more than an average chance of becoming one of the great leavening forces of the world, for it is now being used by an ever increasing multitude of people as a means of guiding them through a world of frenzied hysteria in which the spirit of defeatism threatened, for a time, to bring millions of people to a condition of temporary defeat.

The great North American Continent known as the "New World" was discovered and brought under the influence of civilization as the result of an idea which was born in the mind of a humble sailor and backed by definiteness of purpose. And the time is at hand when that idea, born more than four hundred years ago, may lift our nation to a position where it will become the last frontier of civilization, the only hope of human liberty for all mankind.

Any idea that is held in the mind, emphasized, feared or reverenced, begins at once to clothe itself in the most convenient and appropriate physical form that is available.

That which men believe, talk about and fear, whether it be good or bad, has a very definite way of making its appearance in one form or another. Let those who are struggling to free themselves from the limitations of poverty and misery not forget this great truth, for it applies to an individual just as it does to a nation of people.

SELF-SUGGESTION, THE CONNECTING LINK BETWEEN THE CONSCIOUS AND THE SUBCONSCIOUS MIND

Let us now turn our attention to the working principle through which thoughts, ideas, plans, hopes, and purposes which are placed in the conscious mind find their way into the subconscious section of the mind, where they are picked up and carried out to their logical conclusion, through a law of nature which I shall describe later.

To recognize this principle and understand it is to recognize also the reason why Definiteness of Purpose is the beginning of all achievements.

Transfer of thought from the conscious to the subconscious section of the mind may be hastened by the simple process of "stepping up" or stimulating the vibrations of thought through faith, fear, or any other highly intensified emotion, such as enthusiasm, a burning desire based on definiteness of purpose.

Thoughts backed by faith have precedence over all others in the matter of definiteness and speed with which they are handed over to the subconscious section of the mind and are acted upon. The speed with which the power of faith works has given rise to the belief held by many that certain phenomena are the result of "miracles."

Psychologists and scientists recognize no such phenomenon as a miracle, claiming as they do that everything which happens is the result of a definite cause, albeit a cause which cannot be explained. Be that as it may, it is a known fact that the person who is capable of freeing his mind from all self-imposed limitations, through the mental attitude known as faith, generally finds the solution to all of his problems, regardless of their nature.

Psychologists recognize also that Infinite Intelligence, while it is not claimed to be an automatic solver of riddles, nevertheless carries out to a logical conclusion any clearly defined idea, aim, purpose or desire that is submitted to the subconscious section of the mind in a mental attitude of perfect faith.

However, Infinite Intelligence never attempts to modify, change or otherwise alter any thought that is submitted to it, and it has never been known to act upon a mere wish or indefinite idea, thought or purpose. Get this truth well-grounded in your mind and you will find yourself in possession of sufficient power to solve your daily problems with much less effort than most people devote to worrying over their problems.

So-called "hunches" often are signals indicating that Infinite Intelligence is endeavoring to reach and influence the conscious section of the mind, but you will observe that they usually come in response to some idea, plan, purpose or desire, or some fear that has been handed over to the subconscious section of the mind.

All "hunches" should be treated civilly and examined carefully, as they often convey, either in whole or in part, information of the utmost value to the individual who receives them. These "hunches" often make their appearance many hours, days or weeks after the thought which inspires them has reached the reservoir of Infinite Intelligence. Meanwhile, the individual often has forgotten the original thought which inspired them.

This is a deep, profound subject about which even the wisest of men know very little. It becomes a self-revealing subject only upon meditation and thought.

Understand the principle of mind operation here described and you will have a dependable clue as to why meditation sometimes brings that which one desires, while at other times it brings that which one does not wish.

This type of mental attitude is attained only by preparation and self-discipline attained through a formula I shall describe later.

It is one of the most profound truths of the world that the affairs of men, whether they are circumstances of mass thought or of individual thought, shape themselves to fit the exact pattern of those thoughts.

Successful men become successful only because they acquire the habit of thinking in terms of success.

Definiteness of purpose can, and it should, so completely occupy the mind that one has no time or space in the mind for thoughts of failure.

Another profound truth consists in the fact that the individual who has been defeated and who recognizes himself as a failure may, by reversing the position of the "sails" of his mind, convert the winds of adversity into a power of equal volume which will carry him onward to success, just as,

"One ship sails east, the other west,
Impelled by the self same blow,
It's the set of the sails and not the gales,
That bids them where to go."

To some who pride themselves on being what the world calls "cool-headed, practical business men," this analysis of the principle of Definiteness of Purpose may appear to be abstract or impractical.

There is a power greater than the power of conscious thought, and often it is not perceptible to the finite mind of man. Acceptance of this truth is essential for the successful culmination of any definite purpose based upon the desire for great achievements.

The great philosophers of all ages, from Plato and Socrates on down to Emerson and the moderns, and the great statesmen of our times, from George Washington down to Abraham Lincoln, are known to have turned to the "inner self" in times of great emergency.

We offer no apology for our belief that no great and enduring success has ever been achieved, or ever will be achieved except by those who recognize and use the spiritual powers of the Infinite, as they may be sensed and drawn upon through their "inner selves."

Every circumstance of every man's life is the result of a definite cause, whether it is a circumstance that brings failure or one that brings success.

And most of the circumstances of every man's life are the result of causes over which he has or may have control.

This obvious truth gives importance of the first magnitude to the principle of Definiteness of Purpose. If the circumstances of a man's life are not what he desires he may change them by changing his mental attitude and forming new and more desirable thought habits.

How Definiteness of Purpose Leads to Success

Of all the great American industrialists who have contributed to the development of our industrial system, none was more spectacular than the late Walter Chrysler.

His story should give hope to every young American who aspires to the attainment of fame or fortune, and it serves as evidence of the power one may gain by moving with Definiteness of Purpose.

Chrysler began as a mechanic in a railroad shop in Salt Lake City, Utah. From his savings he had accumulated a little more than $4,000.00, which he intended to use as a fund to set himself up in business.

Looking around diligently he decided that the automobile business was a coming industry, so he decided to go into that field.

His entry into the business was both dramatic and novel.

His first move was one that shocked his friends and astounded his relatives, for it consisted in his investing *all of his savings* in an automobile. When the car arrived in Salt Lake City he gave his friends still another shock by proceeding to take it apart, piece by piece, until the parts were scattered all over the shop.

Then he began to put the parts together again.

He repeated this operation so often that some of his friends thought he had lost his mind. That was because they did not understand his purpose. They saw what he was doing with the automobile, and it looked aimless and without purpose, but what they did not see was the plan which was taking form in Walter Chrysler's mind.

He was making his mind "automobile conscious!" Saturating it with Definiteness of Purpose! He was observing carefully every detail of the car. When he was through with his job of tearing down his automobile and rebuilding it, he knew all of its good points and all of its weak ones.

From that experience he began to design automobiles embodying all of the good points of the car he had bought and omitting all of its weaknesses. He did his job so thoroughly that when the Chrysler automobiles began to reach the market they became the sensation of the entire automobile industry.

His rise to fame and fortune was both rapid and definite, because he knew where he was going before he started, and he prepared himself with painstaking accuracy for the journey.

Observe these men who move with Definiteness of Purpose wherever you find them, and you will be impressed by the ease with which they attract the friendly cooperation of others, break down resistance and get that which they seek.

Analyze Walter Chrysler accurately and observe how definitely he acquired the Twelve Riches of Life and made the most of them.

He began by developing the greatest of all the riches, *a positive mental attitude.*

That provided him with a fertile field in which to plant and germinate the seed of his Definite Major Purpose, the building of fine motorcars.

Then, one by one, he acquired other riches: sound physical health, harmony in human relationships, freedom from fear, hope of achievement, the capacity for faith, willingness to share his blessings, a labor of love, an open mind on all subjects, self-discipline, the capacity to understand people, and last, financial security.

One of the strangest facts concerning the success of Walter Chrysler consists in the simplicity with which he attained it. He had no appreciable amount of working capital with which to begin. His education was a limited one. He had no wealthy backers to set him up in business.

But he did have a practical idea and enough personal initiative to begin, right where he stood, to develop it. Everything he needed to translate his Definite Major Purpose into reality seemed almost miraculously placed in his hands as fast as he was ready for it—a circumstance which is not uncommon to men who move with definiteness of purpose.

When Edward Bok came to the United States, during his early youth, he could not speak our language; he had no money and had to work after school hours to help support his mother and brothers.

Early in life he found out what he wanted and made up his mind to get it. First of all he desired the daughter of Cyrus H. K. Curtis for his wife. Very soon his first desire was attained. The next thing he wanted was to become the editor of the *Ladies' Home Journal*. In a little while he also had that desire fulfilled.

His greatest desire then became his aim—and a very obsessional aim it was—to make the *Ladies' Home Journal* the greatest magazine of its kind in the world. The publishing world is agreed that he attained that aim.

Along with his other aims, Edward Bok desired to be recognized as a truly great American citizen; an ambition that was inspired by the vastness of opportunities which his adopted country had provided him. He also attained that aim.

Now let me call your attention to one very significant fact: Each of Edward Bok's aims was created by himself, in his own mind, and each was attained by his own efforts on sheer merit. He did not depend upon lucky "breaks," did not expect something for nothing, but shaped his own destiny by careful planning based upon Definiteness of Purpose.

And he, like Walter Chrysler, conditioned his mind for success by acquiring all of the Twelve Riches.

Shortly after THINK AND GROW RICH (a one-volume interpretation of a portion of the Andrew Carnegie philosophy of individual achievement) was published, the publisher began to receive telegraphic orders for the book from book stores in and near Des Moines, Iowa.

The orders called for immediate shipment of the book by express. The cause of the sudden demand for the book was a mystery until several weeks later, when the publisher received a letter from Edward P. Chase, a life insurance salesman representing the Sun Life Assurance Company, in which he said:

"I am writing to express my grateful appreciation of your book, 'Think and Grow Rich.' I followed its advice to the letter. As a result I received an idea which resulted in the sale of a two-million-dollar life insurance policy. The largest single sale of its kind ever made in Des Moines."

The key sentence in Mr. Chase's letter is in the second sentence: "I followed its advice to the letter."

He moved on that idea with Definiteness of Purpose, and it helped him to earn more money in one hour than most life insurance men earn in five years of continuous effort.

In one brief sentence Mr. Chase told the entire story of a business transaction which lifted him out of the category of ordinary life insurance salesmen and made him a member of the coveted Million Dollar Round Table.

When he went out to sell a two-million-dollar life insurance policy he took with him a form of Definiteness of Purpose that was supported by faith. He did not merely read the book, as perhaps several million other men had done, and then lay it aside in an attitude of cynicism or doubt, with the thought that the principles it described might work for others but not for him.

He read it with an open mind, in a spirit of expectancy, recognized the power of the ideas it contained, appropriated those ideas, and moved on them with definiteness of purpose.

Somewhere in the book Mr. Chase's mind established contact with the mind of the author of the book, and that contact quickened his own mind so definitely and intensely that an idea was born. The idea was to sell a life insurance policy larger than any he had ever thought of selling. The sale of that policy became his immediate Definite Major Purpose in life. He moved on that purpose without hesitation or delay, and behold! His objective was attained in less than an hour.

As Andrew Carnegie once said, the man who is motivated by definiteness of purpose and moves on that purpose with the spiritual forces of his being, may challenge the man of indecision at the post and pass him at the grandstand. It makes no difference whether he is selling life insurance or digging ditches.

A definite, potent idea, when it is fresh in one's mind, may so change the biochemistry of that mind that it takes on the spiritual qualities which recognize no such reality as failure or defeat.

The major weakness of most men, as Mr. Carnegie so often declared, is that they recognize the obstacles they must surmount without recognizing the spiritual power at their command by which those obstacles may be removed at will.

I recall, as though it were only yesterday, the circumstances of my own awakening to the recognition of the spiritual powers available to me. And strangely enough, that awakening came from the same book that inspired Edward P. Chase to lift himself into the upper brackets of achievement in his chosen profession.

My wife brought the book from the public library and asked me to read it. The moment my hands touched the covers, before the book had been opened, I felt a strange thrill of inspiration which caused me to begin then and there to open the book and read it.

Before I had finished the first chapter I recognized that some strange quirk of fate had caused the book to be placed in my hands. I took it to bed with me and read it from cover to cover before I went to sleep.

The next morning I arose a new man. *I had been literally born again!*

Indecision and doubt were forever gone.

In six brief years that idea enabled me to project my influence for the benefit of millions of people throughout a large portion of the world. At long last I had acquired the blessed art of sharing my riches with others.

And I had acquired the Twelve Riches in their fullest and most bountiful form. Moreover, I had discovered my "other self;" that self I had never known before. I also had discovered the existence of the Eight Princes—the servants of that "other self," which guide me in all that I do.

I was so elated over my changed life that it seemed imperative that I meet the author of the book and thank him in person for my good fortune. Finding him was like searching for the needle in a haystack, for he had retired and was living in seclusion. His publisher could not give me his address, so I traced him from one address to another, until I finally located him, after having crossed the continent three times in my search.

My urge to meet the author was due mainly to a feeling I had that he had not exhausted his entire knowledge on the subject of individual achievement through the pages of "Think and Grow Rich."

In this assumption I was correct, for I discovered that he had mentioned only three of the seventeen principles of individual achievement in this book; that he had written an entirely new course in which the entire philosophy had been presented.

Applying the principle of GOING THE EXTRA MILE— a principle in which I believe devoutly—I induced the author to permit me to carry out a very important portion of my Definite Major Purpose in life—that of assisting in taking this philosophy to an ailing world at a time when it is most needed.

I said to the author, as I now say to you, that I would rather have had the privilege of being the author of that philosophy than to have been President of the United States. And next to that I would rather have the privilege of helping to take it to the world, than to own all the world's wealth.

This privilege has been granted me.

And I shall exercise it in a variety of ways. First, I shall make the philosophy available, although in a brief form, through a series of radio programs which will be presented to the people.

Next, I shall help to make the philosophy available in printed lessons which will be distributed to the people through the newsstands and book stores of the country.

Then I shall aid in having it interpreted through talking pictures suitable for presentation to the workers in industry, and distributed to them through the cooperation of the management of American Industry.

In addition to these sources of outlet for the philosophy I shall aid in the organization of a nationwide series of private study clubs in which the philosophy will be presented by talking pictures and through the printed lessons.

It is my purpose to cooperate with the churches of the nation by helping to provide the means by which the philosophy may be made available to their members.

I have also arranged with the author of the philosophy to write a book for children, in which the philosophy will be interpreted in terms that will grip their imagination. This book will be distributed through the bookstores and it will be translated into talking pictures for use in the public schools.

Beyond this I hope to make other contributions, as opportunities present themselves, leading to the distribution of this philosophy on a scale so vast that it will become available to every person who is searching for his or her place in the world.

Thus do I have the privilege of revealing the inner workings of a mind that has been inspired with a Definite Major Purpose in life, and though the task may seem extensive, let me assure you that my contribution will be truly a labor of love, and my compensation will consist of an ever-increasing reward which is known only to the man who has discovered the blessed privilege of gaining riches by sharing his blessings with others.

Riches—the real riches of life—increase in exact proportion to the scope and extent of the benefit they bring to those with whom they are shared. I know this to be true for I have grown rich by sharing. I have never benefited anyone in any manner whatsoever without having received in return, from one source or another, ten times as much benefit as I have contributed to others.

In sharing my riches with others, I seek no glorification, for my benefactions are made anonymously except in rare instances when my identity must be revealed. Instead of seeking glorification of my name, I prefer to glorify my soul through useful service to others. The riches I give away add to my own estate in Happy Valley.

I wish no monuments built to my name after I am gone. I prefer rather to build my own monuments while I live, in the hearts of my fellowmen—not monuments to my name, but monuments to the spirit of Fellowship which I am endeavoring to promote for the good of mankind.

In this spirit I have created the great estate of Happy Valley; in this spirit I shall maintain the estate as long as I live.

And this is the spirit which I recommend to you who are seeking the path to Happy Valley.

You will find that path most quickly by helping others to find it.

One of the strangest of all truths which have been revealed to me is the fact that the surest way to solve one's personal problems is to find someone with a greater problem and help him to solve it, through some method of application of the habit of GOING THE EXTRA MILE.

This is a simple formula, but it has charm and magic, and it never fails to work.

However, you cannot appropriate the formula by the mere acceptance of my testimony as to its soundness. You must adopt it and apply it in your own way. You will then need no testimony as to its soundness.

You will find that many opportunities surround you.

The destruction wrought by World War II has bewildered and frustrated many millions of people who are now searching for the path to Happy Valley. They need only a spark of human kindness to give them new hope and the courage to carry on. You can supply that spark to those nearest you.

By helping others to find the path *you will find it for yourselves!*

You might begin by organizing a Fellowship Club among your own neighbors or fellow workers, casting yourself for the role of leader and teacher of the group.

Here you will learn another great truth, namely, that the best way to appropriate the principles of the philosophy of individual achievement is by teaching it to others. When a man begins to teach anything he begins also to learn more about that which he is teaching.

You are now a student of this philosophy, but you can become a master of it by teaching it to others. Thus your compensation will be assured you in advance.

If you are a worker in industry here is your big opportunity to find yourself by helping others to adjust their relationships in peace and harmony. For soundness it has never been excelled, for it has been fully verified by the experiences of men in every walk of life.

Labor does not need agitators, but it does need *peacemakers.* It also needs a sound philosophy for the guidance of its following—a philosophy that benefits both the management and the workers. To this end the principles of this philosophy are perfectly suited.

The labor leader who guides his followers by this philosophy will have the *confidence of his followers and the fullest cooperation of their employers.* Is that not obvious? Is it not sufficient promise of reward to justify the adoption of this philosophy?

A labor organization conducted by the principles of this philosophy would benefit everyone whom it affected. Friction would be supplanted by harmony in human relationships. Agitators and exploiters of labor would be automatically eliminated.

The funds of the labor organization could be used for the education of its members and not for political intrigues.

And there would be more profits for distribution as wages— *profits which the management of industry would prefer to give to their workers instead of being forced to use them as a defense fund against the destructive efforts of agitators.*

There is a need for a Fellowship Club in every industry. In the larger industries there is room for many such clubs. The membership should consist of both the workers and the management, for here is a common meeting ground based upon principles on which everyone could agree. And agreement here would mean agreement at the workbench or the lathe.

I have emphasized this particular field of opportunity because I recognize that the chaos existing in the relationship between the management of industry and the workers constitutes *the number one economic problem of this nation.*

If you have not already adopted a Definite Major Purpose in life here is an opportunity for you to do so. You can start right where you are, by helping to teach this philosophy to those who are in need of it.

The time has come when it is not only beneficial to the individual to help his neighbor to solve his personal problems, *but it is imperative that each of us do so as a means of self-preservation.*

If your neighbor's house were on fire you would volunteer to help him put out the fire, even if you were not on friendly terms with him, for common sense would convince you that this would be the means of saving your own house.

In recommending harmony between the management of industry and the workers, I am not thinking of the interests of management alone, for I recognize that if this harmony does not prevail there soon will be neither management nor workers as we know them today.

On the other hand, the man with a sound philosophy of life will find himself surrounded with an abundance of opportunities such as did not exist a decade ago.

The man who tries to get ahead without a Definite Major Purpose will meet with difficulties far greater than the average man can master.

The more lucrative opportunities of the world of today and tomorrow will go to those who prepare themselves for leadership in their chosen calling.

And leadership in any field of endeavor requires a foundation of sound philosophy. The days of the "hit and miss" leadership are gone forever. Skill and technique and human understanding will be required in the changed world we are now approaching.

The foremen and supervisors in industry must take on new responsibilities in the future. They must not only be skilled in the mechanics of their jobs, which is so essential for efficient production, but they must be skilled as well in the production of harmony among the workers for whom they are responsible.

The youngsters of today will become the leaders of our society tomorrow. What are we going to do about them? This is a problem of the first magnitude, and the major portion of the burden of solving it will fall upon the shoulders of the teachers in the public schools.

I mention these obvious facts as evidence that the future holds forth opportunities for useful service such as we have never known before; opportunities born of necessity in a world which has changed so rapidly that some fail to recognize the scope and the nature of the changes which have taken place.

Take inventory, you who are without a Definite Major Purpose; to find out where you fit in this changed world; prepare yourselves for your new opportunities and make the most of them.

If I had the privilege of so doing I could no doubt choose for you a Definite Major Purpose suited in every way to your qualifications and needs, and I might create for you a simple plan by which you could attain the object of that purpose; but I can serve you more profitably by teaching you how to do this for yourself.

Somewhere along the way the idea for which you are searching will reveal itself to you. That has been the experience of most of the students of this philosophy. When the idea comes you will recognize it, for it should come with such force that you cannot escape it. You may be sure of that provided you are sincerely searching for it.

One of the imponderable features of this philosophy is that it inspires the creation of new ideas, reveals the presence of opportunities for self-advancement which had been previously overlooked, and inspires one to move on his own personal initiative in embracing and making the most of such opportunities.

This feature of the philosophy is not the result of chance. It was designed to produce a specific effect, since it is obvious that an opportunity which a man creates for himself, or an idea with which he may be inspired through his own thought, is more beneficial than any he may borrow from others, for the very procedure by which a man creates useful ideas leads him unerringly to the discovery of the source from which he may acquire additional ideas when he needs them.

While it is of great benefit to a man to have access to a source from which he may receive the inspiration necessary to create his own ideas, and self-reliance is an asset of priceless value, there may come a time when he will need to draw upon the resources of other minds. And that time is sure to come to those who aspire to leadership in the higher brackets of personal achievement.

Presently I shall reveal to you the means by which personal power may be attained, through the consolidation of many minds directed to the achievement of definite ends.

It was by this same means that Andrew Carnegie ushered in the great steel age and gave America its greatest industry, although he had no capital with which to begin, and very little education.

And it was by this means that Thomas A. Edison became the greatest inventor of all times, although he had no personal knowledge of physics, mathematics, chemistry, electronics or many other scientific subjects, all of which were essential in his work as an inventor.

It should give you hope to know that lack of education, lack of working capital, and lack of technical skill need not discourage you from establishing, as your major goal in life, any purpose you may choose, for this philosophy provides a way by which any goal within reason may be attained by any man of average ability.

The one thing it cannot do for you is to choose your goal for you!

But, once you have established your own goal, this philosophy can guide you unerringly to its attainment. That is a promise without qualifications.

We cannot tell you what to desire, or how much success to hope for, but we can and we shall reveal to you the formula by which successes may be attained.

Your major responsibility right now is to find out what you desire in life, where you are going, and what you will do when you get there. This is one responsibility which no one but you can assume, and it is a responsibility ninety-eight out of every hundred people never assume. *That is the major reason why only two out of every hundred people can be rated as successful.*

Success begins through Definiteness of Purpose!

If this fact has seemed to be overemphasized it is because of the common trait of procrastination which influences ninety-eight out of every hundred people to go all the way through life without choosing a Definite Major Purpose. Singleness of purpose is a priceless asset—priceless because so few possess it.

Yet it is an asset which one may appropriate on a second's notice.

Make up your mind what you desire of life, decide to get just that, without substitutes, and lo! You will have taken possession of one of the most priceless of all assets available to human beings.

But your desire must be no mere wish or hope!

It must be a *burning desire,* and it must become so definitely an obsessional desire that you are willing to pay whatever price its attainment may cost. The price may be much or it may be little, but you must condition your mind to pay it, regardless of what the cost may be.

The moment you choose your Definite Major Purpose in life you will observe a strange circumstance, consisting in the fact that ways and means of attaining that purpose will begin immediately to reveal themselves to you.

Opportunities you had not expected will be placed in your way.

The cooperation of others will become available to you, and friends will appear as if by a stroke of magic. Your fears and doubts will begin to disappear and self-reliance will take their place.

This may seem, to the uninitiated, a fantastic promise, but not so to the man who has done away with indecision and has chosen a definite goal in life. I speak not from the observation of other men alone, but from my own personal experience. I have transformed myself from a dismal failure to an outstanding success, and I have therefore earned the right to give you this assurance of what you may expect if you follow the roadmap provided by this philosophy.

When you come to that inspiring moment when you choose your Definite Major Purpose, do not become discouraged if relatives or friends who are nearest you call you a dreamer."

Just remember that the dreamers have been the forerunners of all human progress.

They have given us the great American System of Free Enterprise.

They have given us our greatest asset, the privilege of enjoying personal liberty and the right to dream when we choose.

They have given us the greatest air force and the greatest navy in the world.

They have pushed back the frontiers of civilization and have made of the American way of life a glorious pattern which is the envy of the rest of the world.

Christopher Columbus dreamed of an unknown world, set sail on an uncharted ocean and discovered a new world.

Copernicus dreamed of an unseen world, and with the aid of an improvised telescope revealed it, thus setting civilization ahead ten thousand years in the mastery of fear and superstition.

Thomas A. Edison dreamed of a lamp that could be lighted by electricity, went to work on his dream, and despite the fact that he met with ten thousand failures he gave the world that lamp.

So, let no one discourage you from dreaming, but make sure you back your dreams with action based on Definiteness of Purpose. Your chances for success are as great as have been those of anyone who has preceded you. In many ways your chances are greater, for you now have access to the knowledge of the principles of individual achievement which millions of successful men of the past had to acquire the long and hard way.

Wise men share most of their riches generously. They share their confidences sparingly, and take great care not to misplace them. And when they talk of their aims and plans they generally do it by actions rather than by words.

Wise men listen much and speak with caution, for they know that a man may always be in the way of learning something of value when he is listening, while he may learn nothing when he is speaking, unless it be the folly of talking too much!

There is always an appropriate time for one to speak and an appropriate time for one to remain silent. Wise men, when in doubt as to whether to speak or remain silent, give themselves the benefit of the doubt by keeping quiet.

Exchange of thought, through intercourse of speech, is one of the more important means by which men gather useful knowledge, create plans for the attainment of their Definite Major Purpose and find ways and means of carrying out these plans. And the "round table" discussions are an outstanding feature among men in the higher brackets of achievement. But these are far different from the idle discussions in which some men open their minds to anyone who wishes to enter.

Presently I shall reveal to you a safe method by which you may exchange thoughts with other men, with a reasonable assurance that you will get as much as you give, or more. By this method you may not only speak freely of your most cherished plans, but it will be profitable for you to so do.

I shall reveal to you an important intersection at which you may leave the bypath you are following on your way to Happy Valley, and get on the main highway! The way will be clearly marked so that you shall not miss it.

This intersection of which I speak is the point at which men in the higher brackets of achievement come to a parting of the ways with many of their former associates and confidants, and join company with men who are prepared to give them a lift on their journey to Happy Valley.

5
THE HABIT OF GOING THE EXTRA MILE

An important principle of success in all walks of life and in all occupations is a willingness to GO THE EXTRA MILE; which means the rendering of more and better service than that for which one is paid, and giving it in a positive mental attitude.

Search wherever you will for a single sound argument against this principle, and you will not find it; nor will you find a single instance of enduring success which was not attained in part by its application.

The principle is not the creation of man. It is a part of Nature's handiwork, for it is obvious that every living creature below the intelligence of man is forced to apply the principle in order to survive.

Man may disregard the principle if he chooses, but he cannot do so and at the same time enjoy the fruits of enduring success.

Observe how Nature applies this principle in the production of food that grows from the soil, where the farmer is forced to GO THE EXTRA MILE by clearing the land, plowing it, and planting the seed at the right time of the year, for none of which he receives any pay in advance.

But, observe that if he does his work in harmony with Nature's laws, and performs the necessary amount of labor, Nature takes over the job where the farmer's labor ends, germinates the seed he plants and develops it into a crop of food.

And, observe thoughtfully this significant fact: For every grain of wheat or corn he plants in the soil Nature yields him perhaps a hundred grains, thus enabling him to benefit by the law of increasing returns.

Nature GOES THE EXTRA MILE by producing enough of everything for her needs, together with a surplus for emergencies and waste; for example, the fruit on the trees, the bloom from which the fruit is grown, frogs in the pond and fish in the seas.

Nature GOES THE EXTRA MILE by producing enough of every living thing to insure the perpetuation of the species, allowing for emergencies of every kind. If this were not true the species of all living things would soon vanish.

Some believe that the beasts of the jungle and the birds of the air live without labor, but thoughtful men know that this is not true. It is true that Nature provides the sources of supply of food for every living thing, but every creature must labor before it may partake of that food.

Thus we see that Nature discourages the habit which some men have acquired of trying to get something for nothing.

The advantages of the habit of GOING THE EXTRA MILE are definite and understandable. Let us examine some of them and be convinced:

The habit brings the individual to the favorable attention of those who can and will provide opportunities for self-advancement.

It tends to make one indispensable, in many different human

relationships, and it therefore enables him to command more than average compensation for personal services.

It leads to mental growth and to physical skill and perfection in many forms of endeavor, thereby adding to one's earning capacity.

It protects one against the loss of employment when employment is scarce, and places him in a position to command the choicest of jobs.

It enables one to profit by the law of contrast since *the majority* of *people do not practice the habit.*

It leads to the development of a positive, pleasing mental attitude, which is essential for enduring success.

It tends to develop a keen, alert imagination because it is a habit which inspires one continuously to seek new and better ways of rendering service.

It develops the important quality of personal initiative.

It develops self-reliance and courage.

It serves to build the confidence of others in one's integrity.

It aids in the mastery of the destructive habit of procrastination.

It develops definiteness of purpose, insuring one against the common habit of aimlessness.

There is still another, and a greater reason for following the habit of GOING THE EXTRA MILE. *It gives one the only logical reason* for *asking for increased compensation.*

If a man performs no more service than that for which he is being paid, then obviously he is receiving all the pay to which he is entitled.

He must render as much service as that for which he is being paid, in order to hold his job, or to maintain his source of income, regardless of how he earns it.

But he has the privilege always of rendering an over-plus of service as a means of accumulating a reserve credit of goodwill, and to provide a just reason for demanding more pay, a better position, or both.

Every position based upon a salary or wages provides one with an opportunity to advance himself by the application of this principle, and it is important to note that the great American System of Free Enterprise is operated on the basis of providing every worker in industry with a proper incentive to apply the principle.

Any practice or philosophy which deprives a man of the privilege of GOING THE EXTRA MILE is unsound and doomed to failure, for it is obvious that this principle is the stepping-stone of major importance by which an individual may receive compensation for extraordinary skill, experience and education; and it is the one principle which provides the way of self-determination, regardless of what occupation, profession or calling the individual may be engaged in.

In America, under our System of Free Enterprise, anyone may earn a living without the habit of GOING THE EXTRA MILE. And many do just that, but economic security and the luxuries available under the great American way of life are available only to the individual who makes this principle a part of his philosophy of life and lives by it as a matter of daily habit.

Every known rule of logic and common sense forces one to accept this as true. And even a cursory analysis of men in the higher brackets of success will prove that it is true.

The leaders of the American System of Free Enterprise are adamant in their demands that every worker be protected in his right to adopt and apply the principle of GOING THE EXTRA MILE, for they recognize from their own experience that the future leadership in industry is dependent upon men who are willing to follow this principle.

It is a well-known fact that Andrew Carnegie developed

more successful leaders of industry than has any other great American industrialist. Most of them came up from the ranks of ordinary day laborers, and many of them accumulated personal fortunes of vast amounts, more than they could have acquired without the guidance of Mr. Carnegie.

The first test that Mr. Carnegie applied to any worker whom he desired to promote was that of determining to what extent the worker was willing to GO THE EXTRA MILE.

It was this test that led him to the discovery of Charles M. Schwab. When Mr. Schwab first came to Mr. Carnegie's attention he was working as a day laborer in one of the steel master's plants. Close observation revealed that Mr. Schwab always performed more and better service than that for which he was paid. Moreover, he performed it in a pleasing mental attitude which made him popular among his fellow workers.

He was promoted from one job to another until at long last he was made president of the great United States Steel Corporation, at a salary of $77,000.00 a year!

Not through all the ingenuity of man, or all the schemes that men resort to in order to get something for nothing, could Charles M. Schwab, the day laborer, have earned as much as $77,000.00 during his entire lifetime if he had not willingly adopted and followed the habit of GOING THE EXTRA MILE.

On some occasions Mr. Carnegie not only paid Mr. Schwab's salary, which was generous enough, but he gave him as much as $1,000,000.00 as a bonus in addition to his regular salary.

When Mr. Carnegie was asked why he gave Mr. Schwab a bonus so much greater than his salary he replied in words that every worker, regardless of his job or wages, might well ponder. "I gave him his salary for the work he actually performed," said Mr. Carnegie, "and the bonus for his willingness to GO THE EXTRA MILE, thus setting a fine example for his fellow workers."

Think of that! A salary of $77,000.00 a year, paid to a man

who started as a day laborer, and a bonus of more than ten times that amount for a good disposition expressed by a willingness to do more than he was paid for.

Verily it pays to GO THE EXTRA MILE, for every time an individual does so he places someone else under obligation to him. Enough of such obligations make a Charles M. Schwab, an Andrew Carnegie, a Henry Ford, or a Thomas A. Edison!

No one is compelled to follow the habit of GOING THE EXTRA MILE, and seldom is anyone ever requested to render more service than that for which he is paid. Therefore, if the habit is followed it must be adopted on one's own initiative.

But, the Constitution of the United States (as it was originally written) guarantees every man this privilege, and the American System of Free Enterprise provides rewards and bonuses for those who follow this habit, and makes it impossible for a man to adopt the habit without receiving appropriate compensation.

The compensation may come in many different forms. Increased pay is a certainty. Voluntary promotions are inevitable. Favorable working conditions and pleasant human relationships are sure. And these lead to economic security which a man may attain on his own merits.

There is still another benefit to be gained by the man who follows the habit of GOING THE EXTRA MILE: *It keeps him on good terms with his own conscience and serves as a stimulant to his own soul!* Therefore it is a builder of sound character which has no equal in any other human habit.

You who have young boys and girls growing into adulthood might well remember this for their sake! Teach a child the benefits of rendering more service and better service than that which is customary, and you will have made contributions of character to that child which will serve him or her all through life.

The philosophy of Andrew Carnegie is essentially a philosophy of economics. But it is more than that! It is also a philosophy of ethics in human relationships. It leads to harmony and understanding and sympathy for the weak and the unfortunate. It teaches one how to become his brother's keeper, and at the same time rewards him for so doing.

The habit of GOING THE EXTRA MILE is only one of the seventeen principles of the philosophy which Mr. Carnegie has recommended to those who are seeking riches, but let us consider how directly it is related to each of the Twelve Riches.

First, this habit is inseparably related to the development of the most important of the Twelve Riches, a *POSITIVE MENTAL ATTITUDE.* When a man becomes the master of his own emotions, and learns the blessed art of self-expression through useful service to others, he has gone far toward the development of a positive mental attitude.

With a positive mental attitude as a builder of the proper thought pattern, the remainder of the Twelve Riches fall into that pattern as naturally as night follows day, and as inevitably. Recognize this truth and you will understand why the habit of GOING THE EXTRA MILE provides benefits far beyond the mere accumulation of material riches. You will understand also why this principle has been given first place in Mr. Carnegie's philosophy of individual achievement.

Let us now observe that the admonition to render more service and better service than that for which one is paid, is paradoxical because *it is impossible* for *anyone to render such service without receiving appropriate compensation.* The compensation may come in many forms and from many different sources, some of them strange and unexpected sources, but come it will.

The worker who renders this type of service may not always receive appropriate compensation from the person to whom he renders the service, but this habit will attract to him many opportunities for self-advancement, among them new and more favorable sources of employment. Thus his pay will come to him indirectly.

Ralph Waldo Emerson had this truth in mind when he said (in his essay on Compensation), "If you serve an ungrateful master, serve him the more. Put God in your debt. Every stroke shall be repaid. The longer the payment is withholden, the better for you; *for compound interest on compound interest* is *the rate and usage of this exchequer."*

Speaking once more in terms that seem paradoxical, be reminded that the most profitable time a man devotes to labor is that for which he receives no direct or immediate financial compensation. For it must be remembered that there are two forms of compensation available to the man who works for wages. One is the wages he receives in money. *The other is the skill he attains from his experiences;* a form of compensation which often exceeds monetary remuneration, for skill and experience are the worker's most important stock and trade through which he may promote himself to higher pay and greater responsibilities.

The attitude of the man who follows the habit of GOING THE EXTRA MILE is this: *He recognizes the truth that he is receiving pay for schooling himself for a better position and greater pay!*

This is an asset of which no worker can be cheated, no matter how selfish or greedy his immediate employer may be. It is the "compound interest on compound interest" which Emerson mentioned.

It was this very asset which enabled Charles M. Schwab to climb, step by step, from the lowly beginning as a day laborer to the highest position his employer had to offer; and it was this asset as well which brought Mr. Schwab a bonus of more than ten times the amount of his salary.

The million-dollar bonus which Mr. Schwab received was his payoff for having put his best efforts into every job he performed—a circumstance, let us remember, which he controlled entirely. And it was a circumstance that could not have happened if he had not followed the habit of GOING THE EXTRA MILE.

Mr. Carnegie had but little, if anything, to do with the circumstance. It was entirely out of his hands. Let us be generous by assuming that Mr. Carnegie paid off because he knew Mr. Schwab had earned the additional pay which had not been promised him. But the actual fact may be that he paid off rather than lose so valuable a man.

And here let us note that the man who follows the habit of GOING THE EXTRA MILE thereby places the purchaser of his services under a double obligation to pay a just compensation; one being an obligation based upon his sense of fairness, the other based on his sense of fear of losing a valuable man.

Thus we see that no matter how we view the principle of GOING THE EXTRA MILE, we come always to the same answer, that it pays "compound interest on compound interest" to all who follow the habit.

And we understand, too, what a great industrial leader had in mind when he said: *"Personally I am not so much interested in a forty hours per week minimum work law as I am in finding how I can crowd forty hours into a single day."*

The man who made that statement has an abundance of the Twelve Riches, and he freely admits that he attained his riches mainly by working his way up from a lowly beginning, applying the habit of GOING THE EXTRA MILE every step of the way.

It was this same man who said, "If I were compelled to risk my chances of success upon but one of the seventeen principles of achievement, I would, without hesitancy, stake everything on the principle of GOING THE EXTRA MILE."

Fortunately, however, he was not obligated to make this choice, for the seventeen principles of individual achievement are related to each other like the links of a chain. Therefore they blend into a medium of great power through coordination of their use. The omission of any one of these principles would weaken that power, just as the removal of a single link would weaken the chain.

The power of the seventeen principles consists not in the principles, but in their *application* and use! When the principles are applied they change the "chemistry" of the mind from a negative to a positive mental attitude. It is this positive mental attitude which attracts success by leading one to the attainment of the Twelve Riches.

Each of these principles represents, through its use, a definite, positive quality of the mind, and every circumstance that draws upon the power of thought calls for the use of some combination of the principles.

The seventeen principles may be likened to the twenty-six letters of the alphabet through the combinations of which all human thought may be expressed. The individual letters of the alphabet convey little or no meaning, but when they are combined into words they may express any thought one can conceive.

The seventeen principles are the "alphabet" of individual achievement, through which all talents may be expressed in their highest and most beneficial form, and they are the medium of expression which bas been responsible for the great American System of Free Enterprise, the American form of Government, and the American way of life in general. Hence they provide the means by which one may attain the great Master Key to Riches.

6
LOVE, THE TRUE EMANCIPATOR OF MANKIND!

Love is man's greatest experience. It brings one into communication with Infinite Intelligence.

When it is blended with the emotions of sex and romance it may lead one to the higher mountain-peaks of individual achievement through *creative vision.*

The emotions of love, sex and romance are the three sides of the eternal triangle of achievement known as genius. Nature creates geniuses through no other media.

Love is an outward expression of the spiritual nature of man.

Sex is purely biological, but it supplies the springs of action in all creative effort, from the humblest creature that crawls to the most profound of all creations, man.

When love and sex are combined with the spirit of romance the world may well rejoice, for these are the potentials of the great leaders who are the profound thinkers of the world.

Love makes all mankind akin!

It clears out selfishness, greed, jealousy, and envy, and makes right royal kings of the humblest of men. True greatness will never he found where love does not abide.

The love of which I speak must not be confused with the emotions of sex, for love in its highest and purest expression is a combination of the eternal triangle, *yet it is greater than any one of its three component parts.*

The love to which I refer is the "elan vital"—the life-giving factor, the spring of action—of all the creative endeavors which have lifted mankind to his present state of refinement and culture.

It is the one factor which draws a clear line of demarcation between man and all of the creatures of the earth below him. It is the one factor which determines for every man the amount of space he shall occupy in the hearts of his fellowmen.

Love is the solid foundation upon which the first of the Twelve Riches may be built, *a positive mental attitude,* and let us take heed that no man may ever become truly rich without it.

Love is the warp and the woof of all the remaining eleven riches. It embellishes all riches and gives them the quality of endurance, evidence of which may be revealed by cursory observation of all who have acquired material riches but have not acquired love.

The *habit* of GOING THE EXTRA MILE leads to the attainment of that spirit of love, for there can be no greater expression of love than for the benefit of others.

Emerson had the vision of the kind of love to which I refer when he said: *"Those who are capable of humility, of justice, of love, of aspiration, are already on the platform that commands the sciences and arts, speech and poetry, action and grace.* For who so dwells in this mortal beatitude does already anticipate those special powers which men prize so highly."

"The magnanimous know very well that they who give time, or money, or shelter, to the stranger—so it be done for love, and not for ostentation—do, as it were, put God under obligation to them, so perfect are the compensations of the universe. In some way the time they seem to lose, is redeemed and the pains they take, remunerate themselves. These men fan the flame of human love and raise the standard of civic virtue among mankind."

The great minds of every age have recognized love as the eternal elixir that binds the heart-wounds of mankind and makes men their brothers' keepers. One of the greatest minds this nation ever produced expressed his views on love in a classic that shall live as long as time endures. He said:

"Love is the only bow on life's dark cloud.

"It is the morning and the evening star.

"It shines upon the babe, and sheds its radiance on the quiet tomb.

"It is the mother of art, inspirer of poet, patriot and philosopher.

"It is the air and light of every heart-builder of every home, kindler of every fire on every hearth.

"It was the first to dream of immortality.

"It fills the world with melody—for music is the voice of love.

"Love is the magician, the enchanter, that changes worthless things to joy, and makes right royal kings and queens of common clay.

"It is the perfume of that wondrous flower, the heart, and without that sacred passion, that divine swoon, we are less than beasts; but with it, earth is heaven and we are gods.

"Love is transfiguration. It ennobles, purifies and glorifies.

"Love is a revelation, a creation. From love the world borrows its beauty and the heavans their glory.

"Without love all glory fades, the noble falls from life, art dies, music loses meaning and becomes mere motions of the air, and virtue ceases to exist."

If a man is truly great he will love all mankind!

He will love the good and the bad among all humanity. The good he will love with *pride* and *admiration* and *joy*. The bad he will love with *pity* and *sorrow*, for he will know, if he be truly great, that both good and bad qualities in man often are but the results of circumstances over which they have, because of their ignorance, little control.

If a man be truly great he will be compassionate, sympathetic and tolerant. When he is compelled to pass judgment upon others he will temper justice with tender mercy, throwing himself always on the side of the weak, the uninformed and the poverty-stricken.

Thus he will not only GO THE EXTRA MILE in a true spirit of Fellowship, but he will go *willingly and graciously.* And if the second mile be not enough he will go the third and the fourth, and as many additional miles as may be necessary.

Some Who Have Benefited by the Habit of GOING THE EXTRA MILE.

No one ever does anything voluntarily without a motive. Let us see if we can reveal a sound motive that will justify the habit of GOING THE EXTRA MILE by observing a few who have been inspired by it.

Many years ago an elderly lady was strolling through a Pittsburgh Department Store, obviously killing time. She passed counter after counter without anyone paying any attention to her. All of the clerks had spotted her as an idle "looker" who had no intention of buying. They made it a point of looking in another direction when she stopped at their counters.

What *costly business* this neglect turned out to be!

Finally the lady came to a counter that was attended by a young clerk who bowed politely and asked if he might serve her. "No," she replied, "I am just killing time, waiting for the rain to stop so I can go home."

"Very well, Madam," the young man smiled, "may I bring out a chair for you? And he brought it without waiting for her answer. After the rain slacked the young man took the old lady by the arm, escorted her to the street and bade her good-bye. As she left she asked him for his card.

Several months later the owner of the store received a letter, asking that this young man be sent to Scotland to take an order for the furnishings of a home. The owner of the store wrote back that he was sorry, but the young man did not work in the house furnishings department. However, he explained that he would be glad to send an "experienced man" to do the job.

Back came a reply that no one would do except this particular young man. The letters were signed by Andrew Carnegie, and the "house" he wanted furnished was Skibo Castle in Scotland. The elderly lady was Mr. Carnegie's mother. The young man was sent to Scotland. He received an order for several hundred thousand dollars worth of household furnishings, and with it a partnership in the store. He later became the owner of a half interest in the store.

Verily it pays to GO THE EXTRA MILE.

Some years ago the editor of *The Golden Rule Magazine* was invited to deliver a speech at the Palmer School in Davenport, Iowa. He accepted the invitation on his regular fee basis, which was $100.00 and traveling expenses.

While the editor was at the college he picked up enough editorial material for several stories for his magazine. After he had delivered the speech and was ready to return to Chicago he was told to turn in his expense account and receive his check.

He refused to accept any money for either his address or his expenses, explaining that he had already been paid adequately by the material he had procured for his magazine. He took the train back to Chicago feeling well repaid for his trip.

The following week he began to receive from Davenport many subscriptions to his magazine. By the end of the week he had received over $6,000.00 in cash subscriptions. Then followed a letter from Dr. Palmer explaining that the subscriptions had come from his students, who had been told of the editor's refusal to accept money which he had been promised and which he had earned.

During the following two years the students and the graduates of the Palmer School sent in more than $50,000.00 in subscriptions to *The Golden Rule Magazine*. The story was so impressive that it was written up in a magazine that had a circulation throughout the English-speaking world, and the subscriptions came from many different countries.

Thus, by rendering $100.00 worth of service without collecting, the editor had started the law of increasing returns to work in his behalf, and it yielded him a return of over 700 times his investment. The habit of GOING THE EXTRA MILE is no pipedream. It pays, and pays handsomely!

Moreover, it never forgets! Like other types of investments, the habit of GOING THE EXTRA MILE often yields dividends throughout one's lifetime.

Let us look at what happened when one neglected an opportunity to GO THE EXTRA MILE. Late one rainy afternoon an automobile "salesman" sat at his desk in the show room of the New York branch of an expensive automobile. The door opened and in walked a man jauntily swinging a cane.

The "salesman" looked up from the reading of the afternoon paper, took a swift glance at the newcomer, and immediately spotted him as another of those Broadway "window shoppers" who do nothing but waste one's valuable time. He went ahead with his newspaper, not taking the trouble to rise from his chair.

The man with the cane walked through the show room, looking first at one car and then another. Finally he walked over to where the "salesman" was sitting, teetered on his cane, and nonchalantly asked the price of three different automobiles on the floor. Without looking up from his newspaper, the "salesman" gave the prices and went on with his reading.

The man with the cane walked back over to the three automobiles at which he had been looking, kicked the tires of each one, then returned to the busy man at the desk and said, "Well, I hardly know whether I shall take this one, that one, the other one over there; or whether I shall buy all three."

The busy man at the desk responded with a sort of smirky, wiseacre smile, as much as to say, "Just as I thought!"

Then the man with the cane said, "Oh, I guess I will buy one of them. Send that one with the yellow wheels up to my house tomorrow. And, by the way, how much did you say it was?"

He took out his checkbook, wrote out a check, handed it to the "salesman," and walked out. When the "salesman" saw the name on the check, he turned fourteen different shades of pink and almost swooned from heart failure. The man who signed the check was Harry Payne Whitney, and the "salesman" knew that if he had only taken the time to get up from his chair he might have sold all three automobiles without any effort.

Withholding anything short of the best service of which one is capable is costly business—a fact which many have learned too late.

The right of personal initiative is not worth much to the fellow who is too indifferent or too lazy to exercise it. Many people are in this class without recognizing the reason they never accumulate riches.

Over forty years ago a young salesman in a hardware store

observed that the store had a lot of odds and ends which were out of date and not selling. Having time on his hands, he rigged up a special table in the middle of the store. He loaded it with some of this unsalable merchandise, marking it at the bargain price of a dime an article. To his surprise and that of the owner of the store, the gadgets sold like hot cakes.

Out of that experience grew the great F. W. Woolworth Five and Ten Cent chain store system. The young man who stumbled upon the idea by GOING THE EXTRA MILE was Frank W. Woolworth. That idea yielded him a fortune estimated at more than $70,000,000.00. Moreover, the same idea made several other persons rich, and applications of the idea are at the heart of many of the more profitable merchandising systems in America.

No one told young Woolworth to exercise his right to personal initiative. No one paid him for doing so; yet his action led to ever-increasing returns for his efforts. Once he put the idea into practice, increasing returns nearly ran him down.

There is something about this habit of doing more than one is paid for which works in one's behalf even while he sleeps. Once it begins to work, it piles up riches so fast that it seems like queer magic which, like Aladdin's Lamp, draws to one's aid an army of genii which come laden with bags of gold.

Some thirty odd years ago a young newspaper reporter was sent to interview Andrew Carnegie for the purpose of writing a story about his stupendous achievements in the industrial world.

During the interview Mr. Carnegie let drop a hint that if the reporter had the vision to GO THE EXTRA MILE to the tune of about twenty years of unprofitable labor, he might do a job that would make him richer by far than the great steel master.

The reporter accepted that challenge and went to work. After twenty years of "unprofitable" labor, almost to the day, the reporter gave the world the net results of what he had learned about Andrew Carnegie's methods of accumulating riches, as well as what he had learned of the methods of some five hundred other successful men who had accumulated great riches by the simple expedient of GOING THE EXTRA MILE.

Today that information is being circulated in practically every English-speaking country of the world, where it is serving many millions of people who wish to learn the secret of achievement through the exercise of personal initiative. It has been translated into many foreign languages. It is designed to help those who are not afraid of doing more than they are paid for and who wish to convert their share of American opportunity into some form of riches.

The compensation this former newspaper reporter is now receiving for his twenty years of "unprofitable" labor affords him riches sufficient for all his needs. Among the greatest of these are peace of mind, priceless friendships throughout the world, and that form of enduring happiness which is the lot of every man who has found his work, likes it, and is busily engaged in performing it.

Some thirty years ago Charles M. Schwab's private railroad car was switched onto the siding at his steel plant in Pennsylvania. It was a cold, frosty morning. As he alighted from the car he was met by a young man with a stenographer's notebook in his hands who hurriedly explained that he was a stenographer in the general office of the steel company, and that he had come down to meet the car to see if Mr. Schwab needed any letters written, or any telegrams sent.

"Who asked you to meet me?" Mr. Schwab queried. "No one," the young man replied. "I saw the telegram coming through announcing your arrival, so I came down to meet you, hoping I might be of some service."

Think of that! He came down hoping he might be able to find something to do for which he was not paid. And he came on his own initiative without being told.

Mr. Schwab thanked him politely for his thoughtfulness, but said he had no need for a stenographer at the moment. After carefully noting the young man's name, he sent the lad back to his work.

That night, when the private car was hitched to the night train for its return to New York City it carried the young stenographer. He had been assigned, at Mr. Schwab's request, for service in New York as one of the steel magnate's assistants. The lad's name was Williams. He remained in Mr. Schwab's services for several years, during which opportunity after opportunity for promotion came to him unsolicited.

It is peculiar how opportunities have a way of trailing the people who make it their business to GO THE EXTRA MILE, but they do very definitely. Finally an opportunity came to young Williams which he could not ignore. He was made president and a large stockholder in one of the largest drug concerns in the United States—a job which yielded him a fortune far greater than his needs.

This incident is clear evidence of what can happen, and of what has been happening all down through the years under the American way of life.

The habit of GOING THE EXTRA MILE is one that does not confine its rewards to wage earners. It works as well for an employer as it does for an employee, as one merchant whom we knew quite well gratefully testified.

His name was Arthur Nash. His business was merchant tailoring. Some years ago Mr. Nash found his business just one step ahead of the sheriff. The first World War and other conditions over which he seemed to have no control had brought him to the brink of financial ruin.

One of his most serious handicaps was that his employees had caught his spirit of defeatism and they expressed it in their work by slowing down and becoming disgruntled. His situation became desperate. Something had to be done, and it had to be done quickly if he were to continue in business.

Out of sheer desperation he called his employees together and told them the condition. While he was speaking, an idea occurred to him. He said he had been reading a story in *The Golden Rule Magazine* which told how its editor had GONE THE EXTRA MILE by rendering service for which he refused to accept pay, only to be voluntarily rewarded with more than $6,000.00 worth of subscriptions to his magazine.

He wound up by suggesting that if he and all of his employees caught that spirit and began to GO THE EXTRA MILE they might save the business.

He promised his employees that if they would join with him in an experiment he would endeavor to carry on the business, with the understanding that everyone would forget wages, forget working hours, pitch in and do his best, and take chances on receiving pay for work. If the business could be made to pay every employee would receive back wages with a bonus thrown in for good measure.

The employees liked the idea and agreed to give it a trial. The next day they began to come in with their meager savings, which they voluntarily loaned to Mr. Nash.

Everyone went to work with a new spirit, and the business began to show signs of new life. Very soon it was back on a paying basis. Then it began to prosper as it had never prospered before.

Ten years later the business had made Mr. Nash rich. The employees were more prosperous than they had ever been, and everyone was happy.

Arthur Nash passed on, but today the business continues as one of the more successful merchant tailoring businesses of America.

The employees took over the business when Mr. Nash laid

it down. Ask any one of them what he thinks of this business of GOING THE EXTRA MILE, and you will get the answer!

Moreover, talk with one of the Nash salesmen, wherever you meet one, and observe his spirit of enthusiasm and his self-reliance. When this "extra mile" stimulant once gets into a man's mind, he becomes a different sort of person. The outlook on the world appears different to him, and he appears different, because he is different.

Here is the appropriate place to remind you of an important thing about the habit of GOING THE EXTRA MILE by doing more than one is paid for. It is the strange influence which it has on the man who does it. The greatest benefit from this habit does not come to those to whom the service is rendered. It comes to the one who renders the service, in the form of a changed "mental attitude," which gives him more influence with other people, more self-reliance, greater initiative, more enthusiasm, more vision and definiteness of purpose. All of these are qualities of successful achievement.

"Do the thing and you shall have the power," said Emerson. Ah yes, *the power*! What can a man do in our world without power? But it must be the type of power which attracts other people instead of repelling them. It must be a form of power which gains momentum from the *law* of *increasing returns* through the operation of which one's acts and deeds come back to him greatly multiplied.

You who work for wages should learn more about this sowing and reaping business. Then you would understand why no man can go on forever sowing the seed of inadequate service and reaping a harvest of full-grown pay. You would know that there must come a halt to the habit of demanding a full day's pay for a poor day's work.

And you who do not work for wages, but who wish to get more of the better things of life! Let us have a word with you.

Why do you not become wise and start getting what you wish the easy and sure way? Yes, there is an easy and a sure way to promote one's self into whatever he wants from life, and its secret becomes known to every person who makes it his business to GO THE EXTRA MILE. The secret can be uncovered in no other manner, for *it is wrapped up in that extra mile.*

The pot of gold at the "end of the rainbow" is not a mere fairy tale! The end of that *extra mile* is the spot where the rainbow ends, and that is where the pot of gold is hidden.

Few people ever catch up with the "end of the rainbow." When one gets to where he thought the rainbow ended he finds it is still far in the distance. The trouble with most of us is that we do not know how to follow rainbows. Those who know the secret know that the end of the rainbow can be reached only by GOING THE EXTRA MILE.

Late one afternoon, some twenty-five years ago, William C. Durant, the founder of General Motors, walked into his bank after banking hours, and asked for some favor which in the ordinary course of business should have been requested during banking hours.

The man who granted the favor was Carol Downes, an under official of the bank. He not only served Mr. Durant with efficiency, but he went the Extra Mile and *added courtesy to the service.* He made Mr. Durant feel that it was a real pleasure to serve him. The incident seemed trivial, and of itself it was of little importance. Unknown to Mr. Downes, this courtesy was destined to have repercussions of a far-reaching nature.

The next day Mr. Durant asked Downes to come to his office. That visit led to the offer of a position which Downes accepted. He was given a desk in a general office where nearly a hundred other people worked, and he was notified that the office hours were from 8:30 a.m. to 5:30 p.m. His salary to begin with was modest.

At the end of the first day, when the gong rang announcing the close of the day's work, Downes noticed that everyone grabbed his hat and coat and made a rush for the door. He sat still, waiting for the others to leave the office. After they had gone he remained at his desk, pondering in his own mind the cause of the great haste everyone had shown to get away on the very second of quitting time.

Fifteen minutes later Mr. Durant opened the door of his private office, saw Downes still at his desk, and asked Downes whether he understood that he was privileged to stop work at 5:30.

"Oh yes," Downes replied, "but I did not wish to be run over in the rush." Then he asked if he could be of any service to Mr. Durant. He was told he might find a pencil for the motor magnate. He got the pencil, ran it through the pencil sharpener and took it to Mr. Durant. Mr. Durant thanked him and said "good night."

The next day at quitting time Downes remained at his desk again after the "rush" was over. This time he waited with purpose aforethought. In a little while Mr. Durant came out of his private office and asked again if Downes did not understand that 5:30 was the time for closing.

"Yes," Downes smiled, "I understand it is quitting time for the others, but I have heard no one say that I have to leave the office when the day is officially closed, so I chose to remain here with the hope that I might be of some slight service to you."

"What an unusual *hope*," Durant exclaimed. "Where did you get the *idea*?

"I got it from the scene I witness here at closing time every day," Downes replied. Mr. Durant grunted some reply which Downes did not hear distinctly and returned to his office.

From then on Downes always remained at his desk after closing time until he saw Mr. Durant leave for the day. He was not paid to remain over time. No one told him to do it. No one promised him anything for remaining, and as far as the casual observer might know, he *was wasting his time.*

Several months later Downes was called into Mr. Durant's office and informed that he had been chosen to go out to a new plant that had been purchased recently to supervise the installation of the plant machinery. Imagine that! A former bank official becoming a machinery expert in a few months.

Without quibbling, Downes accepted the assignment and went on his way. He did not say, "Why, Mr. Durant, I know nothing about the installation of machinery." He did not say, "That's not my job," or "I'm not paid to install machinery." No, he went to work and did what was requested of him. Moreover, he went at the job with a pleasant "mental attitude."

Three months later the job was completed. It was done so well that Mr. Durant called Downes into his office and asked him where he learned about machinery. "Oh," Downes explained, "I never learned, Mr. Durant. I merely looked around, found men who knew how to get the job done, put them to work, and they did it."

"Splendid!" Mr. Durant exclaimed. "There are two types of men who are valuable. One is the fellow who can do something and do it well, without complaining that he is being overworked. The other is the fellow who can get other people to do things well, without complaining. You are both types wrapped into one package."

Downes thanked him for the compliment and turned to go.

"Wait a moment," Durant requested. "I forgot to tell you that you are the new manager of the plant you have installed, and your salary to start with is $50,000.00 a year."

The following ten years of association with Mr. Durant was worth between ten and twelve million dollars to Carol Downes. He became an intimate advisor of the motor king and made himself rich as a result.

The main trouble with so many of us is that we see men who have "arrived" and we weigh them in the hour of their triumph without taking the trouble to find out how or why they "arrived."

There is nothing very dramatic about the story of Carol Downes. The incidents mentioned occurred during the day's business, without even a passing notice by the average person who worked along with Downes. And we doubt not that many of these fellow workers envied him because they believed he had been favored by Mr. Durant, through some sort of pull or luck, or whatever it is that men who do not succeed use as an excuse to explain their own lack of progress.

Well, to be candid, Downes did have an inside "pull" with Mr. Durant!

He created that "pull" on his own initiative.

He created it by GOING THE EXTRA MILE in a matter as trivial as that of placing a neat point on a pencil when nothing was requested except a plain pencil.

He created it by remaining at his desk "with the hope" that he might be of service to his employer after the "rush" was over at 5:30 each evening.

He created it by using his right of personal initiative by finding men who understood how to install machinery instead of asking Durant where or how to find such men.

Trace down these incidents step by step and you will find that Downes' success was due solely to his own initiative. Moreover, the story consists of a series of little tasks well performed, in the right "mental attitude."

Perhaps there were a hundred other men working for Mr. Durant who could have done as well as Downes, but the trouble with them was that they were searching for the "end of the rainbow" by running away from it in the 5:30 rush each afternoon.

Long years afterward a friend asked Carol Downes how he got his opportunity with Mr. Durant. "Oh," he modestly replied,

"I just made it my business to get in his way, so he could see me. When he looked around, wanting some little service, he called on me because I was the only one in sight. In time he got into the habit of calling on me."

There you have it! Mr. Durant "got into the habit" of calling on Downes. Moreover, he found that Downes could and would assume responsibilities by GOING THE EXTRA MILE.

What a pity that all of the American people do not catch something of this spirit of assuming greater responsibilities. What a pity that more of us do not begin speaking more of our "privileges" under the American way of life, and less of the lack of opportunities in America.

Is there a man living in America today who would seriously claim that Carol Downes would have been better off if he had been forced, by law, to join the mad rush and quit his work at 5:30 in the afternoon? If he had done so, he would have received the standard wages for the sort of work he performed, but nothing more. Why should he have received more?

His destiny was in his own hands. It was wrapped up in this one lone privilege which should be the privilege of every American citizen: the right of personal initiative through the exercise of which he made it a habit always to GO THE EXTRA MILE. That tells the whole story. There is no other secret to Downes' success. He admits it, and everyone familiar with the circumstances of his promotion from poverty to riches knows it.

There is one thing no one seems to know: Why are there so few men who, like Carol Downes, discover the power implicit in doing more than one is paid for? It has in it the seed of all great achievement. It is the secret of all noteworthy success, and yet it is so little understood that most people look upon it as some clever trick with which employers try to get more work out of their employees.

This spirit of indifference toward the habit of GOING THE

EXTRA MILE was dramatically expressed by a "wise acre," who once applied to Henry Ford for a job. Mr. Ford questioned the man about his experience, his habits, and other routine matters, and was satisfied with the replies.

Then he asked, "How much money do you want for your services?" The man was evasive on this point, so Mr. Ford finally said, "Well, suppose you start in and show us what you can do, *and we will pay you all you are worth* after we have tried you out." Mr. Wiseacre exclaimed, "I'm getting more than that where I am now employed." And we doubt not that he told the truth.

That explains precisely why so many people do not get ahead in life. They are "getting more than they are worth" where they are, and they never learn how to get ahead by becoming worth more!

Just after the end of the Spanish-American War, Elbert Hubbard wrote a story entitled A Message to Garcia. He told briefly how President William McKinley commissioned a young soldier by the name of Rowan to carry a message from the United States Government to Garcia, the Rebel Chieftain, whose exact whereabouts were not known.

The young soldier took the message, made his way through the fastnesses of the Cuban jungle, finally found Garcia, and delivered the note to him. That was all there was to the story—just a private soldier carrying out his orders under difficulties, and getting the job done without coming back with an excuse.

The story fired imaginations and spread all over the world. The simple act of a man doing what he was told, and doing it well, became news of the first magnitude. A Message to Garcia was printed in booklet form and the sales reached an all-time high for such publications, amounting to more than ten million copies. This one story made Elbert Hubbard famous, to say nothing of helping to make him rich.

The story was translated into several foreign languages. The

Japanese Government had it printed and distributed to every Japanese soldier during the Japanese-Russian war. The Pennsylvania Railroad Company presented a copy of it to each of their thousands of employees. The big life insurance companies of America presented it to their salesmen.

Long after Elbert Hubbard went down on the ill-fated *Lusitania* in 1917, A Message to Garcia continued as a bestseller throughout America.

The story was popular because it had in it something of the magic power that belongs to the man who does something, and does it well.

The whole world is clamoring for such men. They are needed and wanted in every walk of life. American Industry has always had princely berths for men who can and will assume responsibilities and who get the job done in the right "mental attitude," by GOING THE EXTRA MILE.

Andrew Carnegie lifted no fewer than forty such men from the lowly station of day laborers to millionaires. He understood the value of men who were willing to GO THE EXTRA MILE. Wherever he found such a man, he brought "his find" into the inner circle of his business and gave him an opportunity to earn "all he was worth."

Charles M. Schwab was one of those who gained the favor of the steel master by the simple expedient of GOING THE EXTRA MILE. He began work with Carnegie in the humble capacity of a stake driver at day wages. But step-by-step he climbed to the top and became Carnegie's right-hand man, with the result that some years his income amounted to more than a million dollars in the form of a bonus.

People do things or refrain from doing them because of a motive. The soundest of motives for the habit of GOING THE EXTRA MILE is the fact that it yields enduring dividends, in ways too numerous to mention, to all who follow the habit.

No one has ever been known to achieve permanent success without doing more than he was paid for. The practice has its counterpart in the laws of nature. It has back of it an impressive array of evidence as to its soundness, supplied by those who have made it a practice of GOING THE EXTRA MILE. It is based on common sense and justice.

The best of all methods of testing the soundness of this principle is that of putting it to work as a part of one's daily habits. Some truths we can learn only through our own experience.

Americans want greater individual shares of the vast resources of this country. That is a healthy desire. The wealth is here in abundance, but let us stop this foolish attempt to get it the wrong way. Let us get our wealth by giving something of value in return for it. That is how Andrew Carnegie, Thomas A. Edison, Henry Ford, and many others of their type have acquired their wealth.

We know the rules by which success is attained. Let us appropriate these rules and use them intelligently, thereby acquiring the personal riches we demand, and adding to the wealth of the nation as well.

Some will say, "I am already doing more than I am paid for, but my employer is so selfish and greedy he will not recognize the sort of service I am rendering." We all know there are greedy men who desire more service than that for which they are willing to pay.

Selfish employers are like pieces of clay in the hands of a potter. Through their greed they can be induced to reward the man who renders them more service than he is paid to render.

Greedy employers do not wish to lose the services of one who makes a habit of GOING THE EXTRA MILE. They know the value of such employees. Here, then, is the crowbar and the fulcrum with which employers can be pried loose from their greed.

Any clever man will know how to use this crowbar, not by withholding the quality or quantity of service he renders, *but by increasing it!*

The clever salesman of his personal services can manipulate a greedy purchaser of his services as easily as a smart woman can influence the man of her choice. The effective technique is similar to that used by clever women in managing men.

The clever man will make it his business to become indispensable to a greedy employer by doing more work and better work than any other employee. Greedy employers will "give their eye teeth" before parting with such a man. Thus the alleged greed of employers becomes a great asset to the man who follows the habit of GOING THE EXTRA MILE.

We have seen this technique applied at least a hundred times as a means of manipulating greedy employers through the use of their own weakness. Not once have we seen it fail to work!

On some occasions the greedy employer failed to move as quickly as expected, but that proved to be his hard luck, because his employee attracted the attention of a competitive employer who made a bid for the services of the employee and secured them.

There is no way to cheat the man who follows the habit of GOING THE EXTRA MILE. If he does not get proper recognition from one source, it comes voluntarily from some other source— usually when it is least expected. It always comes if a man does more than he is paid for.

The man who GOES THE EXTRA MILE and does it in the right kind of "mental attitude" never spends time looking for a job. He does not have to, for the job is always looking for him. Depressions may come and go; business may be good or poor; the country may be at war or at peace; but the man who renders more service and better service than he is paid for becomes indispensable to someone and thereby insures himself against unemployment.

High wages and indispensability are twin-sisters. They always have been and always will be!

The man who is smart enough to make himself indispensable is smart enough to keep himself continuously employed, and at wages which not even the most greedy labor leader would ask.

Henry Ford understands the value of indispensability. He also knows the value of GOING THE EXTRA MILE. That is why 30 years ago he voluntarily raised the wages of his workers to an all-time high minimum daily wage. By that act he did for his employees something that no one forced him to do, and it was a wise move because it insured him against labor troubles for more than a quarter of a century.

Andrew Carnegie understood the value of GOING THE EXTRA MILE. By putting that rule to work he piled up a fortune of more than half a billion dollars.

By some he was accused of being greedy, but he was never accused of being weak in the management of men. If he were greedy, he made wise use of his deficiency by paying some of his men (those who had the good judgment to make themselves indispensable to him by GOING THE EXTRA MILE) as much as a million dollars a year in bonuses.

His policy was to encourage men to become indispensable to him by doing more than they were paid for—a privilege that was always available to his humblest worker—and then insuring himself against their becoming his rivals in business by paying them all or more than they were actually worth.

We do not know what others may think of this principle of doing more than one is paid for, but as for ourselves, we prefer to go along with such men as Henry Ford and Andrew Carnegie, and emulate them instead of criticizing them.

By their recognition of the principle of GOING THE EXTRA MILE these two men added many billions of dollars of additional wealth to the nation, provided profitable employment to many millions of men, and piled up huge fortunes for their own use.

Who among us could have done better? Who among us has a better plan than theirs? No, most of us are not as smart as were Henry Ford and Andrew Carnegie. Instead of emulating their examples and making it our business to GO THE EXTRA MILE, most of us, when asked to do something for which we are not paid, display our brand of wisdom by saying, "I am not paid to do that." Thus do we brand ourselves for what we are.

Time, the great interpreter which stands on the sidelines of life and brands us at our worth, writes "Poor Fool" across our foreheads as we march on, while the Henry Fords and the Andrew Carnegies step out of the line, set their own price tag on themselves, and find their fellowmen ready to pay any price they demand for their services.

Most men spend their lives searching for the "breaks," waiting for opportunities to overtake them, depending upon "luck" to provide them with their needs, but never come within sight of their goal because they have no definite goal. Therefore they have no *motive* to inspire them to form the habit of GOING THE EXTRA MILE. They never recognize:

> *"The Worldly Hope men set their Hearts upon*
> *Turns Ashes-or it prospers; and anon,*
> *Like Snow upon the Desert's dusty face*
> *Lighting a little Hour or two-is gone."*

Their haste becomes waste! For they go 'round and 'round, like goldfish in a bowl, coming back always to the place from whence they started; coming back empty-handed and disappointed.

Riches may be attained by appointment only; by the choice of a definite goal and a definite plan for attaining it; also by the selection of a definite starting point from which to take off.

But, let no one make the mistake of assuming that the habit of GOING THE EXTRA MILE pays off only in terms of material riches. The habit definitely helps one to tap the source of spiritual riches, and to draw upon that source for every human need.

THE REVEALING STORY OF EDWARD CHOATE

Some men who are smart, and others who are wise, have discovered the way to riches by the deliberate application of the principle of GOING THE EXTRA MILE for pecuniary gain.

However, those who are truly wise recognize that the greatest payoff through this principle comes in terms of friendships which endure throughout life, in harmonious human relationships, in a labor of love, in the capacity to understand people, in a willingness to share one's blessings with others, all of which are among the Twelve Riches of Life.

Edward Choate is one who has recognized this truth and has found the Master Key to Riches. His home is in Los Angeles, California, and his business is that of selling life insurance.

At the outset of his career as a life insurance salesman he made a modest living from his efforts, but he broke no records in that field. Through an unfortunate business venture he lost all of his money and found himself at the bottom of the ladder, and was forced to make a new start.

I said "an unfortunate business venture," but perhaps I should have said "a fortunate business venture," for his loss influenced him to stop, look, listen, THINK, and to meditate concerning the fates of men which seem to lift some to high places of achievement but condemn others to temporary defeat or permanent failure.

Through his meditations he became a student of the philosophy of individual achievement which Andrew Carnegie helped to provide through his colorful career. When Mr. Choate reached the lesson on GOING THE EXTRA MILE he was awakened by a keen sense of understanding he had never before experienced, and he recognized that the loss of material riches may lead one to the source of greater riches, consisting of one's spiritual forces.

With this discovery Mr. Choate began to appropriate, one by one, the Twelve Riches of Life, beginning at the head of the list by the development *of positive mental attitude.*

For the time being he ceased to think about the amount of life insurance he might sell, and began to look around for opportunities to be of service to others who were burdened with problems they could not solve.

His first opportunity came when he discovered a young man out in the deserts of California who had failed in a mining venture and was facing starvation. He took the young man into his home, fed him, encouraged him and kept him in his home until he found a good position for him.

In thus casting himself for the role of the good Samaritan, Mr. Choate had no thought of pecuniary gain, for it was obvious that a poverty-stricken, broken-spirited boy might never become a prospective purchaser of life insurance. Then other opportunities to help the less fortunate began to reveal themselves so rapidly that it seemed as if Mr. Choate had made of himself a magnet which attracted only those with difficult problems to be solved.

But the appearance was deceiving, for he was only passing through a testing period by which he might demonstrate his sincerity of purpose in helping others. A period, let us not forget, which everyone who applies the principle of GOING THE EXTRA MILE must experience in one way or another.

Then the scene shifted, and the affairs of Edward Choate began to take a turn he probably had not expected. His life insurance sales began to mount higher and higher, until at last they had reached an all-time high level. And miracle of miracles, one of the largest policies he had ever written up to that time was sold to the employer of the young man of the desert whom he had befriended. The sale was made without Mr. Choate's solicitation.

Other sales began to come his way in the same manner, until he was actually selling more insurance, without any strenuous effort, than he had ever sold previously by the hardest kind of labor.

Moreover, he had tapped a field of life insurance salesmanship in which the policies he sold were of large amounts. Men of great responsibilities and extensive financial affairs began to send for him to counsel them in connection with their life insurance problems.

His business grew until it brought him that goal which is so greatly coveted by all life insurance men—Life Membership in the Million Dollar Round Table. Such a distinction is attained only by those who sell a minimum of a million dollars a year in insurance for three consecutive years.

There had been only fifty-seven men to reach this outstanding achievement during the twenty-six-year period prior to 1943, when this information was revealed.

So, in seeking spiritual riches Edward Choate also found material riches; found them in greater abundance than he had ever anticipated. Six brief years after he had begun to cast himself for the role of the good Samaritan, Mr. Choate wrote more than two million dollars of life insurance during the first four months of the year.

The story of his achievements began to spread throughout the nation. It brought him invitations to speak before life insurance conventions, for other life insurance salesmen desired to know how he had managed to lift himself to so enviable a position in that profession.

He told them! And quite contrary to the usual practice among men who have attained success in the upper brackets of achievement, he revealed the humility of heart by which he is inspired, frankly admitting that his achievements were the result of the application of the philosophy of others.

The average man who is successful has a tendency to try to convey the impression that his success is due to his own smartness or wisdom, but very seldom does he frankly give credit to his benefactors.

What a pity there are not more Edward Choates in the world!

For it is obvious to all who think accurately that no man ever attains a high degree of enduring success without the friendly cooperation of others; nor does any man ever attain enduring success without helping others.

Edward Choate is as rich in material values as he needs to be. He is far richer in spiritual values, for he has discovered, appropriated and made intelligent use of all of the Twelve Riches of Life, of which money is the last *and the least in importance.*

7

THE MASTER MIND

Definition: An alliance of two or more minds, blended in a spirit of perfect harmony and cooperating for the attainment of a definite purpose.

Note well the definition of this principle, for it carries a meaning which provides the key to the attainment of great personal power.

The Master Mind principle is the basis of all great achievements, the foundation stone of major importance in all human progress, whether it be individual progress or collective progress.

The key to its power may be found in the word "harmony"!

Without that element collective effort may constitute cooperation, but it will lack the power which harmony provides through coordination of effort.

The tenets of major importance in connection with the Master Mind principle are these:

1. Premise 1: The Master Mind principle is the medium through which one may procure the full

benefit of the experience, training, education, specialized knowledge and native ability of others, just as completely as if their minds were one's own.

2. Premise 2: An alliance of two or more minds, in a spirit of perfect harmony for the attainment of a definite purpose, stimulates each individual mind with a high degree of inspiration, and may become that state of mind known as Faith! (A slight idea of this stimulation and its power is experienced in the relationship of close friendship and in the relationship of love.)

3. Premise 3: Every human brain is both a broadcasting station and a receiving station for the expression of the vibrations of thought, and the stimulating effect of the Master Mind principle stimulates action of thought, through what is commonly known as telepathy, operating through the sixth sense. In this manner many business and professional alliances are translated into reality, and seldom has anyone ever attained a high station or enduring power without the application of the Master Mind principle through which he secured the benefit of other minds.

   This fact alone is sufficient evidence of the soundness and the importance of the Master Mind principle, and it is a fact which anyone may observe without straining his powers of observation or over-taxing his credulity.

4. Premise 4: The Master Mind principle, when actively applied, has the effect of connecting one with the subconscious section of the mind, and

the subconscious sections of the minds of his allies, a fact which may explain many of the seemingly miraculous results obtained through the
Master Mind.

5. Premise 5: The more important human relationships in connection with which one may apply
beneficially the Master Mind principle are
these:

(a) In marriage
(b) In religion
(c) In connection with one's occupation, profession or calling.

The Master Mind principle made it possible for Thomas A.
Edison to become a great inventor despite his lack of education
and his lack of knowledge of the sciences with which he had to
work—a circumstance which offers hope to all who erroneously
believe themselves to be seriously handicapped by the lack of a
formal education.

With the aid of the Master Mind principle one may understand the history and the structure of this earth on which we live
through the knowledge of skilled geologists.

Through the knowledge and experience of the chemist one
may make practical use of chemistry without being a trained
chemist.

With the aid of scientists, technicians, physicists and practical mechanics one may become a successful inventor without
personal training in any of these fields, as did Mr. Edison.

There are two general types of Master Mind alliances, viz:

1. Alliance, for purely social or personal reasons,
with one's relatives, religious advisors and
friends, where no material gain or objective is

   sought. *The most important of this type of alliance is*
   that of man and wife.
 2. Alliances for business, professional and economic
   advancement, consisting of individuals who
   have a personal motive in connection with the
   object of the alliance.

Now let us consider some of the more important examples of power that have been attained by the application of the Master Mind.

The American form of Government, as it was originally written into the Constitution of the United States, should have first analysis because it is one form of power which vitally affects every citizen of our country, and to a large degree affects the entire world.

Our country is noted for three obvious facts:

 1. It is the richest country of the world.
 2. It is the most powerful nation of the world.
 3. It provides its citizens with more personal freedom than does any other nation.

Riches, freedom and power! What an awe-inspiring combination of realities!

The source of these benefits is not difficult to determine, for it centers in the Constitution of our country and in the American System of Free Enterprise, these having been so harmoniously coordinated that they have provided the people with both spiritual and economic power, such as the world has never before witnessed.

Our form of government is a stupendous Master Mind alliance made up of the harmonious relationship of all the people of the nation, functioning through forty-eight separate groups known as states. (We are here considering the original pattern of our government, as it was provided by the Constitution, and the original relationship of harmony which existed between our government and our System of Free Enterprise, taking no account of the temporary disruption of that harmony, for the reason that *it is only temporary!*)

The central core of our American Master Mind is easily discernible by breaking down our form of government and examining its component parts, all of which are under the direct control of a majority of the people.

These parts are:
1. The executive branch of our government (maintained by a President)
2. The judiciary branch (maintained by the Supreme Court)
3. The legislative branch (maintained by the two Houses of Congress)

Our Constitution has been so wisely constructed that the power behind all three of these branches of government is held by the people. It is a power of which the people cannot be deprived *except by their own neglect to use it!*

Our political power is expressed through our government.

Our economic power is maintained and expressed through our System of Free Enterprise.

And the sum total of the power of these two is always in exact ratio to the degree of *harmony with which the two are coordinated!*

The power thus attained *is the property* of *all the people!*

It is this power which has provided the people with the highest standard of living that civilization has yet evolved, and which has made our nation truly the richest and the freest and the most powerful nation of the world.

We speak of this power as "THE AMERICAN WAY OF LIFE"!

It was this way of life and our desire to maintain it which brought about the consolidation of our forces, both economic and spiritual, in a war that threatened the destruction of civilization as well as our way of life.

The future of mankind may have been determined by the application of our American Master Mind, for it is obvious that ours was the balance of power which turned the tide of war in favor of freedom for all mankind.

Another illustration of the Master Mind applied to industry may be found in the great American Systems of Transportation and Communications. Those who manage our railroads and our airlines, our telephone and telegraph systems, have established a service which has never been equaled in any other country. Their efficiency and the resultant power consist entirely in their application of the Master Mind principle or harmonious coordination of effort.

Still another example of power attained through the Master Mind principle may be found by observing the relationship of our military forces—our Armies, our Navies and our Air Forces. Here, as elsewhere, the keystone to the arch of our power has been harmonious coordination of effort.

The modern football team is an excellent example of power attained through harmony of effort.

The great American System of Chain Store merchandising is still another example of economic power attained through the Master Mind principle.

And every successful industry is the result of application of the Master Mind. The American System of Free Enterprise in its entirety is a marvelous illustration of economic power produced by friendly, harmonious coordination of effort.

Andrew Carnegie frankly admitted that his entire fortune

was accumulated by the application of this principle, through which he brought together one of the greatest industrial organizations this nation has ever witnessed. And let it be remembered that his Master Mind consisted of his entire organization of associate workers, from the humblest to the greatest.

The key men of his Master Mind, his managerial and supervisory staff, were recruited from the rank and file of his workers, and he understood the Master Mind principle so thoroughly that he inspired every worker to make the most of his opportunity by aiming for a higher position.

The man to whom he entrusted the organization of the philosophy of individual achievement had the benefit, through Mr. Carnegie's assistance, of the greatest Master Mind alliance that ever collaborated in such an undertaking.

It consisted of more than five hundred leaders of industry of Mr. Carnegie's caliber, and the alliance continued over a period of twenty years, during which every man in the alliance provided the author of the philosophy with the full benefits of his entire industrial experience.

This alliance provided the world with an astounding demonstration of the power which may be attained through the first three principles of the philosophy: (1) The Habit of GOING THE EXTRA MILE, (2) Definiteness of Purpose, and (3) the Master Mind.

The definite purpose which inspired this work was that of providing all people with a workable philosophy based on the experiences of those who had demonstrated material success. It was an unselfish purpose because it was directed entirely for the benefit of others.

The men behind the purpose were already successful, but they recognized the advantages of sharing their knowledge, and they recognized also the disadvantages of an economic system which benefits a few at the expense of many.

And each man in that alliance demonstrated his understanding of the principle of GOING THE EXTRA MILE; demonstrated it by contributing his time and experience, without money and without price, in order that the people of this nation might enjoy the benefits of a philosophy he knew had been the very foundation of the great American way of life—a foundation which had made ours the richest and the freest country of the world.

In order that we may get a comprehensive understanding of the power and the benefits of this particular Master Mind alliance, imagine what it might mean to you if you had the privilege of choosing five hundred American leaders of industry who would consent to serve as your guides and your instructors for a period of twenty years, without cost or obligation.

You would have, through the collaboration of so large a group of successful men, the full benefit of all the knowledge and experience which have grown out of the development of the American System of Free Enterprise.

If you made the best use of this knowledge your success would be inevitable!

Of course you cannot go to school to these men, for alas! most of them have passed on. But fortunately you may have the full benefit of the riches they laid up for you through the seventeen principles of this philosophy, *and the cost will consist in* the time and thought you devote to putting it to use!

The Master Mind principle is not the exclusive property of the rich and the powerful, but it is the means of major importance by which men may attain desirable ends.

The humblest person may benefit from this principle by forming a harmonious alliance with anyone of their choice.

The most profound, and perhaps the most beneficial application of this principle that anyone may make is the Master Mind alliance in marriage, provided the motive behind that alliance is Love!

This sort of alliance not only coordinates their minds, but it also blends the spiritual qualities of their souls.

The benefits of such an alliance not only bring joy and happiness, but they profoundly bless their children with sound character, and endow them with the fundamentals of a successful life.

Let us turn back the pages of time for nearly half a century and have a look at a family whose Master Mind relationship resulted in the building of a great industrial empire which now gives profitable employment to millions of men and women.

The scene opens in the kitchen of their humble home.

The husband set up a roughly constructed model of a gasoline engine. His wife is feeding gasoline into the engine, a drop at a time, with the aid of an eyedropper. The husband is manipulating the spark plug with which he hopes to ignite the gas. After weeks of tireless effort—tireless because it has been supported with love—the gas ignites and the flywheel of the crude engine begins to turn.

There was no money behind this experiment; nothing behind it except the definiteness of purpose of two people who had formed a Master Mind alliance for the fulfillment of that purpose.

And there was no promise of immediate or direct monetary compensation behind the experiment. It had to be conducted by applying the principle of GOING THE EXTRA MILE.

The model was perfected and the first practical self-propelled vehicle ever built in America became a reality.

Then the Master Mind alliance was extended to include skilled mechanics and a few friends and acquaintances who contributed small amounts of working capital for the production of automobiles.

The production has now reached fantastic proportions in

comparison with the humble beginning, and the product of that two-unit Master Mind now belts the entire earth.

The man behind that production is one of the five hundred from whose life experiences the philosophy of individual achievement was organized, and one hardly needs to be reminded that his name is Henry Ford.

As the Ford production grew the Ford Master Mind was increased until it now includes a veritable army of mechanics, engineers, chemists, researchers, financial experts, salespeople and many other types of skilled labor, all of which are essential for so extensive an operation.

Through his Master Mind alliance Mr. Ford has multiplied his own brain by many thousands. Without this alliance he could not carry on his vast industrial activities. It has endured for nearly half a century and will continue to endure, because the power it provides benefits all whom it affects.

And here let us take notice that no Master Mind alliance can endure unless it benefits all whom it affects.

Look well to the purpose of your Master Mind alliance before you begin it, you who see power through the cooperation of human endeavor. If you would have enduring power, be sure that it is applied to ends that benefit all who are affected by it.

Power may be very dangerous or it may serve to glorify the deeds of men, according to the way it is used. The Master Mind is the way to great power; and like all other forms of power, it is subject to either a positive or a negative application by those who wield it.

This is no mere statement of an obvious truism, for the records of the deeds of mankind all bear witness to its truth. Every great philosopher, from the days of Plato, Aristotle and Socrates on down to the days of William James and Ralph Waldo Emerson, also recognized it and called attention to it.

Electricity will do the work of man provided we adapt ourselves to its nature; but also it may snuff out life if it is applied for that purpose.

The imagination cannot conceive any good that may not be converted to destructive ends. Food is necessary for the maintenance of life, and it is good when properly used. But the wrong use of food, or too much food, will do as much harm as will the most potent poison.

You now have an understandable interpretation of the greatest source of personal power known to men—the Master Mind. The responsibility for its right use is yours.

Use it as Henry Ford has done and you will be blessed, as he has been, with the privilege of occupying great space in the world; space that can be estimated in both geography and in human relationships which are friendly and cooperative, for it is an accepted fact that Mr. Ford occupies more friendly space in the hearts of his fellowmen than does any other industrialist.

Mr. Ford's Master Mind consists not only in his harmonious alliance with his associate workers and his technical staff, but it extends far beyond these and includes the masses of the American people who have stood on the sidelines and watched him go by; people like you and me who recognize sound business and personal philosophy and respect its use wherever it is observed.

We emphasize Mr. Ford's application of the Master Mind because there is not to be found in the entire history of industrial America a finer example than his of individual achievement based on the American way of life. He has benefited almost everyone whose life has been touched by his influence, and it is very doubtful if he himself recognizes the full scope and measure of his influence on American life.

Master Mind power under the control of Henry Ford is a blessing, and not a curse or a danger, as it might be if it were wielded by a man with less vision than he possesses. All of which is an observation of Mr. Ford, not to eulogize him, but to inspire all who seek any form of personal aggrandizement under the American way of life.

In an analysis of Henry Ford and fifty other outstanding Americans, representing a wide variety of occupations, based upon the seventeen principles of this philosophy, Mr. Ford led all the others by a wide margin. On the first three principles—GOING THE EXTRA MILE, Definiteness of Purpose and the Master Mind—he rated 100% plus. The "plus" indicated that he had made extraordinary use of these three principles—a fact that was established by close observation and analysis of his achievements and their influence for good throughout the world.

And let us be reminded that the first member of his Master Mind alliance—his wife—has occupied first place in this alliance all down through the years. Her influence upon him has been continuous and profound! So profound in fact that it might not be an exaggeration to say, had there been no Mrs. Ford, there would have been no great Ford Industrial Empire as the world of today knows it.

Henry Ford has made mistakes. Some of them were the result of errors of judgment; others were the result of causes beyond his control. But those who know all the facts concerning his active life will tell you that he has made only two mistakes of major importance, and these were promptly mended by his own design and personal initiative, as soon as they were discovered.

What a record!

Duplicate it and you will have made indispensable contributions to the American way of life. Moreover, the compensation to you will be measured by compound interest on compound interest for every act and deed.

Do not be afraid to aim high when you establish your goal.

Remember that you live in a land of opportunities where no man is limited in the quality, the quantity or the nature of the riches he may acquire, provided he is willing to give adequate value in return.

Before you fix your goal in life, memorize the following lines and take to heart the lesson they teach:

"I bargained with Life for a penny,
And Life would pay no more,
However I begged at evening
When I counted my scanty store.

"For Life is a just employer,
He gives you what you ask,
But once you have set the wages,
Why, you must bear the task.

"I worked for a menial's hire,
Only to learn, dismayed,
That any wage I had asked of Life,
Life would have willingly paid."

Successful people do not bargain with Life for poverty!

They know that there is a power through which Life may be made to pay off on their own terms. They know that this power is available to every man who comes into possession of the Master Key to Riches. They know the nature of this power and its unlimited scope.

They know it by a name of one word; the greatest word in the English language!

This word is known to all men, but the secrets of its power are understood by few.

8

ANDREW CARNEGIE'S ANALYSIS OF THE MASTER MIND PRINCIPLE

The man who was commissioned by Andrew Carnegie to organize the philosophy of individual achievement asked him to describe the Master Mind principle so it might be appropriated and used by others, for the attainment of their Definite Major Purpose.

"Mr. Carnegie," he requested, "will you define the Master Mind principle as it may be applied through the individual efforts of men and women who are seeking their places in the great American way of life? Describe, if you will, the various forms of application that may be made of this principle by the man of average ability, in his daily efforts to make the most of his opportunities in this country."

And this is Mr. Carnegie's reply:

"The privileges which are available to the American people have back of them a source of great power. But privileges do not spring, mushroom-like, from nothing. They must be created and maintained by the application of power.

"The founders of our American form of Government, through their foresight and wisdom, laid the foundation for all of our American form of liberty, freedom and riches. But, they only laid the foundation. The responsibility of embracing and using this foundation must be assumed by every person who claims any portion of this freedom and wealth.

"I will now describe some of the individual uses of the Master Mind principle, as it may be applied in the development of various human relationships which may contribute to the attainment of one's Definite Major Purpose.

"But first I wish to emphasize the fact that the attainment of one's Definite Major Purpose can be carried out only by a series of steps; that every thought one thinks, every transaction in which one engages, in relationship with others, every plan one creates, every mistake one makes, has a vital bearing on his ability to attain his chosen goal. "The mere choice of a Definite Major Purpose, even though it be written out in clear language and fully fixed in one's mind, will not insure the successful realization of that purpose.

"One's major purpose must be backed up and followed through by continuous effort, *the most important part of which consists in the sort of relationship one maintains with others.*

"With this truth well established in one's mind it will not be difficult for one to understand how necessary it is to be careful in one's choice of associates; especially those with whom one maintains close personal contact in connection with his occupation.

"Here, then, are some of the sources of human relationship, which the man with a Definite Major Purpose must cultivate, organize and use in his progress toward the attainment of his chosen goal:

"*Occupation:* Outside of the relationship of marriage (which is the most important of all Master Mind relationships) there is no form of relationship as important as that which exists between a man and those with whom he works in his chosen occupation.

"Every man has a tendency to take on the mannerisms, beliefs, mental attitude, political and economic viewpoint, as well as other traits of the more outspoken of the men with whom he associates in his daily work.

"The major tragedy of this tendency lies in the fact that not always is the most outspoken among one's daily associates the soundest thinker; and very often he is a man with a grievance, who takes pleasure in airing the grievance among his fellow workers.

"Also, the most outspoken man often is an individual who has no Definite Major Purpose of his own. Therefore he devotes much of his time endeavoring to belittle the man who has such a purpose.

"Men of sound character, who know exactly what they wish, usually have the wisdom to keep their own counsel, and seldom waste any of their time trying to discourage others. They are so busily engaged in promoting their own purpose that they have no time to waste with anyone or anything which does not contribute in one way or another to their benefit.

"Realizing that one may find in almost every group of associates some person whose influence and cooperation may be helpful, the man of keen discrimination, who has a Definite Major Purpose he desires to attain, will prove his wisdom by forming friendships with those who can be, and who are willing to become, mutually beneficial to him. The others he will tactfully avoid.

"Naturally he will seek his closest alliances with men whom he recognizes possess traits of character, knowledge and personality which may become helpful to him; and of course he will not overlook those holding positions of higher rank than his own, keeping his eye on the day when he may not only equal such men, but excel them, remembering meanwhile the words of Abraham Lincoln, who said: 'I will study and prepare myself, and some day my chance will come.'

"The man with a constructive Definite Major Purpose will never envy his superiors, but he will study their methods and learn to acquire their knowledge. You may accept it as a sound prophecy that the man who spends his time finding fault with his superiors will never become a successful leader on his own account.

"The greatest soldiers are those who can take, and carry out, orders of their superiors in rank. Those who cannot or will not do this, never will become successful leaders in military operations. The same rule is true of any man in other walks of life. If he fails to emulate the man above him, in a spirit of harmony, he will never benefit greatly from his association with that man.

"No fewer than a hundred men have risen from the ranks in my own organization, and have found themselves richer than they need be. They were not promoted because of bad dispositions or the habit of finding fault with those above or those below them, but they promoted themselves by appropriating and making practical use of the experience of everyone with whom they came in contact.

'The man with a Definite Major Purpose will take careful inventory of every person with whom he comes in contact in his daily work, and he will look upon every such person as a possible source of useful knowledge or influence which he may borrow and use in his own promotion.

"If a man looks about him intelligently he will discover that his place of daily labor is literally a school room in which he may acquire the greatest of all educations—that which comes from observation and experience.

"'How may one make the most of this sort of schooling?' Some will ask.

"The answer may be found by studying the nine basic motives which move men to voluntary action. Men lend their experience, their knowledge, and they cooperate with other men, because they have been given a sufficient motive to cause them to desire as much. The man who relates himself to his daily associates in a friendly, cooperative way, with the right sort of mental attitude toward them, stands a better chance of learning from them than does the man who is belligerent, irritable, discourteous or neglectful of the little amenities of courtesy which exist between all cultured people.

"The old saying that 'a man can catch more flies with honey than with salt' might well be remembered by the man who wishes to learn of his daily associates who know more about many things than he does, and whose cooperation he needs and seeks.

"*Educational:* No man's education is ever finished.

"The man whose Definite Major Purpose is of noteworthy proportions must remain always a student, and he must learn from every possible source; especially those sources from which he may acquire specialized knowledge and experience related to his major purpose.

"The public libraries are free. They offer a great array of organized knowledge on every subject. They carry, in every language, the total of man's knowledge on every subject. The successful man with a Definite Major Purpose makes it his business and his responsibility to read books relating to that purpose, and thus acquire important knowledge which comes from the experiences of other men who have gone before him.

"It has been said that a man cannot consider himself even a kindergarten student of any subject until he has availed himself, as far as reasonably possible, of all the knowledge on that subject which has been preserved for him through the experience of others.

"A man's reading program should be as carefully planned

as his daily diet, for that too is food, without which he cannot grow mentally.

"The man who spends all of his spare time reading the funny papers and the sex magazines is not headed toward any great achievement.

"The same may be said of the man who does not include in his daily program some form of reading that provides him with the knowledge which he may use in the attainment of his major purpose. Random reading may be pleasant, but it seldom is helpful in connection with one's occupation.

"Reading, however, is not the only source of education. By a careful choice among his daily associates in his occupation, one may ally himself with men from whom he can acquire a liberal education through ordinary conversation.

"Business and professional clubs offer an opportunity for one to form alliances of great educational benefit, provided the man chooses his clubs and his close associates in those clubs with a definite objective in mind. Through this sort of association many men have formed both business and social acquaintances of great value to them in carrying out the object of their major purpose.

"No man can go through life successfully without the habit of cultivating friends. The word 'contact,' as it is commonly used in relationship to personal acquaintanceship, is an important word. If a man makes it a part of his daily practice to extend his list of personal 'contacts' he will find the habit of great benefit to him in ways that cannot be foretold while he is cultivating those acquaintances, but the time will come when they will be ready and willing to render aid to him if he has done a good job of selling himself.

"As I have stated, a man with a Definite Major Purpose should form the habit of establishing 'contacts' through every source possible, using care of course to choose those sources through which he is most likely to meet people who may be helpful to him.

"The church is among the more desirable sources through which one may meet and cultivate people, because it brings people together under circumstances which inspire the spirit of fellowship among men.

"Every man needs some source through which he can associate with his neighbors under circumstances that will enable him to exchange thoughts with them for the sake of mutual understanding and friendship, quite aside from all considerations of pecuniary gain. The man who shuts himself up in his own shell becomes a confirmed introvert, and soon becomes selfish and narrow in his views on life.

"*Political Alliances*: It is both the duty and the privilege of an American citizen to interest himself in politics and thereby exercise his right to help place, through his ballot, worthy men and women in public office.

"The political party to which a man belongs is of much less importance than the question of his exercising his privilege of voting. If politics become smeared with dishonest practices there is no one to blame but the people who have it within their power to keep dishonest, unworthy and inefficient people out of office.

"In addition to the privilege of voting and the duty it carries with it, one should not overlook the benefits which may be gained from an active interest in politics, through 'contacts' and alliances with people who may become helpful in the attainment of one's Definite Major Purpose.

"In many occupations, professions and businesses, political influence becomes a definite and important factor in the promotion of one's interests. Business and professional men and women certainly should not neglect the possibility of promoting their interests through active political alliances.

'The alert individual, who understands the necessity of reaching out in every possible direction for friendly allies whom he can use in attaining his major purpose in life, will make the fullest use of his privilege of voting.

"But, the major reason why every American citizen should take an active interest in politics, and the one which I would emphasize above all others, is the fact that if the better type of citizen fails to exercise his right to vote, politics will disintegrate and become an evil that will destroy this nation.

"The founders of this nation pledged their lives and their fortunes to provide all the people with the privileges of liberty and freedom in the pursuit of their chosen purpose in life. And chief among these privileges is that of helping, by the ballot, to maintain the institution of Government which the founders of this nation established to protect those privileges.

"Everything that is worth having has a definite price.

"You desire personal freedom and individual liberty! Very well, you may protect this right by forming a Master Mind alliance with other honest and patriotic men, and making it your business to elect honest men to public office. And it is no exaggeration to state that this may well be the most important Master Mind alliance that any American citizen can make.

"Your forefathers insured your personal liberty and freedom by their votes. *You should do no less for your offspring and the generations that will follow them!*

"Every honest American citizen has sufficient influence with his neighbors, and his daily associates in connection with his occupation, to enable him to influence at least five other people to exercise their right to vote. If he fails to exercise this influence he may still remain an honest citizen, but he cannot truthfully call himself a patriotic citizen, for patriotism has a price consisting in the obligation to exercise it.

"*Social Alliances:* Here is a fertile, almost unlimited, field for the cultivation of friendly 'contacts.' It is particularly available to the married man whose wife understands the art of making friends through social activities.

"Such a wife can convert her home and her social activities into a priceless asset to her husband, if his occupation is one that requires him to extend his list of friends.

"Many professional men whose professional ethics forbid direct advertising or self-promotion, may make effective use of their social privileges, provided they have wives with a bent for social activities.

"A successful life insurance man sells more than a million dollars a year of insurance, with the aid of his wife, who is a member of several Business Women's Clubs. His wife's part is simple. She entertains her fellow club members in her home from time to time, along with their husbands. In this way her husband becomes acquainted with them under friendly circumstances.

"A lawyer's wife has been credited with helping him to build one of the most lucrative law practices in a middle western city, by the simple process of entertaining, through her social activities, the wives of wealthy business men. The possibilities in this direction are endless.

"One of the major advantages of friendly alliances with people in a variety of walks of life consists in the opportunity such contacts provide for 'round-table' discussions which lead to the accumulation of knowledge one may use in the attainment of his Definite Major Purpose.

"If one's acquaintances are sufficiently numerous and varied, they may become a valuable source of information on a wide range of subjects, thus leading to a form of intellectual intercourse which is essential for the development of flexibility and versatility required in many callings.

"When a group of men get together and enter into a round-table discussion on any subject, this sort of spontaneous expression and interchange of thought enriches the minds of all who participate. Every man needs to reinforce his own ideas and plans with new food for thought, which he can acquire only through frank and sincere discussions with people whose experience and education differ from his own.

"The writer who becomes a 'top-notcher' and remains in that exalted position must add continuously to his own stock of knowledge by appropriating the thoughts and ideas of others, through personal contacts and by reading.

"Any mind that remains brilliant, alert, receptive and flexible must be fed continuously from the storehouse of other minds. If this renewal is neglected the mind will atrophy, the same as will an arm that is taken out of use. This is in accordance with nature's laws. Study nature's plan and you will discover that every living thing, from the smallest insect to the complicated machinery of a human being, grows and remains healthy only by constant use.

"Round-table discussions not only add to one's store of useful knowledge, but they develop and expand the power of the mind. The person who stops studying the day he finishes his formal schooling will never become an educated person, no matter how much knowledge he may acquire while he is going to school.

"Life itself is a great school, and everything that inspires thought is a teacher. The wise man knows this; moreover, he makes it a part of his daily routine to contact other minds, with the object of developing his own mind through the exchange of thoughts.

"We see, therefore, that the Master Mind principle has an unlimited scope of practical use. It is the medium by which the individual may supplement the power of his own mind with the knowledge, experience and mental attitude of other minds.

"As one man so aptly expressed this idea: 'If I give you one of my dollars in return for one of yours, each of us will have no more than he started with; but, if I give you a thought in return for one of your thoughts, each of us will have gained a hundred percent dividend on his investment of time.'

"No form of human relationship is as profitable as that through which men exchange useful thoughts, and it may be surprising but true that one may acquire from the mind of the humblest person ideas of the first magnitude of importance.

"Remember this: Every active brain is a potential source of inspiration from which one may procure an idea, or the mere seed of an idea, of priceless value in the solution of his personal problems, or the attainment of his major purpose in life.

"Sometimes great ideas spring from humble minds, but generally they come from the minds of those closest to the individual, where The Master Mind relationship has been deliberately established and maintained.

"The most profitable idea of my own career came one afternoon when Charlie Schwab and I were walking across a golf course. As we finished our shots on the thirteenth hole, Charlie looked up with a sheepish grin on his face, and said, 'I'm three strokes up on you at this hole, Chief; but I have just thought of an idea that should give you a lot of free time to play golf.'

"Curiosity prompted me to inquire as to the nature of the idea. He gave it to me, in one brief sentence, each word of which was worth, roughly speaking, a million dollars.

" 'Consolidate all your steel plants,' said he, 'into one big corporation and sell it out to Wall Street bankers.'

"Nothing more was said about the matter during the game, but that evening I began to turn the suggestion over in my mind

and think about it. Before I went to sleep that night I had converted the seed of his idea into a Definite Major Purpose. The following week I sent Charlie Schwab to New York City to deliver
a speech before a group of Wall Street bankers, among them,
J. Pierpont Morgan.

"The sum and substance of the speech was a plan for the
organization of the United States Steel Corporation, through
which I consolidated all my steel plants and retired from active
business, with more money than anyone needs.

"Now let me emphasize one point: Charlie Schwab's idea
might never have been born, and I never would have received
the benefit of it if I had not made it my business to encourage
in my associates the creation of new ideas. This encouragement
was provided through a close and continuous Master Mind alliance with the members of my business organization, among
whom was Charlie Schwab.

"Contact, let me repeat, is an important word!

"It is much more important if we add to it the word 'harmonious'! Through harmonious relationships with the minds
of others an individual may have the full use of his capacity to
create ideas. The man who overlooks this great fact thereby con-
demns himself eternally to penury and want.

"No man is smart enough to project his influence very far
into the world without the friendly cooperation of other men.
Drive this thought home in every way you can, for it is sufficient
unto itself to open the door to success in the higher brackets of
individual achievement.

"Too many people look for success in the distance, far
from where they are; and altogether too often they search for
it through complicated plans based upon a belief in luck or in
'miracles' which they hope may favor them.

"As Russell Conwell so effectively stated the matter in his
lecture, some people seem to think the grass is greener on the

other side of the fence from where they stand, and they pass up the 'Acres of Diamonds' in the form of ideas and opportunities which are available to them through the minds of their daily associates.

"I found my 'Acres of Diamonds' right where I stood, while looking into the glow of a hot steel blast furnace. I remember well the first day I began to sell myself the idea of becoming a leader in the great steel industry instead of remaining a helper in another man's 'Acres of Diamonds.'

"At first the thought was not very definite. It was a wish I more than it was a definite purpose. But I began to bring it back into my mind and to encourage it to take possession of me, until there came the day when the idea began to drive me instead of my having to drive it.

"That day I began with earnestness to work my own 'Acres of Diamonds,' and I was surprised to learn how quickly a Definite Major Purpose may find a way to translate itself into its physical equivalent.

"The main thing of importance is to know what one wants.

"The next thing of importance is to begin digging for diamonds right where one is, using whatever tools may be at hand, even if they be only the tools of thought. In proportion to the faithful use a man makes of the tools at hand, other and better tools will be placed in his hands when he is ready for them.

"The man who understands the Master Mind principle and makes use of it will find the necessary tools much more quickly than will the fellow who knows nothing of this principle.

"Every mind needs friendly contact with other minds, for the food of expansion and growth. The discriminating person who has a Definite Major Purpose in life chooses, with the greatest of care, the types of minds with whom he associates most intimately, because he recognizes that he will take on a definite portion of the personality of every person with whom he thus associates.

"I wouldn't give much for a man who does not make it his business to seek the company of people who know more than he. A man rises to the level of his superiors or falls to the level of his inferiors, according to the class he emulates through his choice of associates.

"Lastly, there is one other thought which every man who works for wages or a salary should recognize and respect. It lies in the fact that his job is, and should be, a schooling for a higher station in life, for which he is being paid in two important ways; first, by the wages he receives directly, and secondly, by the experience he gains from his work. And it frequently becomes true that a man's greatest pay consists not in his pay envelope, but in the experience he gains from his work!

"This overplus pay a man may gain from his experience depends largely for its value upon the mental attitude in which he relates himself to his associate workers; both those above him and those beneath him. If his attitude is positive and cooperative, and he follows the habit of GOING THE EXTRA MILE, his advancement will be both sure and rapid.

"Thus we see that the man who gets ahead not only makes practical use of the principle of the Master Mind, but he also applies the principle of GOING THE EXTRA MILE, and the principle of Definiteness of Purpose; the three principles which are inseparably associated with successful men in all walks of life.

"*Marriage:* This is by far the most important alliance any man ever experiences during his entire life.

"It is important financially, physically, mentally and spiritually, for it is a relationship bound together by all of these.

"The home is the place where most Master Mind alliances should begin, and the man who has chosen his mate wisely will, if he is wise in an economic sense, make his wife the first member of his personal Master Mind group.

"The home alliance should include not only man and wife,

but it should include other members of the family if they live in the same household, particularly children.

"The Master Mind principle brings into action the spiritual forces of those who are thus allied for a definite purpose; and spiritual power, while it may seem intangible, is nevertheless the greatest of all power.

"The married man who is on the right terms with his wife— terms of complete harmony, understanding, sympathy and singleness of purpose in which each is interested—has a priceless asset in this relationship which may lift him to great heights of personal achievement.

"Inharmony between a man and his wife is unpardonable, no matter what may be the cause. It is unpardonable because it may destroy a man's chances of success, even though he has every attribute necessary for success.

"And may I here interpolate a suggestion for the benefit of the wives of men?

"The suggestion may, if it is heeded and followed, make just the difference between a lifetime of poverty and misery and a lifetime of opulence and plenty.

"The wife has more influence over her husband than has any other person. That is, she has this superior influence if she has made the most of her relationship to her husband. He chose her in marriage in preference to all other women of his acquaintance, which means that she has his love and his confidence.

"Love heads the list of the nine basic motives of life which inspire all voluntary actions of people. Through the emotion of love the wife may send her husband to his daily labor in a spirit which knows no such reality as failure. But remember that 'nagging,' jealousy, fault-finding and indifference do not feed the emotion of love. They kill it.

"If a wife is wise she will arrange with her husband for a regular Master Mind hour each day; a period during which they will pool all of their mutual interests and discuss them in detail, in a spirit of love and understanding. The periods most suited for this Master Mind talk are those following the morning meal and just before retiring at night.

"And every meal hour should be a period of friendly inter-action between the wife and her husband. They should not be converted into periods of inquisition and fault-finding, but rather should be converted into periods of family worship, during which there will be good cheer, and the discussion of pleasant subjects of mutual interest to the husband and wife.

"More family relationships are wrecked at the family meal hour than at any other time, for this is the hour which many families devote to settling their family differences of opinion, or to disciplining the children.

"It has been said that a man's stomach is the way to his heart. Therefore the meal hour provides an excellent opportunity for a wife to reach her husband's heart with any idea she desires to plant there. But the approach must be based on love and affec-tion; not upon negative habits of discipline and faultfinding.

"The wife can coax her husband to do many things!

"The wife should take a keen interest in her husband's oc-cupation. She should become familiar with every feature of it, and never overlook an opportunity to express a keen interest in everything that concerns the source from which he earns his livelihood. And above all, she should not he one of those wives who say to their husbands, by inference if not by words, 'You bring home the money and I will spend it, but don't bother me with the details as to how you earn it, for I am not interested in that.'

"If a wife takes that attitude, the time will come when her husband will not be interested as to how much money he brings home, and the time may come when he will not bring it all home!

"I think that wives who are wise will understand just what I mean.

"When a woman marries she becomes the majority stockholder in the firm. If she relates herself to her husband by a true application of the Master Mind principle she will continue, as long as the marriage exists, to vote that stock as she pleases.

"The wife who is wise will manage the firm's business by a carefully prepared budget, taking care not to spend more than the income will allow. Many marriages go on the rocks because the firm runs out of money. And it is no mere axiom to say that when poverty knocks on the front door, love takes to its heels and runs out through the back door. Love, like a beautiful picture, requires the embellishment of an appropriate frame and proper lighting. It requires cultivation and food, just as does the physical body. Love does not thrive on indifference, nagging, faultfinding or domineering by either party.

"Love thrives best where a man and his wife feed it through singleness of purpose. The wife who remembers this may remain forever the most influential person in the life of her husband. The wife who forgets it may see the time when her husband begins to look around for an opportunity 'to trade her in on a newer model,' to use the phraseology of the automobile industry.

"The husband has the responsibility of earning the living, but the wife may have the responsibility of softening the shocks and the resistances which he will meet in connection with his occupation—a responsibility which the wife can discharge by planning a pleasant home-life, through whatever social activities may be fitting to her husband's calling.

"The wife should see to it that the home is the one place where her husband may lay aside his business or occupational cares and enjoy the ecstasies which only the love and affection and understanding of a wife can provide. The wife who follows this policy will be as wise as the sages, and richer—in the ways that count most—than most queens.

"I would also caution a wife against allowing her maternal instinct to supplant her love for her husband, by transferring all of her love and attention to her children. This mistake has wrecked many homes, and it might well wreck any home if the wife neglects to guard against the error so many wives make of switching their love from their husbands to their children.

"A woman's love, if it be the right kind of love, is sufficient in abundance to serve both the children and her husband; and it is a happy wife who sees to it that her love is sufficient to serve her husband and the children generously, without unfair preference in favor of either.

"Where love abounds as the basis of the family Master Mind relationship the family finances will not be likely to give cause for disturbance, for love has a way of surmounting all obstacles, meeting all problems and overcoming all difficulties.

"Family problems may arise, and they do in every family, but love should be the master of them. Keep the light of love shining brightly and everything else will shape itself to the pattern of your most lofty desires.

"I know this counsel is sound as I have followed it in my own family relationship, *and I can truthfully say that it has been responsible* for *whatever material success I have achieved.*"

(Author's note: Mr. Carnegie's frank admission becomes impressive when one considers the fact that he accumulated a fortune of more than $500,000,000.00. Mr. Carnegie made a huge fortune, but those who knew of his relationship with his wife know that *Mrs. Carnegie* made him!)

Taking up the subject of family Master Mind relationships where Andrew Carnegie left it, this seems an appropriate place to call attention to the fact that his experience is by no means an isolated one.

It is no secret among the personal friends of Henry Ford and his wife that the Master Mind relationship between them has been an important factor in the building of the great Ford industrial empire. The public hears very little of Mrs. Ford, but the fact remains that she has been a powerful influence in Mr. Ford's life, from the early days of their marriage up to the present.

The late Thomas A. Edison freely admitted that Mrs. Edison was the major source of his inspiration. They held their Master Mind meetings daily, usually at the close of Mr. Edison's day's work. And nothing was permitted to interfere with these meetings. Mrs. Edison saw to that, for she recognized the value of her keen interest in all of Mr. Edison's experimental work.

Mr. Edison often worked late into the night, but his homecoming found his wife awaiting him in keen anticipation of hearing him tell of his successes and failures during the day.

She was familiar with every experiment he conducted and took an interest in them.

She served as a sort of "sounding board" for Mr. Edison, through whom he had the privilege of looking at his work from the sidelines, and it has been said that she often supplied the missing link to many of his unsolved problems.

It is believed by many that Mrs. Edison was responsible for the Master Mind alliance that was maintained between Mr. Edison, Henry Ford, Harvey Firestone and John Burroughs, the naturalist, of which the public heard often through the newspaper accounts of their meetings once a year.

If the Master Mind relationship was considered to be of value to men of this caliber, surely it should be regarded as such by men who are struggling to find their places in the world.

The Princes of Love and Romance have played an important role in the lives of all truly great leaders. The story of Robert and Elizabeth Browning is replete with evidence that these unseen entities, which they recognized and respected, were largely responsible for the inspirational literary works of these great poets.

John Wanamaker, the Philadelphia "Merchant Prince," as he was known to thousands of people, gave credit to his wife for his rise from poverty to fame and fortune. Master Mind meetings were a part of their daily routine, every evening being set aside in part for these meetings—usually just before they retired.

Robert G. LeTourneau gives generous credit to his wife for his astounding achievements in industry, and it has been said that Mrs. LeTourneau knows as much about the production of earth-moving equipment as does her famous husband, who has achieved such outstanding success in this field. She is a member of his Board of Directors, takes an active interest in the management of his huge industrial enterprises, and assumes the responsibility for his comfort in his home life.

History attributes the rise to military power of Napoleon Bonaparte to the inspirational influence of his first wife, Josephine. Napoleon's military successes began to wane when he allowed his ambition for power to cause him to put Josephine aside, and his defeat and banishment to the lonely island of St. Helena was not far ahead of this act.

It may not be amiss to mention the fact that many a modern-times business "Napoleon" has met with the same kind of defeat for the same reason. Men often maintain their Master Mind relationships with their wives until they attain power, fame and fortune, then "trade them in for newer models," as Andrew Carnegie expressed it.

Charles M. Schwab's story was different. He too gained fame and fortune through his Master Mind alliance with Andrew Carnegie, aided by a similar relationship with his wife, who was an invalid during the major portion of their married life. He did not put her away on that account, but stood loyally by her until her death, because he believed that loyalty is the first requirement of sound character.

While we are on the subject of loyalty, it may not be out of place to suggest that the lack of loyalty among people in business Master Mind relationships is among the more frequent causes of business failure. As long as associates in business maintain the spirit of loyalty between one another, they generally find a way to bridge their defeats and overcome their handicaps.

It has been said that the first trait of character which Andrew Carnegie looked for in the young men whom he raised from the ranks of his workers to highly paid executive positions, was the trait of loyalty. He often said that if a man did not have inherently the quality of loyalty, he did not have the proper foundation for a sound character in other directions.

His methods of testing men for loyalty were both ingenious and multiple in scope. The testing took place before promotions were made and afterward, until such time as there no longer remained any doubt as to a man's loyalty. And it is a tribute to the deep understanding of men, which Mr. Carnegie possessed, that he made but few mistakes in judging men of loyalty.

Do not reveal the purpose of your Master Mind alliance to those outside of the alliance, and make sure that the members of your alliance refrain from so doing, because the idle, the scoffers and the envious stand on the sidelines of life, looking for an opportunity to sow the seeds of discouragement in the minds of those who are excelling them. Avoid this pitfall by keeping your plans to yourself, except insofar as they may be revealed by your actions and achievements.

Do not go into your Master Mind meetings with your mind filled with a negative mental attitude. Remember, if you are the leader of your Master Mind group it is your responsibility to keep every member of the alliance aroused to a high degree of

interest and enthusiasm. You cannot do this when you are negative. Moreover, men will not follow with enthusiasm the man
who has a tendency toward doubt, indecision or lack of faith
in the object of his Definite Major Purpose. Keep your Master
Mind allies keyed up to a high degree of enthusiasm by keeping
yourself keyed up in the same manner.

Do not neglect to see that each member of your Master Mind
alliance receives adequate compensation, in one form or another,
in proportion to the contributions each person makes to your
success. Remember that no one ever does anything with enthusiasm unless he benefits thereby. Familiarize yourself with the
nine basic motives which inspire all voluntary action, and see
that each of your Master Mind allies is properly motivated to
give you his loyalty, enthusiasm and complete confidence.

If you are related to your Master Mind allies by the motive
of desire for financial gain, be sure that you give more than you
receive, by adopting and following the principle of GOING THE
EXTRA MILE. Do this voluntarily, before you are requested to
do so, if you wish to make the most of the habit.

Do not place competitors in your Master Mind alliance, but
follow the Rotary Club policy of surrounding yourself with
people who have no reason to feel antagonistic toward each
other—people who are not in competition with one another.

Do not try to dominate your Master Mind group by force,
fear or coercion, but hold your leadership by diplomacy based
upon a definite motive for loyalty and cooperation. The day of
leadership by force is gone. Do not try to revive it, for it has no
place in civilized life.

Do not fail to take every step necessary to create the spirit
of fellowship among your Master Mind allies, for friendly teamwork will give you power attainable in no other way.

The most powerful Master Mind alliance in the history of

mankind was formed by the United Nations during World War II. Its leaders announced to the whole world that their

Definite Major Purpose was based upon the determination to establish human liberty and freedom for all the peoples of the world, *both the victors and the vanquished alike!*

That pronouncement was worth a thousand victories on the fields of battle, for it had the effect of establishing confidence in the minds of people who were affected by the outcome of that war. Without confidence there can be no Master Mind relationship, either in the field of military operations or elsewhere.

Confidence is the basis of all harmonious relationships. Remember this when you organize your Master Mind alliance if you wish that alliance to endure and to serve your interests effectively.

I have now revealed to you the working principle of the greatest of all the sources of personal power among men—the Master Mind.

By the combination of the first four principles of this philosophy—the Habit of GOING THE EXTRA MILE, Definiteness of Purpose, the Master Mind, and the one which follows—one may acquire a clue as to the secret of the power which is available through the Master Key to Riches—that mysterious key which opens the final gate to the Estate of Happy Valley.

Therefore, it is not out of place for me to warn you to approach the analysis of our next chapter in a state of expectancy, for it may well mark the most important turning-point of your life.

I shall now reveal to you the true approach to a full understanding of a power which has defied analysis by the entire world of science. Moreover, I shall hope to provide you with the formula by which you may appropriate this power and use it for the attainment of your Definite Major Purpose in life.

9

APPLIED FAITH

Faith is a royal visitor which enters only the mind that has been properly prepared for it; the mind that has been set in order through self-discipline.

In the fashion of all royalty, Faith commands the best room; nay, the finest suite, in the mental dwelling place.

It will not be shunted into servant's quarters, and it will not associate with envy, greed, superstition, hatred, revenge, vanity, doubt, worry or fear.

Get the full significance of this truth and you will be on the way to an understanding of that mysterious power which has baffled the scientists down through the ages.

Then you will recognize the necessity for conditioning your mind, through self-discipline, before expecting Faith to become your permanent guest.

Recalling the words of the sage of Concord, Ralph Waldo Emerson, who said, "In every man there is something wherein I may learn of him, and in that I am his pupil."

I shall now introduce a man who has been a great benefactor of mankind, so that you may observe how one goes about the conditioning of his mind for the expression of Faith.

Let him tell his own story:

"During the business depression which began in 1929 I took a post-graduate course in the University of Hard Knocks, the greatest of all schools.

"It was then I discovered a hidden fortune which I possessed, but had not been using.

"I made the discovery one morning when a notice came that my bank had closed its doors, possibly never to be reopened again, for it was then that I began to take inventory of my intangible, unused assets.

"Come with me while I describe what the inventory revealed. Let us begin with the most important item on the list, *unused Faith!*

"When I searched deeply into my own heart I discovered, despite my financial losses, I had an abundance of Faith left in Infinite Intelligence and Faith in my fellowmen.

"With this discovery came another of still greater importance; the discovery that *Faith can accomplish that which not all the money of the world can achieve.*

"When I possessed all the money I needed I made the grievous error of believing money to be a permanent source of power. Now came the astonishing revelation that money, without Faith, is nothing but so much inert matter, *of itself possessed of no power whatsoever.*

"Recognizing, perhaps for the first time in my life, the stupendous power of enduring Faith, I analyzed myself carefully to determine just how much of this form of riches I possessed. The analysis was both surprising and gratifying.

"I began the analysis by taking a walk into the woods. I

wished to get away from the crowd, away from the noise of the city, away from the disturbances of civilization and the fears of men, that I might meditate in silence.

"Ah! What gratification there is in that word 'silence.'

"On my journey I picked up an acorn and held it in the palm of my hand. I found it near the roots of the giant oak tree from which it had fallen. I judged the age of the tree to have been so great that it must have been a fair-sized tree when George Washington was but a small boy.

"As I stood there looking at the great tree, and its small embryonic offspring which I held in my hand, I realized that the tree had grown from a small acorn. I also realized that all the men living could not have built such a tree.

"I was conscious of the fact that some form of intangible Intelligence created the acorn from which the tree grew, and caused the acorn to germinate and begin its climb up from the soil of the earth.

"Then I realized that the greatest powers are the intangible powers, and not those which consist in bank balances or material things.

"I picked up a handful of black soil and covered the acorn with it. I held in my hand the *visible portion* of the substance out of which that magnificent tree had grown.

"At the root of the giant oak I plucked a fern. Its leaves were beautifully designed—yes, designed—and I realized as I examined the fern that it, too, was created by the same Intelligence which had produced the oak tree.

"I continued my walk in the woods until I came to a running brook of clear, sparkling water. By this time I was tired, so I sat near the brook to rest and listen to its rhythmic music, as it danced on its way back to the sea.

"The experience brought back memories of my youth. I remembered playing by a similar brook. As I sat there listening to

the music of the water I became conscious of an unseen being—
an Intelligence—which spoke to me from within and told me the
enchanting story of the water, and this is the story it told:

"'Water! Pure sparkling water. The same has been rendering
service ever since this planet cooled off and became the home of
man, beast and vegetation.

"'Water! Ah, what a story you could tell if you spoke man's
language. You have quenched the thirst of endless millions of
earthly wayfarers; fed the flowers; expanded into steam and
turned the wheels of man-made machinery, condensing and going back again to your original form. You have cleaned the sewers,
washed the pavements, rendered countless services to man and
beast, returning always to your source in the seas, there to become
purified and start your journey of service once again.

"'When you move you travel in one direction only; toward
the seas from whence you came. You are forever going and coming, but you always seem to he happy at your labor.

"'Water! Clean, pure, sparkling substance. No matter how
much dirty work you perform, you cleanse yourself at the end
of your labor.

"'You cannot be created, nor can you he destroyed. You are
akin to all life. Without your beneficence no form of life on this
earth would exist!'

"And the water of the brook went rippling, laughing, on its
way back to the sea.

"The story of water ended, but I had heard a great sermon;
I had been close to the greatest of all forms of Intelligence. I felt
evidence of that same Intelligence which had created the great
oak tree from a tiny acorn; the Intelligence which had fashioned
the leaves of the fern with mechanical and esthetic skill such as
no man could duplicate.

"The shadows of the trees were becoming longer; the day
was coming to a close.

"As the sun slowly descended beyond the western horizon I realized that it, too, had played a part in that marvelous sermon which I had heard.

"Without the beneficent aid of the sun there could have been no conversion of the acorn into an oak tree. Without the sun's help the sparkling water of the flowing brook would have remained eternally imprisoned in the oceans, and life on this earth could never have existed.

"These thoughts gave a beautiful climax to the sermon I had heard; thoughts of the romantic affinity existing between the sun and the water and all life on this earth, beside which all other forms of romance seemed incomparable and unimportant.

"I picked up a small white pebble which had been neatly polished by the waters of the running brook. As I held it in my hand I received, from within, a still more impressive sermon.

"The Intelligence which conveyed that sermon to my mind seemed to say:

"'Behold, mortal, a miracle which you hold in your hand.

"'I am only a tiny pebble of stone, yet I am, in reality, a small universe in which there is everything that may be found in the more expanded portion of the universe which you see out there among the stars.

"'I appear to be dead and motionless, but the appearance is deceiving. I am made of molecules. Inside my molecules are myriads of atoms, each a small universe unto itself. Inside the atoms are countless numbers of electrons which move at an inconceivable rate of speed.

"'I am not a dead mass of stone, but an organized group of units of ceaseless energy.

"'I appear to be a solid mass, but the appearance is an illusion, for my electrons are separated one from another by a distance greater than their mass.

"'Study me carefully, O humble earthly wayfarer, and remember that the great powers of the universe are the intangibles; that the values of life are those which cannot be added by bank balances.'

"The thought conveyed by that climax was so illuminating that it held me spellbound, for I recognized that I held in my hand an infinitesimal portion of the energy which keeps the sun, the stars and the earth, on which we live for a brief period, in their respective places in relation to one another.

"Meditation revealed to me the beautiful reality that there is law and order, even in the small confines of a tiny pebble of stone. I recognized that within the mass of that tiny pebble the romance and the reality of nature were combined. I recognized that within that small pebble fact transcended fancy.

"Never before had I felt so keenly the significance of the evidence of natural law and order and purpose which reveal themselves in everything the human mind can perceive. Never before had I felt myself so near the source of my Faith in Infinite Intelligence.

"It was a beautiful experience, out there in the midst of Mother Nature's family of trees and running brooks, where the very calmness of the surroundings bade my weary soul be quiet and rest awhile, so that I might look, feel and listen while Infinite Intelligence unfolded to me the story of its reality.

"Never, in all my life, had I previously been so overwhelmingly conscious of the real evidence of Infinite Intelligence, or of the source of my Faith.

"I lingered in this newly found paradise until the Evening Star began to twinkle; then reluctantly I retraced my footsteps back to the city, there to mingle once again with those who are driven by the inexorable rules of civilization, in a mad scramble to gather up material things they do not need.

"I am now back in my study, with my books and my typewriter, on which I am recording the story of my experience. But I am swept by a feeling of loneliness and a longing to be out there by the side of that friendly brook where, only a few hours ago, I had bathed my soul in the satisfying realities of Infinite Intelligence.

"I know that my Faith in Infinite Intelligence is real and enduring. It is not a blind Faith; it is one based on close examination of the handiwork of Infinite Intelligence, and as such has been expressed in the orderliness of the universe.

"I had been looking in the wrong direction for the source of my Faith. I had been seeking it in the deeds of men, in human relationships, in bank balances and material things.

"I found it in a tiny acorn, a giant oak tree, a small pebble or stone, the leaves of a simple fern and the soil of the earth; in the friendly sun which warms the earth and gives motion to the waters; in the Evening Star; in the silence and calm of the great outdoors.

"And I am moved to suggest that Infinite Intelligence reveals itself through silence more readily than through the boisterousness of men's struggles, in their mad rush to accumulate material things.

"My bank account vanished, my bank collapsed, but I was richer than most millionaires, because I had discovered a direct approach to Faith. With this power behind me I can accumulate other bank balances sufficient for my needs.

"Nay, I am richer than are most millionaires, because I depend upon a source of inspired power which reveals itself to me from within, while many of the more wealthy find it necessary to turn to bank balances and the stock ticker for stimulation and power.

"*My source of power is as free as the air I breathe,* and as *limitless!* To avail myself of it I have only to turn on my Faith, and this I have in abundance.

"Thus, once again I learned the truth that every adversity carries with it the seed of an equivalent benefit. My adversity cost me my bank balance. It paid off through the revelation of the means to all riches!"

Stated in his own words, you have the story of a man who has discovered how to condition his mind for the expression of Faith.

And what a dramatic story it is! Dramatic because of its simplicity.

Here is a man who found a sound basis for an enduring Faith; not in bank balances or material riches, but in the seed of an oak tree, the leaves of a fern, a small pebble, and a running brook; things which everyone may observe and appreciate.

But his observation of these simple things led him to recognize that the greatest powers are intangible powers which are revealed through the simple things around us.

I have related this man's story as I wished to emphasize the manner in which one may clear his mind, even in the midst of chaos and insurmountable difficulties, and prepare it for the expression of Faith.

The most important fact which this story reveals is this:

When the mind has been cleared of a negative mental attitude the power of Faith moves in and begins to take possession!

Surely no student of this philosophy will he unfortunate enough to miss this important observation.

Let us turn now to an analysis of Faith, although we must approach the subject with full recognition that Faith is a power which has defied analysis by the entire scientific world.

Faith has been given fourth place in this philosophy because it comes near to representing the "fourth dimension," although it is presented here for its relationship to personal achievement.

Faith is a state of mind which might properly be called the

"mainspring of the soul" through which one's aims, desires and purposes may be translated into their physical or financial equivalent.

Previously we observed that great power may be attained by the application of (1) the habit of GOING THE EXTRA MILE, (2) Definiteness of Purpose, and (3) the Master Mind. But that power is feeble in comparison with that which is available through the combined application of these principles with the state of mind known as Faith.

We have already observed that capacity for faith is one of the Twelve Riches. Let us now recognize the means by which this "capacity" may be filled with that strange power which has been the main bulwark of civilization, the chief cause of all human progress, the guiding spirit of all constructive human endeavor.

Let us remember, at the outset of this analysis, that Faith is a state of mind which may be enjoyed only by those who have learned the art of taking full and complete control of their minds! This is the one and only prerogative right over which an individual has been given complete control.

Faith expresses its powers only through the mind that has been prepared for it. But the way of preparation is known and may be attained by all who desire to find it.

The fundamentals of Faith are these:

a. Definiteness of Purpose supported by personal initiative or action.
b. The habit of GOING THE EXTRA MILE in all human relationships.
c. A Master Mind alliance with one or more people who radiate courage based on Faith, and who are suited spiritually and mentally to one's needs in carrying out a given purpose.

d. A positive mind, free from all negatives, such as fear, envy, greed, hatred, jealousy and superstition. (A positive mental attitude is the first and the most important of the Twelve Riches.)

e. Recognition of the truth that every adversity carries with it the seed of an equivalent benefit; that temporary defeat is not failure until it has been accepted as such.

f. The habit of affirming one's Definite Major Purpose in life, in a ceremony of meditation, at least once daily.

g. Recognition of the existence of Infinite Intelligence which gives orderliness to the universe; that all individuals are minute expressions of this Intelligence, and as such the individual mind has no limitations except those which are accepted and set up by the individual in his own mind.

h. A careful inventory (in retrospect) of one's past defeats and adversities, which will reveal the truth that all such experiences carry the seed of an equivalent benefit.

i. Self-respect expressed through harmony with one's own conscience.

j. Recognition of the oneness of all mankind.

These are the fundamentals of major importance which prepare the mind for the expression of Faith. Their application calls for no degree of superiority, but application does call for intelligence and a keen thirst for truth and justice.

Faith fraternizes only with the mind that is positive!

It is the "elan vital" that gives power, inspiration and action to a positive mind. It is the power that causes a positive mind to act as an "electromagnet," attracting to it the exact physical counterpart of the thought it expresses.

Faith gives resourcefulness to the mind, enabling the mind to make "grist of all that comes to its mill." It recognizes favorable opportunities, in every circumstance of one's life, whereby one may attain the object of Faith, going so far as to provide the means by which failure and defeat may be converted into success of equivalent dimensions.

Faith enables man to penetrate deeply into the secrets of Nature and to understand Nature's language as it is expressed in all natural laws.

From this sort of revelation have come all the great inventions that serve mankind, and a better understanding of the way to human freedom through harmony in human relationships, such as was provided by the Constitution of the United States.

Faith makes it possible to achieve that which man can *conceive* and *believe!*

Thomas *A.* Edison *believed* he could perfect a practical incandescent electric lamp, and despite the fact that he failed more than 10,000 times that Faith carried him to the discovery of the secret for which he was searching.

Signor Marconi *believed* the energy of the ether could be made to carry the vibrations of sound without the use of wires. His Faith carried him through endless failures until at long last he was rewarded by triumph.

Christopher Columbus *believed* the earth was round; that he would find land in an uncharted ocean if he sailed on. Despite the rebellious protests of his *unbelieving* sailors he sailed on and on until he was rewarded for his Faith.

Helen Keller *believed* she would learn to speak, although she had lost the power of speech, her hearing, and her eyesight as well. Her Faith restored her speech and provided her with the equivalent of hearing, through the sense of touch, thus proving that Faith can and will find a way to the realization of human desires.

If you would have Faith, keep your mind on that which you desire. And remember that there is no such reality as a "blanket" faith, for faith is the outward demonstration of definiteness of purpose.

Faith is guidance from within! The guiding force is Infinite Intelligence directed to definite ends. It will not bring that which one desires, but it will guide one to the attainment of the object of desire.

HOW TO DEMONSTRATE THE POWER OF FAITH

a. Know what you want and determine what you have to give in return for it.

b. When you affirm the objects of your desires, through prayer, inspire your imagination to see yourself already in possession of them, and act precisely as if you were in the physical possession thereof. (Remember, the possession of anything first takes place mentally, in the mind.)

c. Keep the mind open at all times for *guidance from within*, and when you are inspired by "hunches" to modify your plans or to move on a new plan, move without hesitancy or doubt.

d. When overtaken by temporary defeat, as you may be overtaken many times, remember that man's Faith is tested in many ways, and your defeat may be only one of your "testing periods." Therefore, accept defeat as an inspiration to greater effort and carry on with *belief* that you will succeed.

e. Any negative state of mind will destroy the capacity for faith and result in a negative climax of any affirmation you may express. Your state of mind is everything; therefore take possession of your mind and clear it completely of all unwanted interlopers that are unfriendly to Faith, and keep it cleared, no matter what may be the cost in effort.

f. Learn to give expression to your power of Faith by writing out a clear description of your Definite Major Purpose in life and using it as the basis of your daily meditation.

g. Associate with your Definite Major Purpose as many as possible of the nine basic motives, described previously.

h. Write out a list of all the benefits and advantages you expect to derive from the attainment of the object of your Definite Major Purpose and call these into your mind many times daily, thereby making your mind "success conscious." (This is commonly called autosuggestion.)

i. Associate yourself, as far as possible, with people who are in sympathy with your Definite Major Purpose; people who are in harmony with you, and inspire them to encourage you in every way possible.

j. Let not a single day pass without making at least one definite move toward the attainment of your Definite Major Purpose. Remember, "Faith without works is dead."

k. Choose some prosperous person of self-reliance and courage as your "pace-maker," and make up your mind not only to keep up with that person, but to excel him. Do this silently, without mentioning your plan to anyone. (Boastfulness will be fatal to your success, as Faith has nothing in common with vanity or self-love.)

l. Surround yourself with books, pictures, wall mottoes and other suggestive reminders of self-reliance founded upon Faith as it has been demonstrated by other people, thus building around yourself an atmosphere of prosperity and achievement. This habit will be fruitful of stupendous results.

m. Adopt a policy of never evading or running away from unpleasant circumstances, but recognize such circumstances and build a counter-fire against them right where they overtake you. You will discover that recognition of such circumstances, without fear of their consequence, is nine-tenths of the battle in mastering them.

n. Recognize the truth that everything worth having has a definite price. The price of Faith, among other things, is eternal vigilance in carrying out these simple instructions.

Your watchword must be PERSISTENCE!

These are the steps that lead to the development and the maintenance of *a positive mental attitude,* the only one in which Faith will abide. They are steps that lead to riches of both mind and spirit as well as riches of the purse. Fill your mind with this kind of mental food.

These are the steps by which the mind may be prepared for the highest expressions of the soul.

Feed your mind on such mental food and it will be easy for you to adopt the habit of GOING THE EXTRA MILE.

It will be easy for you to keep your mind attuned to that which you desire, with assurance that it shall become yours.

"The key to every man," said Emerson, "is his thought."

That is true. Every man today is the result of his thoughts of yesterday!

It would be difficult for one to imagine Henry Ford fearing anything, for his life work and his achievements are the handiwork of Faith.

And it would be difficult to imagine Henry Ford accepting as impossible any end he might desire to attain.

He gave the whole world notice of his Faith some years ago, when he desired to have the Ford automobile engine blocks cast in one piece. He instructed his engineers to draw up a model for the casting.

"Impossible," they cried!

"You use that word carelessly," exclaimed Ford. "Go ahead and try!"

They went ahead, but proceeded without Ford's Faith!

In a little while they reported back to Mr. Ford that they had tried without success.

"Try again," Mr. Ford requested, "and keep on trying until you succeed."

They tried again, again, and again, until eventually they found the method they were seeking. Ford's Faith had won again.

Thomas A. Edison desired to create a machine that would record and reproduce the sound of the human voice. No one had ever seen such a machine, and no one but Edison *believed* it could be produced. His *belief* was more than a desire, for he backed it with Faith, and Faith put in action becomes Wisdom. He went to work on the machine, and lo! His first model justified his Faith, for it worked.

James J. Hill sat with his hand on a telegraph key, waiting for an "open line." But he was not idle. His imagination was at work, building a great Transcontinental Railway System through which he hoped to tap the vast resources of the undeveloped western portion of the United States.

He had no money. He had no influential friends. He had no record of great achievement to give him prestige. But he did have Faith, that irresistible power that recognizes no such reality as "impossible."

He reduced his Definite Major Purpose to writing, omitting no detail.

On a map of the United States he sketched the course of his proposed railroad.

He slept with that map under his pillow. He carried it with him wherever he went. He fed his mind on his desire for the fulfillment of his "dream" until he made that dream a reality.

The morning after the great Chicago fire had laid waste the business portion of the city, Marshall Field came down to the site where, the day before, his retail store stood.

All around him were groups of other merchants whose stores had also been destroyed. He listened in on their conversations and learned that they had given up hope and many of them had already decided to move on further West and start over again.

Calling the nearest groups to him Mr. Field said:

"Gentlemen, you may do as you please, but as for me I intend to stay right here. Over there where you see the smoking remains of what was once my store I shall build the world's greatest retail store."

The store that Mr. Field built on Faith still stands on that spot, in Chicago. It is recognized the world over as the greatest retail store on earth.

These men and others like them have been the pioneers who produced our great American way of life.

They gave us the American System of Free Enterprise that inspires every worker of industry to express his personal initiative backed by Faith.

They gave us our system of railroads and our system of communications.

They gave us the talking pictures; the talking machines; the airplanes; the skyscrapers skeletoned with steel; the automobile; the improved highways; the household electrical appliances; the electric power installations; the x-ray; the banking and investment institutions; the great life insurance companies; the strongest Navy in the world; yes, and more important than all these, they prepared the way, through their Faith, for the freedom each and every one of us enjoys as an American citizen.

Human progress is no matter of accident or luck!

But it is the result of applied faith, expressed by those who have conditioned their minds, through the seventeen principles of this philosophy, for the expression of Faith.

Verily, the United States is a nation founded on Faith and maintained by Faith. Moreover, it provides all the essentials that inspire Faith, so that the humblest citizen may attain the highest ambitions of his heart and soul.

Therefore, our nation is justly known as a "land of opportunity"; the richest and the freest nation of the world!

And all freedom and riches have their roots in an abiding Faith.

The space that every man occupies in the world is measured by the Faith he expresses in connection with his aims and purposes.

Let us remember this, we who aspire to enjoy freedom and riches.

Let us remember, too, that Faith fixes no limitations of

freedom or riches, but it guides every man to the realization of his desires whether they be great or small, according to his expression of it.

And though Faith is the one power which defies the scientists to analyze it, the procedure by which it may be applied is simple and within the understanding of the humblest, thus it is the common property of all mankind.

All that is known of this procedure has been simply stated in this chapter, and not a single step of it is beyond the reach of the humblest person.

Faith begins with definiteness of purpose functioning in a mind that has been prepared for it by the development of a positive mental attitude. It attains its greatest scope of power by physical action directed toward the attainment of a definite purpose.

All voluntary physical action is inspired by one or more of the nine basic motives. It is not difficult for one to develop Faith in connection with the pursuit of one's desires.

Let a man be motivated by LOVE and see how quickly this emotion is given wings for action through Faith. And action in pursuit of the objective of that love quickly follows. The action becomes a labor of love, which is one of the Twelve Riches.

Let a man set his heart upon the accumulation of material riches and see how quickly his every effort becomes a labor of love. The hours of the day are not long enough for his needs, and though he labors long he finds that fatigue is softened by the joy of *self-expression*, which is another of the Twelve Riches.

Thus, one by one the resistances of life fade into nothingness for the man who has prepared his mind for self-expression through Faith. Success becomes inevitable. Joy crowns his every effort. He has no time or inclination for hatred. *Harmony in human relationships* comes naturally to him. His *hope of achievement* is high and continuous, for he sees himself already in possession

of the object of his definite purpose. Intolerance has been supplanted by an *open mind.*

And *self-discipline* becomes as natural as the eating of food.
He *understands people* because he loves them, and because of this
love he is willing to *share his blessings. Of fear he knows nothing,*
for all his fears have been driven away by his Faith. The Twelve
Riches have become his own!

Faith is an expression of gratitude for man's relationship to
his Creator. Fear is an acknowledgment of the influences of evil
and it connotes a lack of *belief* in the Creator.

The greatest of life's riches consist in the understanding of
the four principles which I have mentioned. These principles
are known as the "Big Four" of this philosophy, because they
are the warp and the woof and the major foundation stones of
the Master Key to the power of thought and the inner secrets
of the soul.

Use this Master Key wisely and you shall be free!

Some to Whom the Master Key Has Been Revealed

In a one-room log cabin, in Kentucky, a small boy was lying on
the hearth, learning to write, using the back of a wooden shovel as
a slate, and a piece of charcoal as a pencil.

A kindly woman stood over him, encouraging him to keep
on trying. The woman was his mother! The boy grew into man-
hood without having shown any promise of greatness.

He took up the study of law and tried to make a living at that
profession, but his success was meager.

He tried storekeeping, but the sheriff soon caught up with
him.

He entered the Army, but he made no noteworthy record
there. Everything to which he turned his hand seemed to wither
and disappear into nothingness.

Then a great love came into his life. It ended with the death
of the one and only woman he ever loved, but the sorrow over

that death reached deeply into the man's soul and there it made contact with the secret power that comes from within.

He seized that power and began to put it to work. It made him President of the United States. It wiped out the curse of slavery in America. And it saved the Union from dissolution in the time of a great national emergency.

The great Emancipator is now a citizen of the universe, but the spirit of his great soul—a spirit that was set free by the secret power from within his own mind—goes marching on.

That spirit has helped to make the United States the freest country of the world.

So, this power that comes to men from within knows no social caste! It is as available to the poor and the humble as it is to the rich and the powerful. It need not be passed on from one person to another. It is possessed by all who think. It cannot be put into effect for you by any one except yourself. It must be acquired from within, and it is free to all who will appropriate it.

What strange fear is it that gets into the minds of men and short-circuits their approach to this secret power from within, and when it is recognized and used lifts men to great heights of achievement? How and why do the vast majority of the people of the world become the victims of a hypnotic rhythm which destroys their capacity to use the secret power of their own minds? How can this rhythm be broken?

The approach to the source of all genius has been charted. It is the self-same path that was followed by Thomas A. Edison, Henry Ford, Andrew Carnegie, Dr. Alexander Graham Bell, and the other great leaders who have contributed, from their rich experiences, to the establishment of the American way of life.

"How may one tap that secret power that comes from within?" some will wish to ask! Let us see how others have drawn upon it.

A young clergyman by the name of Frank Gunsaulus had long desired to build a new type of college. He knew exactly what he wanted, but the hitch came in the fact that it required a million dollars in cash.

He made up his mind to get the million dollars! Definiteness of decision, based upon definiteness of purpose, constituted the first step of his plan.

Then he wrote a sermon entitled "WHAT I WOULD DO WITH A MILLION DOLLARS!" and announced in the newspapers that he would preach on that subject the following Sunday morning.

At the end of the sermon a strange man whom the young preacher had never seen before, arose, walked down to the pulpit, extended his hand and said, "I like your sermon, and you may come down to my office tomorrow morning and I will give you the million dollars you desire."

The man was Philip D. Armour, the packinghouse founder of Armour & Company. His gift was the beginning of the Armour School of Technology, one of the great schools of the country.

This is the sum and the substance of what happened. What went on in the mind of the young preacher, that enabled him to contact the secret power that is available through the mind of man, is something with which we can only conjecture, but the modus operandi by which that power was stimulated was applied Faith!

Shortly after birth Helen Keller was stricken by a physical affliction which deprived her of sight, hearing and speech. With two of the more important of the five physical senses stilled forever she faced life under difficulties such as most people never know throughout their lives.

With the aid of a kindly woman who recognized the existence of that secret power which comes from within, Helen Keller began to contact that power and use it. In her own words, she gives a definite clue as to one of the conditions under which the power may be revealed.

"Faith," said Miss Keller, "rightly understood, is active not passive! Passive faith is no more a force than sight is in an eye that does not look or search out. Active faith knows no fear. It denies that God has betrayed His creatures and given the world over to darkness. It denies despair. Reinforced with faith, the weakest mortal is mightier than disaster."

Faith, backed by action, was the instrument with which Miss Keller bridged her affliction so that she was restored to a useful life.

Through applied faith she learned to speak.

Through her faith she substituted the sense of touch to do the work of the sense of hearing and the sense of sight, thus proving that no matter how great may be one's physical handicaps, there always is a means by which they may be eliminated or bridged.

The way may be found through that secret power from within one's mind, the approach to which must be discovered by the individual himself.

Go back through the pages of history and you will observe that the story of civilization's unfoldment leads inevitably to the works of men and women who opened the door to that secret power from within, with applied faith as the master key! Observe, too, that great achievements always are born of hardship and struggle and barriers which seem insurmountable; obstacles which yield to nothing but an indomitable will backed by an abiding faith!

And here, in one short phrase—indomitable will backed by an abiding faith—you have the approach of major importance that leads to the discovery of the door of the mind, behind which the secret power from within is hidden!

Men who penetrate that secret power and apply it in the solution of personal problems sometimes are called "dreamers"! But, observe that they back their dreams with action, thus proving the soundness of Helen Keller's statement that "Faith, rightly understood, is active, not passive."

One of the strange features of "faith, rightly understood," is that it generally appears because of some emergency which forces men to look beyond the power of ordinary thought for the solution of their problems.

It is during these emergencies that we draw upon that secret power from within which knows no resistance strong enough to defeat it. Such emergencies, for example, as that faced by the fifty-six men who gave birth to this nation when they signed their names to the most profound document of all times—the Declaration of Independence.

That was "active faith, rightly understood" for each man who signed that document knew that it might become his own death-warrant! Fortunately it became a license to liberty for all mankind claiming its protection, and it may well prove yet to be a license to liberty for the entire world.

The benefits of the document were proportionate to the risk assumed by those who signed it. The signers pledged their lives, their fortunes and their rights to liberty, the greatest privileges of a civilized people, and they made the pledge without mental reservations.

Here, then, is the suggestion of a test by which men may measure their capacity for active faith! To be effective it must be based on a willingness to risk whatever the circumstances demand; liberty, material fortune, and life itself. Faith without risk is a passive faith which, as Helen Keller stated, "is no more a force than sight is in an eye that does not look or search out."

And let us examine the records of some of the great leaders who came after the signers of the Declaration of Independence, for theirs was also an active faith. The men who gave us the American way of life and the American standard of living, the highest the world has ever known.

They, too, discovered that secret power that comes from within, drew upon it, applied it and converted a vast wilderness into the "cradle of democracy," which is now the envy of the rest of the world.

Such men as James J. Hill, who pushed back the frontiers of the West and brought the Atlantic and Pacific Oceans into easy access of the people, through a great transcontinental railroad system.

And Andrew Carnegie, who perfected the manufacture and distribution of steel products until that metal served to advance American industry in a thousand ways which had been prohibited because of high costs.

And Henry Ford, who supplanted the horse and buggy mode of travel with a more rapid means of transportation that is within the means of the humblest person. As a result this country was covered with a network of improved highways that added immeasurable wealth to the sections through which they pass.

And Lee De Forest, who perfected the mechanical means by which the boundless force of the ether has been harnessed and made to serve as a means of instantaneous communication between the peoples of the world, through the radio.

And Thomas A. Edison, who pushed civilization ahead by thousands of years, with the perfection of the incandescent electric lamp, the talking machine, the moving picture and scores of other useful inventions which lighten the burdens of mankind and add to his pleasure and education.

These, and others of their type, were men of active faith! We sometimes call them "geniuses," but they disclaimed the right to the honor because they recognized that their achievements came as the result of that secret power from within which is available to everyone who will embrace it and use it.

We all know of the achievements of these great leaders; we know the rules of their leadership; we recognize the nature and the scope of the blessings their labors have conferred upon the people of this nation, and, thanks to the vision of Andrew

Carnegie, we have preserved for the people the philosophy of individual achievement through which these men helped to make this the world's richest and freest country.

But, unfortunately, not all of us recognize the handicaps under which they worked, the obstacles they had to overcome, and the spirit of active faith in which they carried on their work.

Of this we may be sure, however: Their achievements were in exact proportion to the emergencies they had to overcome!

They met with opposition from those who were destined to benefit most by their struggles; people who, because of the lack of active faith, always view with skepticism and doubt that which is new and unfamiliar.

The emergencies of life often bring men to the crossroads, where they are forced to choose their direction, one road being marked Faith and another Fear!

What is it that causes the vast majority to take the Fear road? The choice hinges upon one's mental attitude!

The man who takes the Faith road is the man who has conditioned his mind to believe; conditioned it little at a time, by prompt and courageous decisions in the details of his daily experiences. The man who takes the Fear road does so because he has neglected to condition his mind to be positive.

In Washington, a man sits in a wheel chair with a tin cup and a bunch of pencils in his hands, gaining a meager living by begging. The excuse for his begging is that he lost the use of his legs, through Infantile Paralysis. His brain has not been affected.

He is otherwise strong and healthy. But, his choice led him to accept the Fear road when the dreaded disease overtook him, and his mind atrophies through disuse.

In another part of the same city was another man who was afflicted with the same handicap. He, too, had lost the use of his legs, but his reaction to his loss was far different. When he came to the crossroads at which he was forced to make a choice, he took the Faith road, and it led straight to the White House and the highest position within the gift of the American people.

That which he lost through incapacity of his limbs, he gained in the use of his brain and his will, and it is a matter of record that his physical affliction did in no way hinder him from being one of the most active men who ever occupied the position of President.

The difference in the stations of these two men was very great! But, let no one be deceived as to the cause of this difference, for it is entirely a difference of mental attitudes. One man chose Fear as his guide. The other chose Faith.

And, when you come right down to the circumstances which lift some men to high stations in life and condemn others to penury and want, the likelihood is that their widely separated positions reflect their respective mental attitudes. The high man chooses the high road of Faith, the low man chooses the low road of Fear, and education, experience, and personal skill are matters of secondary importance.

When Thomas A. Edison's teacher sent him home from school, at the end of the first three months, with a note to his parents saying he had an "addled" mind and could not be taught, he had the best of excuses for becoming an outcast, a do-nothing, a nobody, and that is precisely what he proceeded to become for a time. He did odd jobs, sold newspapers, tinkered with gadgets and chemicals until he became what is commonly known as a "jack of all trades" and not very good at any.

Then something took place in the mind of Thomas A. Edison that was destined to make his name immortal. Through some strange process which he never fully disclosed to the world, he discovered that secret power from within, took possession of it, organized it and lo! Instead of being a man with an "addled" brain he became the outstanding genius of invention of all time.

And now, wherever we see an electric light, or hear a phonograph, or see a moving picture we should be reminded that we are observing the product of that secret power from within which is as available to us as it was to the great Edison. Moreover, we should feel sorely ashamed if, by neglect or indifference, we are making no appropriate use of this great power.

One of the strange features of this secret power from within is that it aids men in procuring whatever they set their hearts upon, which is but another way of saying it translates into reality one's dominating thoughts.

In the little town of Tyler, Texas, more than a quarter of a century ago, a boy still in his teens walked into a grocery store where some loafers were sitting by a stove. One of the men looked at the youth, grinned broadly and said, "Say, Sonny, what are you going to be when you are a man?"

"I'll tell you what I'm going to be," the boy shouted! "I'm going to be the best lawyer in the world—that's what I'm going to be if you wish to know."

The loafers yelled with laughter! The boy picked up his groceries and quietly walked out of the store.

Later, when the loafers laughed, it was in a different vein, for that boy had become a recognized authority in the legal world and his skill at law was so great that he was earning more than the President of the United States.

His name is Martin W. Littleton. He, too, discovered the secret power within his own mind and that power enabled him to set his own price on his services and get it.

As far as knowledge of the law is concerned there are thousands of lawyers who perhaps are as skilled at law as Martin W. Littleton, but few of them are making more than a living from their profession because they have not discovered there is something that brings success in the legal profession which is not taught in law schools.

The illustration might be extended to cover every profession and all human endeavor. In every calling there are a few who rise to the top while all around them are others who never get beyond mediocrity.

Those who succeed usually are called "lucky." To be sure they are lucky! But, learn the facts and you will discover that their "luck" consists of that secret power from within, which they have applied through a positive mental attitude; a determination to follow the road of Faith instead of the road of Fear and self-limitation.

The power that comes from within recognizes no such reality as permanent barriers.

It converts defeat into a challenge to greater effort.

It removes self-imposed limitations such as fear and doubt.

And, above all else let us remember that it makes no black marks against any man's record which he cannot erase.

If approached through the power from within, every day brings forth a newly born opportunity for individual achievement which need not in any way whatsoever be burdened by the failures of yesterday.

It favors no race or creed, and it is bound by no sort of arbitrary consistency compelling man to remain in poverty because he was born in poverty.

The power from within is the one medium through which the effects of Cosmic Habit force may be changed from a negative to a positive application, instantaneously.

It recognizes no precedent, follows no hard and fast rules, and makes royal kings of the humblest of men at will—THEIR WILL!

It offers the one and only grand highway to personal freedom and liberty.

It restores health where all else fails, in open defiance of all the rules of modern medical science.

It heals the wounds of sorrow and disappointment regardless of their cause.

It transcends all human experience, all education, all knowledge available to mankind.

And its only fixed price is that of an unyielding faith! An active applied faith!

It was the inspiration of the poet who wrote:

"Isn't it strange that princes and kings
And clowns that caper in sawdust rings;
And common folks, like you and me,
All are builders for eternity.

"To each is given a book of rules,
A block of stone and a bag of tools;
And each must shape ere time has flown,
A stumbling block or a stepping stone."

Search until you find the point of approach to that secret power from within, and when you find it you will have discovered your true self—that "other self" which makes use of every experience of life.

Then, whether you build a better mousetrap, or write a better book, or preach a better sermon, the world will make a beaten path to your door, recognize you and adequately reward you, no matter who you are or what may have been the nature and scope of your failures of the past.

What if you have failed in the past?

So did Edison, Henry Ford, the Wright Brothers, Andrew Carnegie, and all the other great American leaders who have helped to establish the American way of life. They all met with failure in one way or another, but they didn't call it by that name; they called it "temporary defeat."

With the aid of the light that shines from within, these and all truly great men have recognized temporary defeat for exactly what it is—a challenge to greater effort backed by greater faith!

Anyone can quit when the going is hard!

Anyone can feel sorry for himself when temporary defeat overtakes him, but self-coddling was no part of the character of those whom the world has recognized as great.

The approach to that power from within cannot be made by self-pity. It cannot be made through fear and timidity. It cannot be made through envy and hatred. It cannot be made through avarice and greed.

No, your "other self" pays no heed to any of these negatives! It manifests itself only through the mind that has been swept clean of all negative mental attitudes. It thrives in the mind that is guided by faith!

It is not a new philosophy of achievement that the world needs!

But it is a re-dedication of the old and tried principles which led unerringly to the discovery of that power from within which "moves mountains."

The power that has brought forth great leaders in every walk of life and in every generation is still available. Men of vision and faith, who have pushed back the frontiers of ignorance and superstition and fear, have given the world all that we know as civilization.

The power is clothed in no mystery and it performs no miracles, but it works through the daily deeds of men, and reflects itself in every form of service rendered for the benefit of mankind.

It is called by myriad names, but its nature never changes, no matter by what name it is known.

It works through but one medium, and that is the mind.

It expresses itself in thoughts, ideas, plans and purposes of men, and the grandest thing to be said about it is that it is as free as the air we breathe and as abundant as the scope and space of the universe.

10

THE LAW OF COSMIC HABIT FORCE

Habit is a cable; we weave a thread of it every day, and at last we cannot break it.

—HORACE MANN

So, we come now to the analysis of the greatest of all of Nature's laws, the law of Cosmic Habit force!

Briefly described, the law of Cosmic Habit force is Nature's method of giving fixation to all habits so that they may carry on automatically once they have been set into motion—the habits of men the same as the habits of the universe.

Every man is where he is and what he is because of his established habits of thoughts and deeds. The purpose of this entire philosophy is to aid the individual in the formation of the kind of habits that will transfer him from where he is to where he wishes to be in life.

Every scientist, and many laymen, knows that Nature maintains a perfect balance between all the elements of matter and energy throughout the universe; that the entire universe is operated through an inexorable system of orderliness and habits which never vary, and cannot be altered by any form of human endeavor; that the five known realities of the universe are (1) Time, (2) Space, (3) Energy, (4) Matter, and (5) Intelligence, which shape the other known realities into orderliness and system based upon fixed habits.

These are Nature's building blocks with which she creates a grain of sand or the largest stars that float through space, and every other thing known to man, or that the mind of man can conceive.

These are the known realities, but not every one has taken the time or the interest to ascertain the fact that Cosmic Habit force is the particular application of Energy with which Nature maintains the relationship between the atoms of matter, the stars and the planets in their ceaseless motion onward toward some unknown destiny, the seasons of the year, night and day, sickness and health, life and death. Cosmic Habit force is the medium through which all habits and all human relationships are maintained in varying degrees of permanence, and the medium through which thought is translated into its physical equivalent in response to the desires and purposes of individuals.

But these are truths capable of proof, and one may count that hour sacred during which he discovers the inescapable truth that man is only an instrument through which higher powers than his own are projecting themselves. This entire philosophy is designed to lead one to this important discovery, and to enable him to make use of the knowledge it reveals, by placing himself in harmony with the unseen forces of the universe which may carry him inevitably into the success side of the great River of Life.

The hour of this discovery should bring him within easy reach of the Master Key to all Riches!

Cosmic Habit force is Nature's Comptroller through which all other natural laws are coordinated, organized and operated through orderliness and system. Therefore it is the greatest of all natural laws.

We see the stars and the planets move with such precision that the astronomers can predetermine their exact location and their relationship to one another scores of years hence.

We see the seasons of the year come and go with a clock like regularity.

We know that an oak tree grows from an acorn, and a pine tree grows from the seed of its ancestor; that an acorn never makes a mistake and produces a pine tree; nor does a pine seed produce an oak tree. We know that nothing is ever produced that does not have its antecedents in something similar which preceded it; that the nature and the purpose of one's thoughts produce fruits after their kind, just as surely as fire produces smoke.

Cosmic Habit force is the medium by which every living thing is forced to take on and become a part of the environmental influences in which it lives and moves. Thus it is clearly evident that success attracts more success, and failure attracts more failure—a truth that has long been known, although but few have understood the reason for this strange phenomenon.

It is known that the person who has been a failure may become a most outstanding success by close association with those who think and act in terms of success, but not every one knows that this is true because the law of Cosmic Habit force transmits the "success consciousness" from the mind of the successful man to the mind of the unsuccessful one who is closely related to him in the daily affairs of life.

Whenever any two minds contact each other there is born of that contact a third mind patterned after the stronger of the two. Most successful men recognize this truth and frankly admit that their success began with their close association with some person whose positive mental attitude they either consciously or unconsciously appropriated.

Cosmic Habit force is silent, unseen and unperceived through any of the five physical senses. That is why it has not been more widely recognized, for most men do not attempt to understand the intangible forces of Nature, nor do they interest themselves in abstract principles. However, these intangibles and abstractions represent the real powers of the universe, and they are the real basis of everything that is tangible and concrete, the source from which tangibility and concreteness are derived.

Understand the working principle of Cosmic Habit force and you will have no difficulty in interpreting Emerson's essay on Compensation, for he was rubbing elbows with the law of Cosmic Habit force when he wrote this famous essay.

And Sir Isaac Newton likewise came near to the complete recognition of this law when he made his discovery of the law of gravitation. Had he gone but a brief distance beyond where his discovery ended he might have helped to reveal the same law which holds our little earth in space and relates it systematically to all other planets in both Time and Space; the same law that relates human beings to each other and relates every individual to himself through his thought habits.

The term "Habit force" is self-explanatory. It is a force which works through established habits. And every Living thing below the intelligence of man lives, reproduces itself and fulfills its earthly mission in direct response to the power of Cosmic Habit force through what we call "instinct."

Man alone has been given the privilege of choice in connection with his living habits, and these he may fix by the patterns of his thoughts—the one and only privilege over which any individual has been given complete right of control.

Man may think in terms of self-imposed limitations of fear and doubt and envy and greed and poverty, and Cosmic Habit force will translate these thoughts into their material equivalent. Or he may think in terms of opulence and plenty, and this same law will translate his thoughts into their physical counterpart.

In this manner may one control his earthly destiny to an astounding degree—simply by exercising his privilege of shaping his own thoughts. But once these thoughts have been shaped into definite patterns they are taken over by the law of Cosmic Habit force and are made into permanent habits, and they remain as such unless and until they have been supplanted by different and stronger thought patterns.

Now we come to the consideration of one of the most profound of all truths; the fact that most men who attain the higher brackets of success seldom do so until they have undergone some tragedy or emergency which reached deeply into their souls and reduced them to that circumstance of life which men call "failure."

The reason for this strange phenomenon is readily recognized by those who understand the law of Cosmic Habit force, for it consists in the fact that these disasters and tragedies of life serve to break up the established habits of man—habits which have led him eventually to the inevitable results of failure—and thus break the grip of Cosmic Habit force and allow him to formulate new and better habits.

We see the same phenomenon in the results of warfare!

When nations or large groups of people so relate themselves that their efforts do not harmonize with the Divine Plan of Nature, they are forced to break up their habits, by warfare or some other equally disturbing circumstances, such as business depressions or epidemics of disease, so that a new start may be made which conforms more nearly to Nature's ultimate and overall scheme.

This conclusion is not intended to provide a justification for warfare, but rather to serve as an indictment of mankind on the charge of ignorance of a law which, if it were universally understood and respected would make warfare unnecessary and impossible!

Wars grow out of maladjustments in the relationships of men! These maladjustments are the results of the negative thoughts of men which have grown until they assume mass proportions. The spirit of any nation is but the sum total of the dominating thought-habits of its people.

And the same is true of individuals, for here too the spirit of the individual is determined by his dominating thought habits. Most individuals are at war, in one way or another, throughout their lives. They are at war with their own conflicting thoughts and emotions. They are at war in their family relationships and in their occupational and social relationships.

Recognize this truth and you will understand the real power and the benefits which are available to those who live by the Golden Rule, *for this great rule will save you from the conflicts of personal warfare.*

Recognize it and you will understand also the real purpose and benefits of a Definite Major Purpose, for once that purpose has been fixed in the consciousness, by one's thought habits, it will be taken over by Cosmic Habit force and carried out to its logical conclusion, *by whatever practical means that may be available.*

Cosmic Habit force does not suggest to an individual what he shall desire, or whether his thought habits shall be positive or negative, but it does act upon all his thought habits by crystallizing them into varying degrees of permanency and translating them into their physical equivalent, through inspired motivation to action.

It not only fixes the thought-habits of individuals, but it fixes also the thought-habits of groups and masses of people, according to the pattern established by the preponderance of their individual dominating thoughts. For example, the whole world began, soon after the end of World War I, to speak of "the next war," until that war was crystallized into action.

In a similar manner, epidemics of disease are thought and talked into existence. When the Department of Health of a city begins posting large red-lettered signs, warning people to be on the lookout for the measles, or diphtheria, or some other disease, an epidemic of that particular disease is the very next manifestation of this expression of thought. It is almost sure to follow.

Here too the same rule applies to the individual who thinks and talks of disease. At first he is regarded as a hypochondriac— one who suffers with imaginary illness—but when the habit is maintained the disease thus manifested, or one very closely akin to it, generally makes its appearance. Cosmic Habit force attends to this! For it is true that any thought held in the mind through repetition begins immediately to translate itself into its physical equivalent, by every practical means that may be available.

It is a sad commentary on the intelligence of people to observe that more than three-fourths of the people who have the full benefits of a great country such as ours, should go all the way through life in poverty and want, but the reason for this is not difficult to understand if one recognizes the working principle of Cosmic Habit force.

Poverty is the direct result of a "poverty consciousness" which results from thinking in terms of poverty, fearing poverty, and talking of poverty.

It would be difficult to imagine Henry Ford thinking in terms of that which he does not want, or in terms of poverty! He lives on the side of the street opposite the things he does not want, but he never crosses over, and that is why he is carried onward to success by the positive side of the great River of Life!

His education and general ability have nothing to do with

his success, for he has less of each than have millions of men who remain poverty-stricken all their lives, some of them men with a string of college degrees after their names.

The world has thought and spoken of cancer as an incurable disease for so long that Cosmic Habit force has transmuted this thought-pattern into a major fixation which is difficult to break. But the time is at hand when groups of the better-informed people are beginning to set up thought patterns which may serve as an antidote for this disease.

When this kind of "mass thinking" becomes sufficiently extensive cancer will go the way of all human ills which have been starved to death because people stopped talking and thinking of them. And let us all join in the hope that the time will come, and soon, when people will stop "enjoying poor health," and will regard the admission of sickness as a disgrace rather than something to serve as the major topic of polite conversation wherever friends and acquaintances meet.

Sound health is the result of a carefully cultivated "health consciousness" that has been created by constant thoughts of sound health and is made permanent by the law of Cosmic Habit force. If you desire sound health, give orders to your subconscious mind to create it and Cosmic Habit force will carry out the order.

If you desire opulence, give orders to your subconscious mind to produce opulence, thus developing a "prosperity consciousness," and see how quickly your economic condition will improve.

First comes the "consciousness" of that which you desire; then follows the physical or mental manifestation of your desires. The "consciousness" is your responsibility. It is something you must create by your daily thoughts, or by meditation if you prefer to make known your desires in that manner. In this manner one may ally himself with no less a power than that of the Creator of all things.

"I have come to the conclusion," said a great philosopher,

"that the acceptance of poverty, or the acceptance of ill health, is an open confession of the lack of Faith."

We do a lot of proclaiming of Faith, but our actions belie our words. Faith is a state of mind that may become permanent only by actions. Belief alone is not sufficient.

The law of Cosmic Habit force is Nature's own creation. It is the one universal principle through which order and system and harmony are carried out in the entire operation of the universe, from the largest star that hangs in the heavens to the smallest atoms of matter.

It is a power that is equally available to the weak and the strong, the rich and the poor, the sick and the well. It provides the solution to all human problems.

The major purpose of the seventeen principles of this philosophy is that of aiding the individual to adapt himself to the power of Cosmic Habit force by self-discipline in connection with the formation of his habits of thought.

Let us turn now to a brief review of these principles, so that we may understand their relationship to Cosmic Habit force. Let us observe how these principles are so related that they blend together and form the Master Key which unlocks the doors to the solution of all problems.

The analysis begins with the first principle of the philosophy:

a. THE HABIT OF GOING THE EXTRA MILE.
   This principle is given first position because it aids in conditioning the mind for the rendering of useful service. And this conditioning prepares the way for the second principle—

b. DEFINITENESS OF PURPOSE.
   With the aid of this principle one may give organized direction to the principle of Going The

Extra Mile, and make sure that it leads in the
direction of his major purpose and becomes
cumulative in its effects. These two principles
alone will take anyone very far up the ladder of
achievement, but those who are aiming for the
higher goals of life will need much help on the
way, and this help is available through the application of the third principle—

c. THE MASTER MIND.

Through the application of this principle one
begins to experience a new and a greater sense
of power which is not available to the individual
mind, as it bridges one's personal deficiencies
and provides him, when necessary, with any
portion of the combined knowledge of mankind
which has been accumulated down through the
ages. But this sense of power will not be complete
until one acquires the art of receiving guidance
through the fourth principle—

d. APPLIED FAITH.

Here the individual begins to tune in on the
powers of Infinite Intelligence, which is a benefit that is available only to the person who has
conditioned his mind to receive it. Here the individual begins to take full possession of his own
mind by mastering all fears, worries and doubts,
by recognizing his oneness with the source of all
power.

These four principles have been rightly called
the "Big Four" because they are capable of providing more power than the average man needs
to carry him to great heights of personal achievement. But they are adequate only for the very

few who have other needed qualities of success,
such as those which are provided by the fifth
principle—

e. PLEASING PERSONALITY.

A pleasing personality enables a man to sell
himself and his ideas to other men. Hence it is an
essential for all who desire to become the guiding
influence in a Master Mind alliance. But observe
carefully how definitely the four preceding principles tend to give one a pleasing personality.
These five principles are capable of providing one
with stupendous personal power, but not enough
power to insure him against defeat, for defeat is a
circumstance that every man meets many times
throughout his lifetime; hence the necessity of
understanding and applying the sixth principle—

f. HABIT OF LEARNING FROM DEFEAT.

Notice that this principle begins with the word
"habit," which means that it must be accepted
and applied as a matter of habit, under all the
circumstances of defeat. In this principle may be
found hope sufficient to inspire a man to make a
fresh start when his plans go astray, as go astray
they must at one time or another.

Observe how greatly the source of personal
power has increased through the application of
these six principles. The individual has found
out where he is going in life; he has acquired the
friendly cooperation of all whose services are
needed to help him reach his goal; he has made
himself pleasing, thereby insuring for himself
the continued cooperation of others; he has acquired the art of drawing upon the source of

Infinite Intelligence and of expressing that power
through applied faith; and he has learned to
make stepping stones of the stumbling blocks of
personal defeat. Despite all of these advantages,
however, the man whose Definite Major Purpose
leads in the direction of the higher brackets of
personal achievement will come many times to
the point in his career when he will need the benefits of the seventh principle—

g. CREATIVE VISION.

This principle enables one to look into the future
and to judge it by a comparison with the past,
and to build new and better plans for attaining
his hopes and aims through the workshop of his
imagination. And here, for the first time perhaps,
a man may discover his sixth sense and begin
to draw upon it for the knowledge which is
not available through the organized sources of
human experience and accumulated knowledge.
But, in order to make sure that he puts this benefit to practical use he must embrace and apply
the eighth principle—

h. PERSONAL INITIATIVE.

This is the principle that starts action and keeps
it moving toward definite ends. It insures one
against the destructive habits of procrastination,
indifference and laziness. An approximation of the
importance of this principle may be had by recognizing that it is the "habit-producer" in connection
with the seven preceding principles, for it is obvious that the application of no principle may become a habit except by the application of personal
initiative. The importance of this principle may be

further evaluated by recognition of the fact that it is the sole means by which a man may exercise full and complete control over the only thing that the Creator has given him to control, the power of his own thoughts.

Thoughts do not organize and direct themselves. They need guidance, inspiration and aid which can be given only by one's personal initiative.

But personal initiative is sometimes misdirected. Therefore it needs the supplemental guidance that is available through the ninth principle—

i. ACCURATE THINKING.

Accurate thinking not only insures one against the misdirection of personal initiative, but it also insures one against errors of judgment, guesswork and premature decisions. It also protects one against the influence of his own undependable emotions by modifying them through the power of reason commonly known as the "head."

Here the individual who has mastered these nine principles will find himself in possession of tremendous power, but personal power may be, and often it is, a dangerous power if it is not controlled and directed through the application of the tenth principle—

j. SELF-DISCIPLINE.

Self-discipline cannot be had for the mere asking, nor can it be acquired quickly. It is the product of carefully established and carefully maintained habits which in many instances can be acquired only by many years of painstaking effort. So

we have come to the point at which the power
of the will must be brought into action, for self-
discipline is solely a product of the will.

Numberless men have risen to great power by
the application of the preceding nine principles,
only to meet with disaster, or they carry others to
defeat by their lack of self-discipline in the use of
their power.

This principle, when mastered and applied,
gives one complete control over his greatest enemy, himself!

Self-discipline must begin with the application of the eleventh principle—

k. CONCENTRATION OF ENDEAVOR.

The power of concentration is also a product of the
will. It is so closely related to self-discipline that the
two have been called the "twin brothers" of this
philosophy. Concentration saves one from the dissipation of his energies, and aids him in keeping
his mind focused upon the object of his Definite
Major Purpose until it has been taken over by the
subconscious section of the mind and there made
ready for translation into its physical equivalent,
through the law of Cosmic Habit force. It is the
camera's eye of the imagination through which
the detailed outline of one's aims and purposes
are recorded in the subconscious section of the
mind; hence it is indispensable.

Now look again, and see how greatly one's
personal power has grown by the application of
these eleven principles. But even these are not
sufficient for every circumstance of life, for there
are times when one must have the friendly co-

operation of many people, such as customers in business, or clients in a profession, or votes in an election to public office, all of which may be had through the application of the twelfth principle—

l. COOPERATION.

Cooperation differs from the Master Mind principle in that it is a human relationship that is needed, and may be had, without a definite alliance with others, based upon a complete fusion of the minds for the attainment of a definite purpose.

Without the cooperation of others one cannot attain success in the higher brackets of personal achievement, for cooperation is the means of major value by which one may extend the space he occupies in the minds of others, which is sometimes known as "good-will." Friendly cooperation brings the merchant's customers back as repeat purchasers of his wares, and insures a continuance of patronage from the clients of the professional man. Hence it is a principle that belongs definitely in the philosophy of successful men, regardless of the occupation they may follow.

Cooperation is attained more freely and willingly by the application of the thirteenth principle—

m. ENTHUSIASM.

Enthusiasm is a contagious state of mind which not only aids one in gaining the cooperation of others, but more important than this, it inspires the individual to draw upon and use the power of his own imagination. It inspires action also in the expression of personal initiative, and leads to the habit of concentration of endeavor. Moreover, it is one of the qualities of major importance of a pleasing personality, and it makes easy the application of the principle of GOING THE EXTRA MILE. In addition to all these benefits, enthusiasm gives force and conviction to the spoken word.

Enthusiasm is the product of *motive,* but it is difficult of maintenance without the aid of the fourteenth principle—

n. THE HABIT OF HEALTH.

Sound physical health provides a suitable housing place for the operation of the mind; hence it is an essential for enduring success, assuming that the word "success" shall embrace all of the requirements for happiness.

Here again the word "habit" comes into prominence, for sound health begins with a "health consciousness" that can be developed only by the right habits of living, sustained through self-discipline.

Sound health provides the basis for enthusiasm, and enthusiasm encourages sound health; so the two are like the hen and the egg; no one can determine which came into existence first, but everyone knows that both are essential for the production of either. Health and enthusiasm are like that. Both are essential for human progress and happiness.

Now take inventory again and count up the gains in power which the individual has attained by the application of these fourteen principles. It has reached proportions so stupendous that it staggers the imagination. Yet it is not sufficient to

insure one against failure; therefore we shall have
to add the fifteenth principle—

o. BUDGETING TIME AND MONEY.

Oh! What a headache one gets at the mention of
saving of time and the conservation of money.
Nearly everyone wishes to spend both time and
money freely, but budget and conserve them,
never! However, independence and freedom of
body and mind, the two great desires of all mankind, cannot become enduring realities without
the self-discipline of a strict budgeting system.
Hence this principle is of necessity an important
essential of the philosophy of individual achievement.

Now we are reaching the ultimate in the attainment of personal power. We have learned the
sources of power and how we may tap them and
apply them at will to any desired end; and that
power is so great that nothing can resist it save
only the fact that the individual may unwisely
apply it to his own destruction and the destruction of others. Hence, to guide one in the right
use of power it is necessary to add the sixteenth
principle—

p. THE GOLDEN RULE APPLIED.

Observe the emphasis on the word "applied."
Belief in the soundness of the Golden Rule is not
enough. To be of enduring benefit, and in order
that it may serve as a safe guide in the use of
personal power, it must be applied as a matter of
habit, in all human relationships.

Quite an order, this! But the benefits which are
available through the application of this profound

rule of human relationship are worthy of the
efforts necessary to develop it into a habit. The
penalties for failure to live by this rule are too numerous for description in detail.

Now we have attained the ultimate in personal power, and we have provided ourselves
with the necessary insurance against its misuse.
What we need from here on out is the means
by which this power may be made permanent
during our entire lifetime. We shall climax this
philosophy, therefore, with the only known
principle by which we may attain this desired
end—the seventeenth and last principle of this
philosophy—

q. COSMIC HABIT FORCE.

Cosmic Habit force is the principle by which all
habits are fixed and made permanent in varying
degrees. As stated, it is the comptrolling principle of this entire philosophy, into which the
preceding sixteen principles blend and become
a part. And it is the comptrolling principle of all
natural laws of the universe. It is the principle
that gives the fixation of habit in the application
of the preceding principles of this philosophy.
Thus it is the controlling factor in conditioning
the individual mind for the development and
the expression of the "prosperity consciousness"
which is so essential in the attainment of personal success.

Mere understanding of the sixteen preceding principles will
not lead anyone to the attainment of personal power. The princi-

ples must be understood and applied as a matter of strict habit, and habit is the sole work of the law of Cosmic Habit force.

Cosmic Habit force is synonymous with the great River of Life to which frequent references have been made previously, for it consists of a negative and a positive potentiality, as do all forms of energy.

The negative application is called "hypnotic rhythm" because it has a hypnotic effect on everything that it contacts. We may see its effects, in one way or another, on every human being.

It is the sole means by which the "poverty consciousness" becomes fixed as a habit!

It is the builder of all established habits of fear, and envy, and greed, and revenge, and of desire for something for nothing.

It fixes the habits of hopelessness and indifference.

And it is the builder of the habit of hypochondria, through which millions of people suffer all through their lives with imaginary illness.

It is also the builder of the "failure consciousness" which undermines the self-confidence of millions of people.

In brief, it fixes all negative habits, regardless of their nature or effects. Thus it is the "failure" side of the great River of Life.

The "success" side of the River—the positive side—fixes all constructive habits, such as the habit of Definiteness of Purpose, the habit of GOING THE EXTRA MILE, the habit of applying the Golden Rule in human relationships, and all the other habits which one must develop and apply in order to get the benefits of the sixteen preceding principles of this philosophy.

Now let us examine this word "habit"!

Webster's dictionary gives the word many definitions, among them: "Habit implies a settled disposition or tendency due to repetition; custom suggests the fact of repetition rather than the tendency to repeat; usage (applying only to a considerable body of people) adds the implication of long acceptation or standing; both custom and usage often suggest authority; as, we do many things mechanically from force of habit."

Webster's definition runs on into considerable additional detail, but no part of it comes within sight of describing the law that fixes all habits; this omission being due no doubt to the fact that the law of Cosmic Habit force had not been revealed to the editors of this dictionary. But we observe one significant and important word in the Webster definition—the word "repetition." It is important because it describes the means by which any habit is begun.

The habit of Definiteness of Purpose, for example, becomes a habit only by repetition of the thought of that purpose, by bringing the thought into the mind repeatedly; by *repeatedly* submitting the thought to the imagination with a burning desire for its fulfillment, until the imagination creates a practical plan for attaining this desire; by applying the *habit* of Faith in connection with the desire, and doing it so intensely and repeatedly that one may see himself already in possession of the object of his desires, *even before he begins to attain it.*

The building of voluntary positive habits calls for the application of self-discipline, persistence, willpower and Faith, all of which are available to the person who has assimilated the sixteen preceding principles of this philosophy.

Voluntary habit building is self-discipline in its highest and noblest form of application!

And all voluntary positive habits are the products of willpower directed toward the attainment of definite ends. *They originate with the individual, not with Cosmic Habit force.* And they must be grounded in the mind through repetition of thoughts and deeds until they are taken over by Cosmic Habit force and are given fixation, after which they operate automatically.

The word *habit* is an important word in connection with this philosophy of individual achievement, for it represents the real cause of every man's economic, social, professional, occupational and spiritual condition in life. We are where we are and what we are because of our fixed habits. And we may be where we wish to be and what we wish to be only by the development and the maintenance of our *voluntary habits.*

Thus we see that this entire philosophy leads inevitably to an understanding and application of the law of Cosmic Habit force—the power of fixation of all habits!

The major purpose of each of the sixteen preceding principles of this philosophy is that of aiding the individual in the development of a particular, specialized form of habit that is necessary as a means of enabling him *to take full possession of his own mind*! This too must become a habit!

Mind-power is always actively engaged on one side of the River of Life or the other. The purpose of this philosophy is to enable one to develop and maintain habits of thought and of deed which keep his mind concentrated upon the "success" side of the River. This is the sole burden of the philosophy.

Mastery and assimilation of the philosophy, like every other desirable thing, has a definite price which must be paid before its benefits may be enjoyed. That price, among other things, is eternal vigilance, determination, persistence and the will to make Life pay off on one's own terms instead of accepting substitutes of poverty and misery and disillusionment.

There are two ways of relating one's self to Life.

One is that of playing horse while Life rides. The other is that of becoming the rider while Life plays horse. The choice as to whether one becomes the horse or the rider is the privilege of every person, but this much is certain: if one does not choose to become the rider of Life, he is sure to be forced to become the horse. Life either rides or is ridden. It never stands still.

THE RELATIONSHIP OF THE "EGO" AND COSMIC HABIT FORCE

As a student of this philosophy you are interested in the method by which one may transmute the power of thought into its physical equivalent. And you are interested in learning how to relate yourself to others in a spirit of harmony.

Unfortunately our public schools have been silent on both of these important needs.

"Our educational system," said Dr. Henry C. Link, "has concentrated on mental development and has failed to give any understanding of the way emotional and personality habits are acquired or corrected."

His indictment is not without a sound foundation. The public-school system has failed in the obligation of which Dr. Link complains, because the law of Cosmic Habit force was but recently revealed, and even now it has not been recognized by the great mass of educators.

Everyone knows that practically everything we do, from the time we begin to walk, is the result of habit. Walking and talking are habits. Our manner of eating and drinking is a habit. Our sex activities are the results of habit. Our relationships with others, whether they are positive or negative, are the results of habits, but few people understand why or how we form habits.

Habits are inseparably related to the human ego. Therefore, let us turn to the analysis of this greatly misunderstood subject of the ego. But first let us recognize that the ego is the medium through which faith and all other states of mind operate.

Throughout this philosophy great emphasis has been placed upon the distinction between passive faith and active faith. The ego is the medium of expression of all action. Therefore we must know something of its nature and possibilities in order that we may make the best use of it. We must learn how to stimulate the ego to action and how to control and guide it to the attainment of definite ends.

Above all, we must disabuse our minds of the popular error of believing the ego to be only a medium for expression of vanity. The word "ego" is of Latin origin, and it means "I."

But it also connotes a driving force which may be organized and made to serve as the medium for translating desire into faith, through action.

THE MISUNDERSTOOD POWER OF THE EGO

The word ego has reference to all the factors of one's personality!

Therefore it is obvious that the ego is subject to development, guidance and control through voluntary habits—habits which we deliberately and with purpose forethought develop.

A great philosopher who devoted his entire life to the study of the human body and the mind, provided us with a practical foundation for the study of the ego when he stated:

"Your body, whether living or dead, is a collection of millions of little energies that can never die.

"These energies are separate and individual; at times they act in some degree of harmony.

"The human body is a drifting mechanism of life, capable but not accustomed to control the forces within, except as habit, will, cultivation or special excitement (through the emotion) may marshal these forces to the accomplishment of some important end.

"We are satisfied from many experiments that this power of marshalling and using these energies can be, in every person, cultivated to a high degree.

"The air, sunlight, food and water you take, are agents of a force which comes from the sky and earth. You idly float upon the tide of circumstances to make up your day's life, and the opportunities of being something better than you are drift beyond your reach and pass away.

"Humanity is hemmed in by so many influences that, from

time immemorial, no real effort has been made to gain control of the impulses that run loose in the world. It has been, and still is, easier to let things go as they will rather than exert the will to direct them.

"But the dividing line between success and failure is found at the stage where aimless drifting ceases (where Definiteness of Purpose begins).

"We are all creatures of emotions, passions, circumstances and accident. What the mind will be, what the heart will be, what the body will be, are problems which are shaped to the drift of life, even when special attention is given to any of them.

"If you will sit down and think for a while, *you will be surprised to know how much of your life has been mere drift.*

"Look at any created life, and see its efforts to express itself. The tree sends its branches toward the sunlight, struggles through its leaves to inhale air; and even underground sends forth its roots in search of water and the minerals it needs for food. This you call inanimate life; but it represents a force that comes from some source and operates for some purpose.

"There is no place on the globe where energy is not found.

"The air is so loaded with it that in the cold north the sky shines in boreal rays; and wherever the frigid temperature yields to the warmth, the electric conditions may alarm man. Water is but a liquid union of gases, and is charged with electrical, mechanical and chemical energies, any one of which is capable of doing great service and great damage to man.

"Even ice, in its coldest phase, has energy, for it is not subdued, nor even still; its force has broken mountain rocks into fragments. This energy about us we are drinking in water, eating in food and breathing in air. Not a chemical molecule is free from it; not an atom can exist without it. We are a combination of individual energies."

Man consists of two forces, one tangible, in the form of his physical body, with its myriad individual cells numbering billions, each of which is endowed with intelligence and energy; and the other intangible, in the form of an ego—the organized dictator of the body which may control man's thoughts and deeds.

Science teaches us the tangible portion of a man weighing one hundred and sixty pounds is composed of about seventeen chemical elements, all of which are known.

They are:
97 pounds of oxygen.
38 pounds of carbon.
15 pounds of hydrogen.
4 pounds of nitrogen.
4½ pounds of calcium.
6 ounces of chlorine.
4 ounces of sulphur.
3½ ounces of potassium.
3 ounces of sodium.
¼ ounce of iron.
2½ ounces of fluorin.
2 ounces of magnesium.
1½ ounces of silicon.

Small traces of arsenic, iodine and aluminum.

These tangible parts of man are worth commercially approximately eighty cents, and may be purchased in any modern chemical plant.

Add to these chemical elements a well-developed and properly organized and controlled ego, and they may be worth any price the owner sets upon them. The ego is a power which cannot be purchased at any price, but it can be developed and shaped to fit any desired pattern. The development takes place through organized habits which are made permanent by the law of Cosmic

Habit force, which carries out the thought-patterns one develops through controlled thought.

An Edison develops and guides his ego in the field of creative investigation, and the world finds a genius whose worth cannot be estimated in dollars alone.

A Henry Ford guides his ego in the field of automotive transportation and gives it such a stupendous value that it changes the trend of civilization by removing frontiers and converting mountain trails into public highways.

A Marconi magnetizes his ego with a keen desire to harness the ether and lives to see his wireless communication system evolve into the discovery of radio through which the world becomes akin, through instantaneous exchange of thought.

These men, and all others who have contributed to the march of progress, have given the world a demonstration of the power of a well-developed and carefully controlled ego.

One of the major differences between men who make valuable contributions to mankind and those who merely take up space in the world, is mainly a difference in egos, because the ego is the driving force behind all forms of human action.

Liberty and freedom of body and mind—the two major desires of all people—are available in exact proportion to the development and use one makes of the ego. Every person who has properly related himself to his own ego has both liberty and freedom in whatever proportions he desires.

A man's ego determines the manner in which he relates himself to all other people. More important than this, it determines the policy under which a man relates his own body and mind, wherein is patterned every hope, aim and purpose by which he fixes his destiny in life.

A man's ego is his greatest asset or his greatest liability, according to the way he relates himself to it. The ego is the sum total of one's thought habits which have been fastened upon him through the automatic operation of the law of Cosmic Habit force.

Every highly successful person possesses a well-developed and highly disciplined ego, but there is a third factor associated with the ego which determines its potency for good or evil—the self-control necessary to enable one to transmute its power into any desired purpose.

Autosuggestion (or self-hypnosis) is the medium by which one may attune his ego to any desired rate of vibration and charge it with the attainment of any desired purpose.

Unless you catch the full significance of the principle of auto-suggestion you will miss the most important part of this analysis, because the power of the ego is fixed entirely by the application of self-suggestion.

When this self-suggestion attains the status of faith the ego becomes limitless in its power.

The ego is kept alive and active, and it is given power by constant feeding. Like the physical body, the ego cannot and will not subsist without food.

It must be fed with Definiteness of Purpose.

It must be fed with Personal Initiative.

It must be fed with continuous action, through well-organized plans.

It must be supported with Enthusiasm.

It must be fed by Controlled Attention, directed to a definite end.

It must be controlled and directed through Self-discipline.

And it must be supported with Accurate Thought.

No man can become the master of anything or anyone until he becomes the master of his own ego.

No man can express himself in terms of opulence while most of his thought-power is given over to the maintenance of a "poverty consciousness." Nevertheless, one should not lose sight of the fact that many men of great wealth began in poverty—a fact which suggests that this and all other fears can be conquered and removed from interference with the ego.

In the one word, ego, may be found the composite effects of all the principles of individual achievement described in this philosophy, coordinated into one single unit of power which may be directed to any desired end by any individual who is the complete master of his ego.

We are preparing you to accept the fact that the most important power which is available to you—the one power which will determine whether you succeed or fail in your life's ambition—is that which is represented by your own ego.

We are also preparing you to brush aside that time-worn belief which associates the ego with self-love, vanity and vulgarity, and to recognize the truth that the ego is all there is of a man outside of the eighty cents' worth of chemicals, of which his physical body is composed.

Sex is the great creative force of man. It is definitely associated with and is an important part of one's ego. Both sex and the ego got their bad reputations from the fact that both are subject to destructive as well as constructive application, and both have been abused by the ignorant, from the beginning of the history of mankind.

The egoist who makes himself offensive through the expression of his ego is one who has not discovered how to relate himself to his ego in a manner which gives it constructive use.

Constructive application of the ego is made through the expressions of one's hopes, desires, aims, ambitions and plans, and not by boastfulness or self-love. The motto of the person who has his ego under control is, "Deeds not words."

The desire to be great, to be recognized and to have personal power, is a healthy desire; but an open expression of one's belief in his own greatness is an indication that he has not taken possession of his ego, that he has allowed it to take possession of him; and you may be sure that his proclamations of greatness are but a cloak with which to shield some fear or inferiority complex.

THE RELATIONSHIP BETWEEN THE EGO AND MENTAL ATTITUDE

Understand the real nature of your ego and you will understand the real significance of the Master Mind principle. Moreover, you will recognize that to be of the greatest service to you, the members of your Master Mind alliance must be in complete sympathy with your hopes, aims and purposes; that they must not be in competition with you in any manner whatsoever. They must be willing to subordinate their own desires and personalities entirely for the attainment of your major purpose in life.

They must have confidence in you and your integrity, and they must respect you. They must be willing to pander to your virtues and make allowances for your faults. They must be willing to permit you to be yourself and live your own life in your own way at all times. Lastly, they must receive from you some form of benefit which will make you as beneficial to them as they are to you.

Failure to observe the last mentioned requirement will bring to an end to the power of your Master Mind alliance.

Men relate themselves to one another in whatever capacities they may be associated because of a motive or motives. There can be no permanent human relationship based upon an indefinite or vague motive, or upon no motive at all. Failure to recognize this truth has cost many men the difference between penury and opulence.

The power which takes over the ego and clothes it with the material counterparts of the thoughts which give it shape, is the law of Cosmic Habit force. This law does not give quality or quantity to the ego; it merely takes what it finds and translates it into its physical equivalent.

The men of great achievement are, and they have always been, those who deliberately feed, shape and control their own egos, leaving no part of the task to luck or chance, or to the varying vicissitudes of life.

Every person may control the shaping of his own ego, but from that point on he has no more to do with what happens than does the farmer have anything to do with what happens to the seed he sows in the soil of the earth. The inexorable law of Cosmic Habit force causes every living thing to perpetuate itself after its kind, and it translates the picture which a man paints of his ego into its physical equivalent, as definitely as it develops an acorn into an oak tree, and no outside aid whatsoever is required, except time.

From these statements it is obvious that we are not only advocating the deliberate development and control of the ego, but also we are definitely warning that no man can hope to succeed in any calling without such control over his ego.

So that there may be no misunderstanding as to what is meant by the term "a properly developed ego" we shall describe briefly the factors which enter into its development, viz:

First, one must ally himself with one or more persons who will coordinate their minds with his in a spirit of perfect harmony for the attainment of a definite purpose, and that alliance must be continuous and active.

Moreover, the alliance must consist of people whose spiritual and mental qualities, education, sex and age are suited for aiding in the attainment of the purpose of the alliance. For example, Andrew Carnegie's Master Mind alliance was made up of more than twenty men, each of whom brought to the alliance some quality of mind, experience, education or knowledge which was directly related to the object of the alliance and not available through any of the other members of the alliance.

Second, having placed himself under the influence of the proper associates, one must adopt some definite plan by which to attain the object of the alliance and proceed to put that plan into action. The plan may be a composite plan created by the joint efforts of all the members of the Master Mind group.

If one plan proves to be unsound or inadequate, it must be supplemented or supplanted by others, until a plan is found which will work. But there must be no change in the purpose of the alliance.

Third, one must remove himself from the range of influence of every person and every circumstance which has even a slight tendency to cause him to feel inferior or incapable of attaining the object of his purpose. Positive egos do not grow in negative environments. On this point there can be no excuse for a compromise, and failure to observe it will prove fatal to the chances of success.

The line must be so clearly drawn between a man and those who exercise any form of negative influence over him that he closes the door tightly against every such person, no matter what previous ties of friendship or obligation or blood relationship may have existed between them.

Fourth, one must close the door tightly against every thought of any past experience or circumstance which tends to make him feel inferior or unhappy. Strong, vital egos cannot be developed by dwelling on thoughts of past unpleasant experiences. Vital egos thrive on the hopes and desires of the yet unattained objectives.

Thoughts are the building blocks from which the human ego is constructed. Cosmic Habit force is the cement which binds these blocks together in permanency, through fixed habits. When the job is finished it represents, right down to the smallest detail, the nature of the thoughts which went into the building.

It was Henry Ford's recognition of this truth which prompted him to remove from his business family every person who was out of step with his business policy.

It was Andrew Carnegie's complete understanding of this truth which caused him to insist upon complete harmony between himself and the members of his Master Mind group.

Fifth, one must surround himself with every possible physical means of impressing his mind with the nature and the purpose of the ego he is developing. For example, the author should set up his workshop in a room decorated with pictures and the works of authors in his field whom he most admires. He should fill his bookshelves with books related to his own work. He should surround himself with every possible means of conveying to his ego the exact picture of himself which he expects to express, because that picture is the pattern which the law of Cosmic Habit force will pick up; the picture which it translates into its physical equivalent.

Sixth, the properly developed ego is at all times under the control of the individual. There must be no over-inflation of the ego in the direction of "egomania" by which some men destroy themselves.

Egomania reveals itself by a mad desire to control others by force. Striking examples of such men are Adolph Hitler, Benito Mussolini and William Hohenzollern, the former Kaiser of Germany.

In the development of the ego, one's motto might well be, "Not too much, not too little, of anything." When men begin to thirst for control over others, or begin to accumulate large sums of money which they cannot or do not use constructively, they are treading upon dangerous grounds. Power of this nature grows of its own accord and soon gets out of control.

Nature has provided man with a safety valve through which she deflates the ego and relieves the pressure of its influence when an individual goes beyond certain limits in the development of the ego. Emerson called it the Law of Compensation, but what ever it is, it operates with inexorable definiteness.

Napoleon Bonaparte began to die, because of his crushed ego, on the day he landed on St. Helena Island.

People who quit work and retire from all forms of activity after having led active lives, generally atrophy and die soon thereafter. If they live they are usually miserable and unhappy. A healthy ego is one which is always in use and under complete control.

Seventh, the ego is constantly undergoing changes, for better or for worse, because of the nature of one's thought habits. The two factors which force these changes upon one are Time and the law of Cosmic Habit force.

We are here concerned with the desire to bring to your attention the importance of Time as a significant factor in the operation of Cosmic Habit force. Just as seed which are planted in the soil of the earth require definite periods of Time for their germination, development and growth, so do ideas, impulses of thought and desires which are planted in the mind require definite periods of Time during which the law of Cosmic Habit force gives them life and action.

There is no adequate means of describing or predetermining the exact period of Time which is required for the transformation of a desire into its physical equivalent. The nature of the desire, the circumstances which are related to it, and the intensity of the desire, are all determining factors in connection with the Time required for transformation from the thought stage to the physical stage.

The state of mind known as faith is so favorable for the quick change of desire into its physical equivalent that it has been known to make the change almost instantaneously.

Man matures physically within about twenty years, but mentally—which means the ego—requires from thirty-five to sixty years for maturity. This fact explains why men seldom begin to accumulate material riches in great abundance, or to attain outstanding records of achievement in other directions, until they are about fifty years of age.

The ego which can inspire a man to acquire and retain great material wealth is of necessity one which has undergone self-discipline, through which he acquires self-confidence, definiteness of purpose, personal initiative, imagination, accuracy of judgment and other qualities, without which no ego has the power to procure and hold wealth in abundance.

These qualities come through the proper use of Time. Observe that we did not say they come through the lapse of time.

Through the operation of Cosmic Habit force every individual's thought habits, whether they are negative or positive, whether of opulence or of poverty, are woven into the pattern of his ego, and there they are given permanent form which determines the nature and the extent of his spiritual and physical status.

About the beginning of the 1929 economic depression the owner of a small beauty salon turned over a back room in her place of business to an old man who needed a place to sleep. The man had no money, but he did have considerable knowledge of the methods of compounding cosmetics.

The owner of the salon gave him a place to sleep and provided him with an opportunity to pay for his room by compounding the cosmetics she used in her business.

Soon the two entered into a Master Mind alliance which was destined to bring each of them economic independence. First, they entered into a business partnership, with the object of compounding cosmetics to be sold from house to house; the woman providing the money for the raw materials, the man doing the work

After a few years the Master Mind arrangement between the two had proved so profitable that they decided to make it permanent by marriage, although there was a difference of more than twenty-five years in their ages.

The man had been in the cosmetic business for the better portion of his adult life, but he had never achieved success. The young woman had barely made a living from her beauty salon. The happy combination of the two brought them into possession of a power which neither had known prior to their alliance, and they began to succeed financially.

At the beginning of the depression they were compounding cosmetics in one small room, and selling their products personally from door to door. By the end of the depression, some eight years later, they were compounding their cosmetics in a large factory which they had bought and paid for, and had more than a hundred employees working steadily, and more than four thousand agents selling their products throughout the nation.

During this period they accumulated a fortune of over two million dollars, despite the fact that they were operating during depression years when such luxuries as cosmetics were naturally hard to sell.

They have placed themselves beyond the need for money for the remainder of their lives. Moreover, they have gained financial freedom on precisely the same knowledge and the same opportunities they possessed prior to their Master Mind alliance, when both were poverty-stricken.

We wish the names of these two interesting people could be revealed, but the circumstances of their alliance and the nature of the analysis we shall now present makes this impractical.

Nevertheless we are free to describe what we conceive to be the source of their astounding achievement, viewing every circumstance of their relationship entirely from the viewpoint of an unbiased analyst who is seeking only to present a true picture of the facts.

The motive which brought these two people together in a Master Mind alliance was definitely economic in nature.

The woman had previously been married to a man who failed to earn a living for her and who deserted her when her child was an infant. The man also had been previously married.

There was not the slightest indication of the emotion of love as a motive for their marriage. The motive was entirely a mutual desire for economic freedom.

The business and the elaborate home in which the couple live are entirely dominated by the old man, who, sincerely believes that he is responsible for both.

Their house is expensively furnished, but no one—not even invited guests—is permitted to take a turn at the piano, or to sit in one of the chairs in the living room, without special invitation from the "lord and master" of the household.

The main dining room is equipped with ornate furniture, including a long dining table which is suitable for use on "state" occasions, but the family is never permitted to use it on other occasions. They dine in the breakfast room, and nothing may be served at the table at any time except food of the "master's" choice.

A gardener is employed to attend the gardens, but no one is permitted to cut a flower without special invitation from the head of the house.

Such conversations as are carried on by the family are conducted entirely by the head of the house, and no one may intervene, not even to ask a question or to offer a remark, unless he invites it. His wife never speaks unless she is definitely requested to do so, and then her speech is very brief and carefully weighed so as not to irritate her "master."

Their business is incorporated and the man is the president of the company. He has an elaborate office which is furnished with a large hand-carved desk and overstuffed chairs.

On the wall, directly in front of his desk, is an enormous oil painting of himself at which he gazes, sometimes for an hour at a time, with obvious approval.

When he speaks of the business, and particularly of the unusual success it has enjoyed during the country's worst business depression, the man takes full credit for all that has been accomplished, and he never mentions his wife's name in connection with the business.

While the wife goes to business daily, she has no office and no desk. She is apt to be found strolling around among the workers, or assisting one of the girls in wrapping packages as nonchalantly as if she were an ordinary paid employee.

The man's name is on every package of merchandise which leaves the factory. It is printed in large letters on every delivery truck they operate, and it appears in large type on every piece of sales literature and in every advertisement they publish. The wife's name is conspicuous by its total absence.

The man believes that he built the business; that he operates it; that it could not operate without him. The truth of the matter is precisely the opposite. His ego built the business, runs it, and the business might continue to run as well or better without his presence as with it, for the very good reason that his wife developed that ego, and she could have done the same for any other man under similar circumstances.

Patiently, wisely and with purpose aforethought, this man's wife completely submerged her own personality into that of her husband, and step by step she fed his ego the type of food which removed from it every trace of his former inferiority complex, which was born of a lifetime of deprivation and failure. She hypnotized her husband into believing himself to be a great business tycoon.

Whatever degree of ego this man may have possessed before it came under the influence of a clever woman, had died of starvation. She revived his ego, nurtured it, fed it and developed it into a power of stupendous proportions despite his eccentric nature and his lack of business ability.

In truth every business policy, every business move, and every forward step the business has taken was the result of the wife's ideas, which she so cleverly planted in her husband's mind that he failed to recognize their source. In reality she is the brains of the business, he the mere window dressing; but the combination is unbeatable, as evidenced by their astounding financial achievements.

The manner in which this woman completely effaced herself was not only convincing evidence of her complete self-control, but it was evidence of her wisdom, for she probably knew she could not have accomplished the same results alone, or by any other methods than those she adopted.

This woman has very little formal education, and we have no idea how or where she learned enough about the operation of the human mind to inspire her to merge her entire personality with that of her husband for the purpose of developing in him the ego he now has. Perhaps the natural intuition which many women possess was responsible for her successful procedure. Whatever it was, she did a thorough job, and it sewed the ends she sought by bringing her economic security.

Here then is evidence that the major difference between poverty and riches is merely the difference between an ego that is dominated by an inferiority complex and one that is dominated by a feeling of superiority. This old man might have died a homeless pauper if a clever woman had not blended her mind with his in such a way as to feed his ego with thoughts of, and belief in, his ability to attain opulence.

This is a conclusion from which there is no escape. Moreover, this case is only one of many that could be cited which prove that the human ego must be fed, organized and directed to definite ends if one is to succeed in any walk of life.

The Henry Ford ego—famous because of what the public at large does not know about it—is a combination of his own ego and that of his wife. The definiteness and singleness of purpose, persistence, self-reliance and self-control—so obviously important parts of the Ford ego—can be traced largely to the influence of Mrs. Ford.

The Ford ego—quite unlike that of the cosmetician described—functions without glamour or ostentation of any kind. It functions in an obvious spirit of humility of the heart.

There are no large pictures of Henry Ford hanging on the walls of his office, but make no mistake about this: Mr. Ford's influence is felt by every person associated directly or indirectly with his vast industrial empire, and something of Henry Ford himself goes into every automobile which leaves his factories.

These are the means whereby he expresses his ego:

Through mechanical perfection; through transportation service which is dependable, at a popular price; through the satisfaction he gets from giving employment, directly and indirectly, to millions of men and women.

Mr. Ford is not above appreciating a word of praise, but he has never gone out of his way to attract it. His ego does not require constant pampering such as that which was given the cosmetician by his wife.

Mr. Ford's method of appropriating the knowledge and experience of other men is entirely different from that of Andrew Carnegie and most other business magnates. His ego is so modest and unassuming that he neither encourages favorable comment upon his work nor goes out of his way to express any form of appreciation of the compliments which are paid him.

Henry Ford has one of the truly great minds of the world. He has a great mind because he has learned to recognize the laws of nature and to adapt himself to them in a manner beneficial to himself, but many believe that his greatness is derived in a large measure from the influence of his wife and his association with other great minds, including those of Thomas A. Edison, Luther Burbank, John Burroughs and Harvey Firestone, with whom he had a Master Mind alliance for a great number of years.

For many years these five men left their respective businesses and went away together to some quiet spot where they exchanged thoughts and fed their egos on the food which each needed and craved.

Henry Ford's personality, his business policies, and even his physical appearance began to show a decided improvement from year to year because of his association with these four men. Their influence upon him was definite, deep, profound and enduring.

Henry Ford has his ego completely under his control. By studying men of great achievement one may observe that the space they occupy in the world is in exact proportion to the extent to which they dominate their egos.

The cosmetician occupies and controls only the space bounded by his own business and his household. It does not extend beyond these bounds, and it never can. His own mental attitude has fixed these limits and Cosmic Habit force has made the fixation permanent.

Henry Ford occupies, in one way or another, practically all of the space of the world, and he influences in many ways the entire trend of civilization. Because he is master of his ego, Henry Ford is capable of acquiring any material thing he may set his heart upon. In fact he has already done so.

The cosmetician expresses his ego in many forms of childish, petty, selfishness. Consequently he has limited his influence to the mere accumulation of a few million dollars, and the domination (without their consent) of a few hundred people, including his own household and his employees.

Henry Ford expresses his ego in ever-expanding and increasing terms of benefit to mankind and, without making a bid for it, finds himself an influencing factor throughout the world.

This is an astounding thought!

It provides vitally important suggestions as to the type of ego one should endeavor to develop.

Henry Ford has developed an ego which extends itself into plans which belt the entire earth. He thinks in terms of the manufacture and distribution of millions of automobiles.

He thinks in terms of tens of thousands of men and women working for him.

He thinks in terms of millions of dollars of working capital.

He thinks in terms of a business he dominates by establishing his own policies for procuring working capital by which he keeps his business out of the control of others.

He thinks in terms of economy through efficient coordination of the efforts of the thousands of men and women who work for him, by setting up pay schedules and working conditions far more favorable to his employees than they could reasonably demand.

He thinks in terms of harmonious cooperation between himself and his business associates, and puts his thoughts into action by removing from his organization any man who does not see eye to eye with him.

These are the qualities and traits of character which nourish, feed and maintain the Ford ego. There is nothing about any of these qualities which is difficult to understand. They are qualities which any man may have by simply adopting them and using them.

Turn the spotlight on the many men who began to build automobiles after Henry Ford began; study each of the men carefully and you will learn quickly why one remembers but few of those men, or the brands of automobiles they temporarily produced.

You will discover that every one of the Ford competitors who fell by the wayside did so because of self-imposed limitations or dissipation of the ego. You will also find that practically every one of these forgotten men apparently possessed as much intelligence as Henry Ford. The majority of them not only had better educations than he, but many of them had more dynamic personalities.

The major difference between Henry Ford and his competitors of the past is this: He developed an ego which extended itself far beyond his personal achievements; the others so limited their egos that they soon caught up with them, and their plans went on the rocks for want of that something which an extended, flexible ego does to lead a man forward.

Among the hundreds of Ford competitors who started to make automobiles soon after he began, there was one man who made such rapid progress that he probably would have eclipsed Ford's achievements in the industry if something had not gone wrong with his ego.

That man's outstanding qualities were: a magnetic personality, a well-rounded formal education, marvelous capacity as a salesman and sales organizer, and a record of achievement in a great industrial enterprise outside of the automotive field of such magnitude as to enable him to procure all the working capital he needed.

When he was at the height of his career he was the head of his own company, manufacturing an automobile which led the field in its price class. Even at the outset of his career he had before him a future far more promising than that of Henry Ford. His name was then a national byword in the automotive field.

His ego was dynamic, powerful and ambitious. According to the rules by which men are usually judged, he should have outdistanced Henry Ford in a few more years of operations. But something happened to him at the very height of his career which sent him into financial oblivion and quickly erased his name from the list of automobile manufacturers.

The tragedy which happened was this:

Success went to his head and he allowed his ego to become so greatly over inflated that it literally blew up and burst!

Had he acquired humility of the heart, as did Henry Ford, he would have equaled Ford's achievements, or perhaps he would have excelled them. He had everything which was required for success except the self-discipline necessary to shape his ego and control it. Therefore his ego took possession of him and led him to ruin.

The well-balanced ego is not subject to serious influence by either commendation or condemnation. The man with a well-balanced ego sets his sails in the direction of his Definite Major Purpose, moves on his personal initiative in the direction of that purpose, and never looks to the right or to the left. He accepts both defeat and victory as the natural essentials of life, but he does not allow either to modify his plans.

No one ever heard of Henry Ford spending an evening among social butterflies and cocktail glasses. No one ever read a newspaper account of Ford having boasted of his achievements. The Ford ego was not evolved from such influences, and that is why it became powerful and healthy, hale and rich, at an age when most men consider themselves ready for the scrap heap.

The Ford ego is exactly as Mr. Ford desires it to be. He is in control of it at all times; therefore he occupies more space and carries more influence in the world than any other industrialist. What an astounding fact; and all the more so when one considers the lowly beginning from which Mr. Ford started, with but little education, no working capital, no extensive influence, no credit privileges; with nothing but a Definite Major Purpose plus the qualities he acquired by the application of the seventeen principles of this philosophy. These were enough!

Henry Ford's power and fortune are not based upon knowledge alone. They are not based upon intelligence alone. They are not based upon education. They are in no way associated with luck, good fortune, or his having been born under the "right star." The Ford power is only the expression of the self-made ego which is absolutely free from all manner of fear, and which is not fettered by any self-imposed limitations.

Henry Ford has taken possession of his own mind and has learned to direct it to the attainment of his desires.

When Mr. Ford told a group of newspaper men, who accosted him on a visit to the White House, that he had come to Washington to let the President see a man who did not come to ask any favors and who did not want anything, he was neither egotistical nor facetious. He spoke a truth with stupendous connotations.

Henry Ford can get any material thing he desires, or its adequate equivalent, because he has developed and controls his own ego! There is no other mystery to his great power.

Henry Ford has long been a resident of Happy Valley.

He attained a place in that great estate by the proper organization and usage of his own ego. He developed that ego by the application of the principles of this philosophy, through which he came into possession of the great Master Key to Riches.

And you who are learning to assimilate this philosophy may reach that estate in the same manner. You have, in the seventeen principles of this philosophy, all that is required to place you in possession of the Master Key!

You are now in possession of all the practical knowledge which has been used by successful men from the dawn of civilization to the present.

This is a complete philosophy of life—sufficient for every human need. It holds the secret to the solution of all human problems. And it has been presented in terms which the humblest person may understand.

You may not aspire to become a Henry Ford, or a Thomas A. Edison, but you can and you should aspire to make yourself useful in order that you may occupy as much space in the world as your ego desires.

Every man comes finally to resemble those who make the strongest impression upon his ego. We are all creatures of imitation, and naturally we endeavor to imitate the heroes of our choice. This is a natural and healthful trait.

Fortunate indeed is the man whose hero is a person of great Faith, because hero worship carries with it something of the nature of the hero one worships.

In conclusion let us summarize what has been said on the subject of the ego by calling attention to the fact that it represents the fertile garden spot of the mind wherein one may develop all the stimuli which inspire active Faith, or by neglecting to do so he may allow this fertile soil to produce a negative crop of fear and doubt and indecision which will lead to failure.

You now have at your command a *complete philosophy* of life that is sufficient for the solution of every individual problem.

It is a philosophy of principles, some combination of which has been responsible for every individual success in every occupation or calling, although many may have used the philosophy successfully without recognizing the seventeen principles by the names we have given them.

No essential factor of successful achievement has been omitted. The philosophy embraces them all and describes them in words and similes that are well within the understanding of a majority of the people.

It is a philosophy of concreteness that touches only rarely the abstractions, and then only when necessary. It is free from academic terms and phrases which all too often serve only to confuse the average person.

The overall purpose of the philosophy is to enable one to get from where he stands to where he wishes to be, both economically and spiritually; thus it prepares one to enjoy the abundant life which the Creator intended all people to enjoy.

And it leads to the attainment of "riches" in the broadest and fullest meaning of the word, *including the twelve most important of all riches.*

The world has been greatly enriched by abstract philosophies, from the days of Plato, Socrates, Copernicus, Aristotle and many others of the same profound caliber of thinkers, on down to the days of Ralph Waldo Emerson and William James.

Now the world has the first complete, concrete philosophy of individual achievement that provides the individual with the practical means by which he may take possession of his own mind and direct it to the attainment of peace of mind, harmony in human relationships, economic security, and the fuller life known as happiness.

Not as an apology, but to serve as an explanation, I shall call your attention to the fact that throughout this analysis of the seventeen principles we have emphasized the more important of these principles by continuous reference to them. The repetition was not accidental!

It was deliberate and necessary because of the tendency of all mankind to be unimpressed by new ideas or new interpretations of old truths.

Repetition has been necessary also because of the interrelationship of the seventeen principles, being connected as they are like the links of a chain, each one extending into and becoming a part of the principle preceding it and the principle following it.

And lastly, let us recognize that repetition of ideas is one of the basic principles of effective pedagogy and the central core of all effective advertising. Therefore it is not only justified, but it is definitely necessary as a means of human progress.

When you have assimilated this philosophy you will have a better education than the majority of people who graduate from college with the Master of Arts degree. You will be in possession of all the more useful knowledge which has been organized from the experiences of the most successful men this nation has produced, and you will have it in a form which you can understand and apply.

But remember that the responsibility for the proper use of this knowledge will be yours. The mere possession of the knowledge will avail you nothing. Its use is what will count.

11

SELF-DISCIPLINE

The man who acquires the ability to take full possession of his own mind may take possession of everything else to which he is justly entitled.

—ANDREW CARNEGIE

We shall now reveal the methods by which one may take possession of his own mind.

We begin with a quotation from a man who proved the truth of his statement by his astounding achievements.

Mr. Carnegie not only acquired more material riches than he needed, but he acquired also the other eleven riches, and the more important of the Twelve Riches of Life.

And those who knew him best, who worked with him most closely, say that his most outstanding trait of character consisted in the fact that he took full possession of his own mind at an early age, and never gave up any portion of his right to think his own thoughts.

What an achievement! And what a blessing it would be if every person could truthfully say, "I am the master of my fate; I am the Captain of my soul."

The Creator probably intended it to be so!

If it had been intended otherwise man would not have been limited solely to the right of control over but one power—the power of his own thoughts.

We go all the way through life searching for freedom of body and mind, yet most men never find it! Why? The Creator provided the means by which men may be free, and gave every man access to these means; and also inspired every man with impelling motives for the attainment of freedom.

Why then do men go through life imprisoned in a jail of their own making, when the key to the door is so easily within their reach? The jail of poverty, the jail of ill health, the jail of fear, the jail of ignorance.

The desire for freedom of body and mind is a universal desire among all peoples, but few ever attain it because most men who search for it look everywhere except the one and only source from which it may come—*within their own minds*.

The desire for riches is also a universal desire, but most men never come within sight of the real riches of life because they do not recognize that all riches begin within their own minds.

Men search all their lives for power and fame without attaining either, because they do not recognize that the real source of both is within their own minds.

The mechanism of the mind is a profound system of organized power which can be released only by one means, and that is by strict *self-discipline*.

The mind that is properly disciplined and directed to definite ends is an irresistible power that recognizes no such reality as permanent defeat. It organizes defeat and converts it into victory; makes stepping-stones of stumbling blocks; hitches its wagon to a star and uses the forces of the universe to carry it within easy grasp of its every desire.

And the man who masters himself through self-discipline never can be mastered by others!

Self-discipline is one of the Twelve Riches, but it is much more; it is an important prerequisite for the attainment of all riches, including freedom of body and mind, power and fame, and all the material things that men call wealth.

It is the sole means by which one may focus the mind upon the objective of a Definite Major Purpose until the law of Cosmic Habit force takes over the pattern of that purpose and begins to translate it into its material equivalent.

It is the key to the volitional power of the will and the emotions of the heart, for it is the means by which these two may be mastered and balanced, one against the other, and directed to definite ends in accurate thinking.

It is the directing force in the maintenance of a Definite Major Purpose.

It is the source of all persistence and the means by which one may develop the habit of carrying through his plans and purposes.

It is the power with which all thought habits are patterned and sustained until they are taken over by the law of Cosmic Habit force and carried out to their logical climax.

It is the means by which one may take full and complete control of his mind and direct it to whatever ends he may desire.

It is indispensable in all leadership.

And it is the power through which one may make of his conscience a cooperator and guide instead of a conspirator.

It is the policeman who clears the mind for the expression of Faith, by the mastery of all fears.

It clears the mind for the expression of Imagination and of Creative Vision.

It does away with indecision and doubt.

It helps one to create and to sustain the "prosperity consciousness" that is essential for the accumulation of material riches, and the "health consciousness" necessary for the maintenance of sound physical health.

Also it operates entirely through the functioning system of the mind. Therefore, let us examine this system so that we may understand the factors of which it consists.

The Ten Factors of the "Mechanism" of Thought

The mind operates through ten factors, some of which operate automatically, while others must be directed through voluntary effort. Self-discipline is the sole means of this direction.

These ten factors are:

1. INFINITE INTELLIGENCE: The source of all
    power of thought, which operates automatically,
    but it may be organized and directed to definite
    ends through Definiteness of Purpose.

Infinite Intelligence may be likened to a great reservoir of water that overflows continuously, its branches flowing in small streams in many directions, and giving life to all vegetation and all living things. That portion of the stream which gives life to man supplies him also with the power of thought.

The brain of man may be likened to the water spigot, while the water flowing through the spigot represents Infinite Intelligence. The brain does not generate the power of thought; it merely receives that power from Infinite Intelligence and applies it to whatever ends the individual desires.

And remember, this privilege of the control and the direction of thought is the only prerogative over which an individual has been given complete control. He may use it to build, or he may use it to destroy. He may give it direction, through Definiteness of Purpose, or he may neglect to do so, as he chooses.

The exercise of this great privilege is attained solely by self-discipline.

2. THE CONSCIOUS MIND: The individual mind functions through two departments. One is known as the conscious section of the mind, the other as the subconscious section. It is the opinion of psychologists that these two sections are comparable to an iceberg, the visible portion above the water line representing the conscious section, the invisible portion below the water line representing the subconscious section. Therefore it is obvious that the conscious section of the mind—that portion with which we consciously and voluntarily turn on the power of thought—is but a small portion of the whole, consisting of not more than one-fifth of the available mind Power.

The subconscious section of the mind operates automatically. It carries on all the necessary functions in connection with the building and the maintenance of the physical body; keeps the heart beating to circulate the blood; assimilates the food through a perfect system of chemistry, and delivers the food in liquid form throughout the body; removes worn out cells and replaces them with new cells; removes bacteria which are deleterious to health; creates new physical beings by the blending of the cells of protoplasm (the formative material of animal embryos) contributed by the male and female of living organisms.

These and many other essential functions are performed by the subconscious section of the mind, in addition to which it serves as the connecting link between the conscious mind and Infinite Intelligence.

It may be likened to the spigot of the conscious mind, through which (by its control through self-discipline) more thought power may be turned on. Or it may be likened to a rich garden soot wherein may be planted and germinated the seed of any desired idea.

The importance of the subconscious section of the mind may be estimated by recognition of the fact that it is the only means of voluntary approach to Infinite Intelligence. Therefore it is the medium by which all prayers are conveyed and all answers to prayer are received.

It is the medium that translates one's Definite Major Purpose into its material equivalent, a process which consists entirely in guidance of the individual in the proper use of the natural means of attaining the objects of his desires.

The subconscious section of the mind acts upon all impulses of thought, carrying out to their logical conclusion all thoughts which are definitely shaped by the conscious mind, but it gives preference to thoughts inspired by emotional feeling, such as the emotion of fear or the emotion of Faith; hence the necessity for self-discipline as a means of providing the subconscious mind with only those thoughts or desires which lead to the attainment of whatever one wishes.

The subconscious section of the mind gives preference also to the dominating thoughts of the mind—those thoughts which one creates by the repetition of ideas or desires. This fact explains the importance of adopting a Definite Major Purpose and the necessity of fixing that purpose (through self-discipline) as a dominating thought of the mind.

3. THE FACULTY OF WILL POWER: The power of the will is the "boss" of all departments of the mind. It has the power to modify, change or balance all thinking habits, and its decisions

are final and irrevocable except by itself. It is the power that puts the emotions of the heart under control, and it is subject to direction only by self-discipline. In this connection it may be likened to the Chairman of a Board of Directors whose decisions are final. It takes its orders from the conscious mind, but recognizes no other authority.

4. THE FACULTY OF REASON: This is the "presiding judge" of the conscious section of the mind which may pass judgment on all ideas, plans and desires, and it will do so if it is directed by self-discipline. But its decisions can be set aside by the power of the will, or modified by the power of the emotions when the will does not interfere. Let us here take note of the fact that all accurate thinking requires the cooperation of the faculty of reason, *although it is a requirement which not more than one person in every ten thousand respects.* This explains why there are so few accurate thinkers.

Most so-called thinking is the work of the emotions without the guiding influence of self-discipline, without relationship to either the power of the will or the faculty of reason.

5. THE FACULTY OF THE EMOTIONS: This is the source of most of the actions of the mind, the seat of most of the thoughts released by the conscious section of the mind. The emotions are tricky and undependable and may be very dangerous if they are not modified by the faculty of reason under the direction of the faculty of the will.

However, the faculty of the emotions is not to be condemned because of its undependability, for it is the source of all enthusiasm, imagination and Creative Vision, and it may be directed by self-discipline to the development of these essentials of individual achievement. The direction may be given by modification of the emotions through the faculties of the will and the reason.

Accurate thinking is not possible without complete mastery of the emotions.

Mastery is attained by placing the emotions under the control of the will, thus preparing them for direction to whatever ends the will may dictate, modifying them when necessary through the faculty of reason.

The accurate thinker has no opinions and makes no decisions which have not been submitted to, and passed upon by, the faculties of the will and the reason. He uses his emotions to inspire the creation of ideas through his imagination, but refines his ideas through his will and reason before their final acceptance.

This is self-discipline of the highest order. The procedure is simple but it is not easy to follow; and it is never followed except by the accurate thinker who moves on his own personal initiative.

The more important of the Twelve Riches, such as (1) a positive mental attitude, (2) harmony in human relationships, (3) freedom from fear, (4) the hope of achievement, (5) the capacity for faith, (6) an open mind on all subjects, and (7) sound physical health, *are attainable only by a strict direction and control of all the emotions.* This does not mean that the emotions should be suppressed, but they must be controlled and directed to definite ends.

The emotions may be likened to steam in a boiler, the power of which consists in its release and direction through he mechanism of an engine. Uncontrolled steam has no power, and to be controlled it must be released through a governor, which is a mechanical device corresponding to self-discipline in connection with the control and release of emotional power.

The emotions which are most important and most dangerous are, (1) the emotion of sex, (2) the emotion of love, and (3) the emotion of fear. *These are the emotions which produce the major portion of all human activities.* The emotions of love and sex are creative. When controlled and directed they inspire one with imagination and creative vision of stupendous proportions. If they are not controlled and directed they may lead one to indulge in destructive follies.

6. THE FACULTY OF IMAGINATION: This is the workshop wherein are shaped and fashioned all desires, ideas, plans and purposes, together with the means of attaining them. Through organized use and self-discipline the imagination may be developed to the status of Creative Vision.

But the faculty of the imagination, like the faculty of the emotions, is tricky and undependable if it is not controlled and directed by self-discipline. Without control it often dissipates the power of thought in useless, impractical and destructive activities which need not be here mentioned in detail. Uncontrolled imagination is the stuff that daydreams are made of!

Control of the imagination begins with the adoption of definiteness of purpose based on definite plans. The control is completed by strict habits of self-discipline which give definite direction to the faculty of the emotions, for the power of the emotions is the power that inspires the imagination to action.

7. THE FACULTY OF THE CONSCIENCE: The conscience is the moral guide of the mind, and its

major purpose is that of modifying the individual's aims and purposes so that they harmonize
with the moral laws of nature and of mankind.
The conscience is a twin-brother of the faculty of
reason in that it gives discrimination and guidance to the reason when reason is in doubt.

The conscience functions as a cooperative guide only so long
as it is respected and followed. If it is neglected, or its mandates
are rejected, it finally becomes a conspirator instead of a guide,
and often volunteers to justify man's most destructive habits.
Thus the dual nature of the conscience makes it necessary for
one to direct it through strict self-discipline.

8. THE SIXTH SENSE: This is the "broadcasting
station" of the mind through which one automatically sends and receives the vibrations of
thought commonly known as telepathy. It is the
medium through which all thought impulses
known as "hunches" are received. And it is
closely related to, or perhaps it may be a part of
the subconscious section of the mind.

The sixth sense is the medium through which Creative Vision operates. It is the medium through which all basically new
ideas are revealed. And it is the major asset of the minds of all
men who are recognized as "geniuses."

9. THE MEMORY: This is the "filing cabinet" of the
brain, wherein is stored all thought impulses,
all experiences and all sensations that reach the
brain through the five physical senses. And it
may be the "filing cabinet" of all impulses of

thought which reach the mind through the sixth
sense, although all psychologists do not agree as
to this.

The memory is tricky and undependable unless it is organized and directed by self-discipline.

10. THE FIVE PHYSICAL SENSES: These are the
physical "arms" of the brain through which it
contacts the external world and acquires information therefrom. The physical senses are not
reliable, and therefore they need constant self-
discipline. Under any kind of intense emotional
activity the senses become confused and unreliable.

By the simplest sort of legerdemain the five physical senses
may be deceived. And they are deceived daily by the common
experiences of life. Under the emotion of fear the physical senses
often create monstrous "ghosts" which have no existence except
in the faculty of the imagination, and there is no fact of life
which they will not and do not exaggerate or distort when fear
prevails.

Thus we have briefly described the ten factors which enter
into all mental activities of man. But we have supplied enough
information concerning the "mechanism" of the mind to indicate clearly the necessity for self-discipline in their manipulation
and use.

Self-discipline is attained by the control of thought habits.
And the term "self-discipline" has reference only to the power
of thought, because all discipline of self must take place in the
mind, although its effects may deal with the functions of the
physical body.

You are where you are and what you are because of your habits of thought!

Your thought habits are subject to your control!

They are the only circumstances of your life over which you have complete control, which is the most profound of all the facts of your life because it clearly proves that your Creator recognized the necessity of this great prerogative privilege. Otherwise He would not have made it the sole circumstance over which man has been given exclusive control.

Further evidence of the Creator's desire to give man the unchallengeable right of control over his thought habits has been clearly revealed through the law of Cosmic Habit force—the medium by which thought habits are fixed and made permanent, so that habits become automatic and operate without the voluntary effort of man.

For the present we are interested only in calling attention to the fact that the Creator of the marvelous mechanism known as a brain ingeniously provided it with a device by which all thought habits are taken over and given automatic expression.

Self-discipline is the principle by which one may voluntarily shape the patterns of thought to harmonize with his aims and purposes.

This privilege carries with it a heavy responsibility because it is the one privilege which determines, more than all others, the position in life which each man shall occupy. If this privilege is neglected, by one's failure to voluntarily form habits designed to lead to the attainment of definite ends, then the circumstances of life which are beyond one's control will do the job; and what an extremely poor job it often becomes!

Every man is a bundle of habits. Some are of his own making while others are involuntary. They are made by his fears and doubts and worries and anxieties and greed and superstition and envy and hatred.

Self-discipline is the only means by which one's habits of thought may be controlled and directed until they are taken over and given automatic expression by the law of Cosmic

Habit force. Ponder this thought carefully, for it is the key to your mental, physical and spiritual destiny.

You can make your thought habits to order and they will carry you to the attainment of any desired goal within your reach. Or you can allow the uncontrollable circumstances of your life to make your thought habits for you and they will carry you irresistibly into the failure side of the great River of Life.

You can keep your mind trained on that which you desire from Life and get just that! Or you can feed it on thoughts of that which you do not desire and it will, as unerringly, bring you just that. Your thought habits evolve from the food that your mind dwells upon.

That is as certain as that night follows day!

Awake, arise, and quicken your mind to the attunement of the circumstances of life which your heart craves.

Turn on the full powers of your will and take complete control of your own mind. It is your mind! It was given to you as a servant to carry out your desires. And no one may enter it or influence it in the slightest degree without your consent and cooperation. What a profound fact this is!

Remember this when the circumstances over which you appear to have no control begin to move in and aggravate you. Remember it when fear and doubt and worry begin to park themselves in the spare bedroom of your mind. Remember it when the fear of poverty begins to park itself in the space of your mind that should be filled with a "prosperity consciousness."

And remember, too, that this is self-discipline—the one and only method by which anyone may take full possession of his own mind.

You are not a worm made to crawl in the dust of the earth.

If you were you would have been equipped with the physical means by which you would have crawled on your belly instead of walking on your two legs. Your physical body was designed to enable you to stand and to walk and to think your way to the highest attainment which you are capable of conceiving. Why be contented with less? Why should you insult your Creator by indifference or neglect in the use of His most priceless gift—the power of your own mind?

The potential powers of the human mind are beyond comprehension.

And one of the great mysteries which has endured down through the ages consists in man's neglect to recognize and to use these powers as a means of shaping his own earthly destiny!

The mind has been cleverly provided with a gateway of approach to Infinite Intelligence, through the subconscious section of the mind; and this gateway has been so arranged that it can be opened for voluntary use by preparation through that state of mind known as Faith.

The mind has been provided with a faculty of imagination wherein may be fashioned ways and means of translating hope and purpose into physical realities.

It has been provided with the stimulative capacity of desire and enthusiasm with which one's plans and purposes may be given action.

It has been provided with the power of the will through which both plan and purpose may be sustained indefinitely.

It has been given the capacity for Faith, through which the will and the reasoning faculty may be subdued while the entire machinery of the brain is turned over to the guiding force of Infinite Intelligence; and it has been prepared, through a sixth sense, for direct connection with other minds (under the Master Mind principle) from which it may add to its own power the stimulative forces of other minds which serve so effectively to stimulate the imagination.

It has been given the capacity to reason, through which facts and theories may be combined into hypotheses, ideas and plans.

It has been given the power to project itself into other minds, through what is known as telepathy.

It has been given the power of deduction by which it may foretell the future by analysis of the past. This capacity explains why the philosopher looks backward in order that he may see the future.

It has been provided with the means of selection, modification and control of the nature of its thoughts, thereby giving to man the privilege of building his own character to order, to fit any desired pattern, and the power to determine the kind of thoughts which shall dominate his mind.

It has been provided with a marvelous filing system for receiving, recording and recalling every thought it has expressed, through what is known as a memory, and this marvelous system automatically classifies and files related thoughts in such a manner that the recall of one particular thought leads to the recall of associated thoughts.

It has been provided with the power of emotion through which it can stimulate at will the body for any desired action.

It has been given the power to function secretly and silently, thereby insuring privacy of thought under all circumstances.

It has an unlimited capacity to receive, organize, store and express knowledge on all subjects, in both the fields of physics and metaphysics, the outer world and the inner world.

It has the power to aid in the maintenance of sound physical health, and apparently it is the sole source of cure of physical ills, all other sources being merely contributory; and it maintains a perfect repair system for the upkeep of the physical body—a system that works automatically.

It maintains and automatically operates a marvelous system of chemistry through which it converts food into suitable combinations for the maintenance and repair of the body.

It automatically operates the heart through which the bloodstream distributes food to every portion of the body and removes all waste materials and worn out cells of the body.

It has the power of self-discipline through which it can form any desired habit and maintain it until it is taken over by the law of Cosmic Habit force and is given automatic expression.

It is the common meeting ground wherein man may commune with Infinite Intelligence, through prayer (or any form of expressed desire or definiteness of purpose) by the simple process of opening the gateway of approach through the subconscious section of the mind, by Faith.

It is the sole producer of every idea, every tool, every machine and every mechanical invention created by man for his convenience in the business of living in a material world.

It is the sole source of all happiness and all misery, and of both poverty and riches of every nature whatsoever, and it devotes its energies to the expression of whichever of these that dominates the mind through the power of thought.

It is the source of all human relationships, and all forms of intercourse between men; the builder of friendships and the creator of enemies, according to the manner in which it is directed.

It has the power to resist and defend itself against all external circumstances and conditions, although it cannot always control them.

It has no limitations within reason (no limitations except those which conflict with the laws of nature) save only those which the individual accepts through the lack of Faith!

Truly, "whatever the mind can conceive and believe the mind can achieve."

It has the power to change from one mood to another at will. Therefore it need never be damaged beyond repair by any kind of discouragement.

It can relax into temporary oblivion through sleep, and prepare itself for a fresh start within a few hours.

It grows stronger and more dependable the more it is controlled, directed to definite ends and used voluntarily.

It can convert sound into music that rests and soothes both the body and the soul.

It can send the sound of the human voice around the earth in a fraction of a minute.

It can make two blades of grass grow where but one grew before.

It can build a printing press that receives a roll of paper at one end and turns out a completely printed and bound book at the other end, in a few moments.

It can call back the sunlight at will, at any time of the day, by merely causing the pushing of a button.

It can convert water into steam power and steam into electric power.

The mind can control the temperature of heat at will, and it can create fire by rubbing two sticks together.

It can produce music by drawing a hair from the tail of a horse across strings made from the internals of a cat.

It can accurately locate any position on earth by observation of the position of the stars.

It can harness the law of gravitation and make it do the work of man and beast in ways too numerous for mention.

It can build a machine that will generate electrical power from the air.

It can build an airplane that will safely transport human beings through the air.

It can build a machine that will penetrate the human body with light and photograph the bones and the soft tissues without injury.

It has the power of clairvoyance through which it can discern physical objects not present or visible to the naked eye.

It can clear the jungle and convert the desert into a garden spot of productivity.

It can harness the waves of the oceans and convert them into power for the operation of machinery.

It can produce glass that will not break and convert wood pulp into clothing.

It can transform the stumbling blocks of failure into stepping-stones of achievement.

It can build a machine that can detect falsehoods.

It can accurately measure any circle by the smallest fragment of its arc.

It can produce rubber from chemicals.

It can reproduce a picture of any material object, by television, without the aid of the human eye.

It can determine the size, weight and material contents of the sun, over 93,000,000 miles away, by analysis of the sun's rays of light.

It can create a mechanical eye that can detect the presence of airplanes or submarines, or any other physical object, hundreds of miles distant.

It can seal hermetically any type of food and preserve it indefinitely.

It can record and reproduce any sound, including the human voice, with the aid of a machine and a piece of wax.

It can record and reproduce pictures of any kind of physical motion, with the aid of a piece of glass and a strip of celluloid.

It can build a machine that will travel in the air, on the ground or under the water.

It can build a machine that will plough its way through the thickest forest, smashing trees as if they were cornstalks.

It can build a shovel that will lift as many tons of dirt in a minute as ten men could move in a day.

It can harness the magnetic poles of the northern and southern portions of the earth, with the aid of a compass, and determine direction accurately.

Great and powerful is the mind of man, and it shall yet perform feats which will make all the foregoing seem as trifles by comparison.

And yet, despite all this astounding power of the mind the great majority of the people make no attempt to take control of their minds and they suffer themselves to become cowed by fears or difficulties which do not exist save in their own imaginations.

The arch enemy of mankind is FEAR!

We fear poverty in the midst of an overabundance of riches!

We fear ill health despite the ingenious system nature has provided with which the physical body is automatically maintained, repaired and kept in working order.

We fear criticism when there are no critics save only those which we set up in our own minds through the negative use of our imagination.

We fear the loss of love of friends and relatives although we know well enough that our own conduct may be sufficient to maintain love through all ordinary circumstances of human relationship.

We fear old age whereas we should accept it as a medium of greater wisdom and understanding.

We fear the loss of liberty although we know that liberty is a matter of harmonious relationships with others.

We fear death when we know it is inevitable; therefore beyond our control.

We fear failure, not recognizing that every failure carries with it the seed of an equivalent benefit.

And we feared the lightning until Franklin and Edison and a few other rare individuals, who dared to take possession of their own minds, proved that lightning is a form of physical energy which can be harnessed and used for the benefit of mankind.

Instead of opening our minds for the guidance of Infinite Intelligence, through Faith, we close our minds tightly with every conceivable shade and degree of self-imposed limitation based upon unnecessary fears.

We know that man is the master of every other living creature on this earth, yet we fail to look about us and learn from birds of the air and beasts of the jungle that even the dumb animals have been wisely provided with food and all the necessities of their existence through the universal plan which makes all fears groundless and foolish.

We complain of lack of opportunity and cry out against those who dare to take possession of their own minds, not recognizing that every man who has a sound mind has the right and the power to provide himself with every material thing he needs or can use.

We fear the discomfort of physical pain, not recognizing that pain is a universal language through which man is warned of evils and dangers that need correction.

Because of our fears we go to the Creator with prayers over

petty details which we could and should settle for ourselves, then give up and lose Faith (if we had any Faith to begin with) when we do not get the results we ask for, not recognizing our duty to offer prayers of thanks for the bountiful blessings which we have been provided through the power of our minds.

We talk and preach sermons about sin, failing to recognize that the greatest of all sins is that of the loss of Faith in an all-wise Creator who has provided His children with more blessings than any earthly parent ever thinks of providing for his own children.

We convert the revelations of inventions into the tools of destruction through what we politely call "war," then cry out in protest when the law of compensation pays us off with famines and business depressions.

We abuse the power of the mind in ways too numerous for mention, because we have not recognized that this power can be harnessed through self-discipline, and used to serve our needs.

Thus we go all the way through life, eating the husks and throwing away the kernels of plenty!

SOME OF THE KNOWN FACTS CONCERNING THE NATURE OF THOUGHT

Before leaving the analysis of self-discipline, which deals entirely with the "mechanism" of thought, let us briefly describe some of the known facts and habits of thought in order that we may acquire the art of accurate thinking.

1. All thought (whether it is positive or negative, good or bad, accurate or inaccurate) tends to clothe itself in its physical equivalent, and it does so by inspiring one with ideas, plans, and the means of attaining desired ends, through logical and natural means.

After thought on any given subject becomes a habit and has been taken over by the law of Cosmic Habit force, the subconscious section of the mind proceeds to carry it out to its logical conclusion, through the aid of whatever natural media that may be available.

It may not be literally true that "thoughts are things" but it is true that thoughts create all things, and the things it creates are striking duplicates of the thought patterns from which they are fashioned.

It is believed by some that every thought one releases starts an unending series of vibrations with which the one who releases the thought will later be compelled to contend; that man himself is but a physical reflection of thought put into motion and crystallized into physical form by Infinite Intelligence.

It is also the belief of many that the energy with which man thinks is but a projected minute portion of Infinite Intelligence, appropriated from the universal supply through the equipment of the brain. No thought contrary to this belief has yet been proved sound.

2. Through the application of self-discipline thought can be influenced, controlled and directed through transmutation to a desired end, by the development of voluntary habits suitable for the attainment of any given end.

3. The power of thought (through the aid of the subconscious section of the mind) has control over every cell of the body, carries on all repairs and replacements of injured or dead cells, stimulates their growth, influences the action of all organs of the body and helps them to function by habit and orderliness, and assists in fighting disease through what is commonly called

"body resistance." These functions are carried
on automatically, but many of them may be
stimulated by voluntary aid.

4. All of man's achievements begin in the form of
thought, organized into plans, aims and purposes and expressed in terms of physical action.
All action is inspired by one or more of the nine
basic motives.

5. The entire power of the mind operates through
two sections of the mind, the conscious and the
subconscious. The conscious section is under
the control of the individual; the subconscious is
controlled by Infinite Intelligence and serves as
the medium of communication between Infinite
Intelligence and the conscious mind.

The "sixth sense" is under the control of the subconscious
section of the mind and it functions automatically in certain
fixed fundamentals, but may be influenced to function in carrying out the instructions of the conscious mind.

6. Both the conscious and the subconscious sections of the mind function in response to
fixed habits, adjusting themselves to whatever
thought habits the individual may establish,
whether the habits are voluntary or involuntary.

7. The majority of all thoughts released by the individual are inaccurate because they are inspired by
personal opinions which are arrived at without
the examination of facts, or because of bias, prejudice, fear, and the result of emotional excitement
in which the faculty of the reason has been given
little or no opportunity to modify them rationally.

8. The first step in accurate thinking (a step that is taken by none except those with adequate self-discipline) is that of separating facts from fiction and hearsay evidence. The second step is that of separating facts (after they have been identified as such) into two classes, important and the unimportant. An important fact is any fact which can be used to help one attain the object of his major purpose or any minor purpose leading to his major purpose.

All other facts are relatively unimportant. The average person spends his life in dealing with "inferences" based upon unreliable sources of information and unimportant facts. Therefore he seldom comes within sight of that form of self-discipline which demands facts and distinguishes the difference between important and unimportant facts.

9. Desire, based on a definite motive, is the beginning of all voluntary thought action associated with individual achievement.

The presence in the mind of any intense desire tends to stimulate the faculty of the imagination with the purpose of creating ways and means of attaining the object of the desire.

If the desire is continuously held in the mind (through the repetition of thought) it is picked up by the subconscious section of the mind and automatically carried out to its logical conclusion.

These are some of the more important of the known facts concerning the greatest of all mysteries, the mystery of human thought, and they indicate clearly that accurate thinking is attainable only by the strictest habits of self-discipline.

"Where," some may ask, "and how may one begin the development of self-discipline?"

It might well begin by concentration upon a Definite Major Purpose.

Nothing great has ever been achieved without the power of thought.

The subconscious section of the mind is not subject to control, but it is subject to influence, by the means here described. It acts on its own accord, and voluntarily, although its action may be speeded up by intensifying the emotions, or applying the power of the will in a highly concentrated form.

A burning desire behind a Definite Major Purpose may stimulate the action of the subconscious section of the mind and speed up its operations.

The relationship between the subconscious section of the mind and the six other departments of the mind, is similar in many respects to that of the farmer and the laws of nature through which his crops are grown.

The farmer has certain fixed duties to perform, such as preparing the soil, planting the seed at the right season, and keeping the weeds out, after which his work is finished. From there on out nature takes over, germinates the seed, develops it to maturity and yields a crop.

The conscious section of the mind may be compared with the farmer in that it prepares the way by the formulation of plans and purposes, under the direction of the faculty of the will. If this work is done properly, and a clear picture of that which is desired is created (the picture being the seed of the purpose desired) the subconscious takes over the picture, draws upon the power of Infinite Intelligence for the intelligence needed for the translation of the picture, gets the information necessary and presents it to the conscious section of the mind in the form of a practical plan of procedure.

Unlike the laws of nature which germinate seed and produce a crop for the farmer within a definite, predetermined length of time, the subconscious takes over the seed of ideas or purposes submitted to it and fixes its own time for the submission of a plan for their attainment.

Power of will, expressed in terms of a burning desire, is the one medium by which the action of the subconscious may be speeded up. Thus, by taking full possession of one's own mind, by exercising the power of the will, one comes into possession of power of stupendous proportions.

And the act of mastering the power of the will, so that it may be directed to the attainment of any desired end, is self-discipline of the highest order. Control of the will requires persistence, faith and definiteness of purpose.

In the field of salesmanship, for example, it is a fact well known to all master salesmen, that the persistent salesman heads the list in sales production. In some fields of selling, such as that of life insurance, persistence is the asset of major importance to the salesman.

And persistence, in selling or any other calling, is a matter of strict self-discipline!

In the field of advertising the same rule applies. The most successful advertisers carry on with unyielding persistence, repeating their efforts month after month, year after year, with unabating regularity; and professional advertising experts have convincing evidence that this is the only policy which will produce satisfactory results.

The pioneers who settled America when this country was only a vast wilderness of primitive men and wild animals, demonstrated what can be accomplished when will, power is applied with persistence.

At a later period in the history of our country, after the pioneers had established a semblance of civilized society, George

Washington and his little army of underfed, half-clothed, under-equipped soldiers proved once more that will power applied with persistence is unbeatable.

And the pioneers of American Industry; such men as Henry Ford, Thomas A. Edison, and Andrew Carnegie, gave us another demonstration of the benefits of will-power backed by persistence. These men, and all others of their type who have made great contributions to the American way of life, were men with self-discipline, and they attained it through the power of the will, backed with persistence.

Andrew Carnegie's entire career provides an excellent example of the benefits which are available through self-discipline.

He came to America when he was a very young boy, and began work as a laborer. He had only a few friends; none of them wealthy or influential. But he did have an enormous capacity for the expression of his willpower.

By working at manual labor during the day and studying at night he learned telegraphy, and finally worked his way up to the position of private operator for the Division Superintendent of the Pennsylvania Railroad Company.

In this position he made such effective application of some of the principles of this philosophy, among them the principle of self-discipline, that he attracted the attention of men with money and influence who were in a position to aid him in carrying out the object of his Major Purpose in life.

At this point in his career he had precisely the same advantages that hundreds of other telegraph operators enjoyed, but no more. But he did have one asset which the other operators apparently did not possess: The will to win and a definite idea of what he wanted, together with the persistence to carry on until he got it.

This too was the outgrowth of self-discipline!

Mr. Carnegie's outstanding qualities were will-power and persistence, plus a strict self-discipline through which these traits were controlled and directed to the attainment of a definite purpose. Beyond these he had no outstanding qualities which are not possessed by the man of average intelligence. By exercising his willpower he adopted a Definite Major Purpose and clung to that purpose until it made him America's greatest industrial leader, not to mention the huge personal fortune which he accumulated.

Out of his will-power, properly self-disciplined and directed to the attainment of a definite purpose, came the great United States Steel Corporation which revolutionized the steel industry and provided employment for a huge army of skilled and unskilled workers.

Thus we see that a successful man gets his start through the application of self-discipline, in pursuit of a definite purpose; and he carries on until he attains that purpose, with the aid of that same principle.

Self-discipline is a self-acquired trait of character. It is not one which can be appropriated from the lives of others, nor acquired from the pages of a book. It is an asset which must come from within, by exercise of one's power of will. These self-acquired qualities are just as effective in other forms of application as they are in the attainment of leadership in industry, as we shall observe by considering the achievements of Miss Helen Keller.

With the aid of her will-power and persistence she bridged her afflictions so effectively that she learned to speak, and by her sense of touch she learned to connect her mind with much more of the outside world than the average person with two good eyes ever sees.

With that same power of will she acquired peace of mind far beyond the average, acquired the hope necessary to sustain her in a life of total darkness, and educated herself sufficiently to enable her to perceive the nature of the world around her as well or better than the average person who has all his physical faculties.

When we consider the achievements of this remarkable woman we are forced to the conclusion that the power of the will is an irresistible force capable of enabling one to surmount all the ordinary difficulties of life.

It seems hardly necessary to emphasize the fact that Miss Keller accomplished her astounding feat by the strictest sort of self-discipline, for that is obvious. It may be helpful to some, however, if we call attention to the fact that Miss Keller's entire life has been devoted to some form of service designed to help others. She not only believes in the soundness of the principle of GOING THE EXTRA MILE, but she lives it every minute of her busy life.

When Andrew Carnegie said that "the power of will is an irresistible force which recognizes no such reality as failure," he doubtlessly meant that it is irresistible when it is properly organized and directed to a definite end in a spirit of faith. Obviously he intended to emphasize three important principles of this philosophy as the basis of all self-acquired self-discipline, viz.:

   a. Definiteness of Purpose.
   b. Applied Faith.
   c. Self-Discipline.

It should be remembered, however, that the state of mind which can be developed through these three principles can best be attained, and more quickly, by the application of other principles of this philosophy, among them:

   a. The Master Mind.
   b. A Pleasing Personality.
   c. The Habit of Going The Extra Mile.
   d. Personal Initiative.
   e. Creative Vision.

Combine these five principles with Definiteness of Purpose, Applied Faith and Self-Discipline, and you will have an available source of personal power of stupendous proportions.

The beginner in the study of this may find it difficult to gain control over his power of will without approaching that control step-by-step, through the mastery and application of these eight principles.

Mastery can be attained in one way only, and that is by constant, persistent application of the principles. They must be woven into one's daily habits and applied in all human relationships, and in the solution of all personal problems.

The power of the will responds only to motive persistently pursued!

And it becomes strong in the same way that one's arm may become strong—by systematic use.

Men with willpower which has been self-acquired, through self-discipline, do not give up hope or quit when the going becomes hard. Men without willpower do.

A humble general stood in review before an army of tired, discouraged soldiers who had just been badly defeated during the War Between the States. He too had a reason to be discouraged, for the war was going against him.

When one of his officers suggested that the outlook seemed discouraging, General Grant lifted his weary head, closed his eyes, clenched his fists, and exclaimed: "We will fight it out along these lines if it takes all summer!"

And he did fight it out along the lines he had chosen. Thus it may well be that on this firm decision of one man, backed by an indomitable will, came the final victory which preserved the union of the states.

One school of thought says that, "right makes might"! Another school of thought says that, "might makes right"!

But men who think accurately know that the power of the will makes might, whether right or wrong, and the entire history of mankind backs up this belief.

Study men of great achievement, wherever you find them, and you will find evidence that the power of the will, organized and persistently applied, is the dominating factor in their success. Also, you will find that successful men commit themselves to a stricter system of self-discipline than any which is forced upon them by circumstances beyond their control.

They work when others sleep!

They Go The Extra Mile, and if need be another and still another mile, never stopping until they have contributed the utmost service of which they are capable.

Follow in their footsteps for a single day and you will be convinced that they need no taskmaster to drive them on. They move on their own personal initiative because they direct their efforts by the strictest sort of self-discipline.

They may appreciate commendation, but they do not require it to inspire them to action. They listen to condemnation, but they do not fear it, and they are not discouraged by it.

And they sometimes fail, or suffer temporary defeat, just as others do, but failure only spurs them on to greater effort.

They encounter obstacles, as does everyone, but these they convert into benefit through which they carry on toward their chosen goal.

They experience discouragements, the same as others do, but they close the doors of their minds tightly behind unpleasant experiences and transmute their disappointments into renewed energy with which they struggle ahead to victory.

When death strikes in their families they bury their dead, but not their indomitable wills.

They seek the counsel of others, extract from it that which

they can use and reject the remainder, although the whole world may criticize them on account of their judgment.

They know they cannot control all the circumstances which affect their lives, but they do control their own state of mind and their mental reactions to all circumstances, by keeping their minds positive at all times.

They are tested by their own negative emotions, as are all people, but they keep the upper hand over these emotions by making right royal servants of them.

Let us keep in mind the fact that through self-discipline one may do two important things, both of which are essential for outstanding achievement.

First, one may completely control the negative emotions by transmuting them into constructive effort, using them as an inspiration to greater endeavor.

Secondly, one may stimulate the positive emotions, and direct them to the attainment of any desired end.

Thus, by controlling both the positive and the negative emotions the faculty of reason is left free to function, as is also the faculty of the imagination.

Control over the emotions is attained gradually, by the development of habits of thought which are conducive of control. Such habits should be formed in connection with the small, unimportant circumstances of life, for it is true, as Supreme Court Justice Brandeis once said, that "the brain is like the hand. It grows with use."

One by one the six departments of the mind which are subject to self-discipline can be brought under complete control, but the start should he made by habits which give one control over the emotions first, since it is true that most people are the victims of their uncontrolled emotions throughout their lives. Most people are the servants, not the masters of their emotions, because they have never established definite, systematic habits of control over them.

Every person who has made up his mind to control the six departments of his mind, through a strict system of self-discipline, should adopt and follow a definite plan to keep this purpose before him.

One student of this philosophy wrote a creed for this purpose, which he followed so closely that it soon enabled him to become thoroughly self-discipline conscious. It worked so successfully that it is here presented for the benefit of other students of the philosophy.

The creed was signed, and repeated orally, twice daily; once upon arising in the morning and once upon retiring at night. This procedure gave the student the benefit of the principle of autosuggestion, through which the purpose of the creed was conveyed clearly to the subconscious section of his mind, where it was picked up and acted upon automatically.

The creed follows:

A CREED FOR SELF-DISCIPLINE!

Will-power:
Recognizing that the Power of Will is the Supreme Court over all other departments of my mind, I will exercise it daily, when I need the urge to action for any purpose; and

I will form habits designed to bring the power of my will into action at least once daily.

Emotions:
Realizing that my emotions are both positive and negative I will form daily habits which will encourage the development of the positive emotions, and aid me in

converting the negative emotions into some form of useful action.

Reason:

Recognizing that both my positive emotions and my negative emotions may be dangerous if they are not controlled and guided to desirable ends, I will submit all my desires, aims and purposes to my faculty of reason, and I will be guided by it in giving expression to these.

Imagination:

Recognizing the need for sound plans and ideas for the attainment of my desires, I will develop my imagination by calling upon it daily for help in the formation of my plans.

Conscience:

Recognizing that my emotions often err in their over-enthusiasm, and my faculty of reason often is without the warmth of feeling that is necessary to enable me to combine justice with mercy in my judgments, I will encourage my conscience to guide me as to what is right and what is wrong, but I will never set aside the verdicts it renders, no matter what may be the cost of carrying them out.

Memory:

Recognizing the value of an alert memory, I will encourage mine to become alert by taking care to impress it clearly with all thoughts I wish to recall, and by associating those thoughts with related subjects which I may call to mind frequently.

Subconscious Mind:
Recognizing the influence of my subconscious mind over my power of will, I shall take care to submit to it a clear and definite picture of my Major Purpose in life and all minor purposes leading to my major purpose, and I shall keep this picture constantly before my subconscious mind by repeating it daily.

Signed _____

Discipline over the mind is gained, little by little, by the formation of habits which one may control. Habits begin in the mind; therefore, a daily repetition of this creed will make one habit-conscious in connection with the particular kind of habits which are needed to develop and control the six departments of the mind.

The mere act of repeating the names of these departments has an important effect. It makes one conscious that these departments exist; that they are important; that they can be controlled by the formation of thought-habits; that the nature of these habits determines one's success or failure in the matter of self-discipline.

It is a great day in any person's life when he recognizes the fact that his success or failure throughout life is largely a matter of control over his emotions!

Before one can recognize this truth he must recognize the existence and the nature of his emotions, and the power which is available to those who control them—a form of recognition which many people never indulge in during their entire lifetime.

There is an alliance of men known as Alcoholics Anonymous, with a membership that spreads throughout the nation. These men operate in local Master Mind groups in almost every city of the nation. And they are releasing one another from the evils of alcoholism on a scale which is nothing short of miraculous.

They operate entirely through self-discipline!

The medicine they use is the most powerful known to mankind. It consists of the power of the human mind directed to a definite end; that end being the end of alcoholism.

Here is an achievement which should inspire all men to become better acquainted with the power of their own minds. If the mind can cure alcoholism—and it is doing so—it can cure poverty, and ill health, and fear, and self-imposed limitations!

Alcoholics Anonymous is getting results because its members have been introduced to their "other selves"; those unseen entities which consist in the power of thought; the forces within the human mind which recognize no such reality as the "impossible."

This organization will live and it will grow, as all the forces of good must. The organization will eventually extend its service to include not only the elimination of the evils of alcoholism, but all other evils, such as the evils of fear, and poverty, and ill health, and hatred, and selfishness.

Eventually Alcoholics Anonymous will no doubt adopt the seventeen principles of this philosophy and provide its benefits for every member of that organization, as some of its members have already done with astounding effects.

It is a well-known fact that an enemy which has been recognized is an enemy that is half defeated.

And this applies to enemies which operate within one's own mind as well as to those which operate outside of it; and especially does it apply to the enemies of negative emotions.

Once these enemies have been recognized one begins, almost unconsciously, to set up habits, through self-discipline, with which to counteract them.

This same reasoning applies also to the benefits of positive emotions, for it is true that a benefit recognized is a benefit easily utilized.

The positive emotions are beneficial, for they are a part of the driving force of the mind; but they are helpful only when they are organized and directed to the attainment of definite, constructive ends. If they are not so controlled they may be as dangerous as any of the negative emotions.

The medium of control is self-discipline, systematically and voluntarily applied through the habits of thought.

Take the emotion of Faith, for example:

This emotion, the most powerful of all the emotions, may be helpful only when it is expressed through constructive, organized action based upon Definiteness of Purpose.

Faith without action is useless, because it may resolve itself into mere daydreaming, wishing and faint hopefulness.

Self-discipline is the medium through which one may stimulate the emotion of Faith, through definiteness of purpose persistently applied.

The discipline should begin by establishing habits which stimulate the use of the power of the will, for it is the ego—the seat of the power of the will—in which one's desires originate. Thus, the emotions of desire and Faith are definitely related.

Wherever a burning desire exists, there exists also the capacity for Faith which corresponds precisely with the intensity of the desire. The two are associated always. Stimulate one and you stimulate the other. Control and direct one, through organized habits, and you control and direct the other.

This is self-discipline of the highest order.

Benjamin Disraeli, believed by some to have been the greatest Prime Minister England ever had, attained that high station through the sheer power of his will, directed by Definiteness of Purpose.

He began his career as an author, but he was not highly successful in that field.

He published a dozen or more books, but none of them made any great impression on the public. Failing in this field, he accepted his defeat as a challenge to greater effort in some other field—nothing more.

Then he entered politics, with his mind definitely set upon becoming the Prime Minister of the far-flung British Empire.

In 1837 he became a member of Parliament from Maidstone, but his first speech in Parliament was universally regarded as a flat failure.

Again he accepted his defeat as a challenge to try once more. Fighting on, with never a thought of quitting, he became the leader of the House of Commons by 1878, and later became the Chancellor of the Exchequer. In 1868 he realized his Definite Major Purpose by becoming the Prime Minister.

Here he met with terrific opposition (his "testing time" was at hand), which resulted in his resignation; but far from accepting his temporary defeat as failure, he staged a comeback and was elected Prime Minister a second time, after which he became a great builder of empires, and extended his influence in many different directions.

His greatest achievement perhaps was the building of the Suez Canal—a feat which was destined to give the British Empire unprecedented economic advantages.

The keynote of his entire career was self-discipline!

In summarizing his achievements in one short sentence he said, "The secret of success is constancy of purpose!"

When the going was the hardest Disraeli turned on his willpower to its greatest capacity. It sustained him through the emergencies of temporary defeat, and brought him through to victory.

Here is the greatest of all the danger points of the majority of men!

They give up and quit when the going becomes tough; and often they quit when one more step would have carried them triumphantly to victory.

Will-power is needed most when the oppositions of life are the greatest. And self-discipline will provide it for every such emergency, whether it be great or small.

The late ex-president, Theodore Roosevelt, was another example of what can happen when a man is motivated by the will to win despite great handicaps.

During his early youth he was seriously handicapped by chronic asthma and weak eyes. His friends despaired of his ever regaining his health, but he did not share their views, thanks to his recognition of the power of self-discipline.

He went West, joined a group of hard-hitting outdoor workers, and placed himself under a definite system of self-discipline, through which he built a strong body and a resolute mind. Some doctors said he could not do it—but he refused to accept their verdict.

In his battle to regain his health he acquired such perfect discipline over himself that he went back East, entered politics, and kept on driving until his will to win made him President of the United States.

Those who knew him best have said that his outstanding quality was a will which refused to accept defeat as anything more than an urge to greater effort. Beyond this his ability, his education, his experience were in no way superior to similar qualities possessed by men all around him of whom the public heard little or nothing.

While he was President some army officials complained of an order he gave them to keep physically fit. To show that he knew what he was talking about he rode horseback a hundred miles, over rough Virginia roads, with the army officials trailing after him, trying hard to keep pace.

Behind all this physical action was an active mind which was determined not to be handicapped by physical weakness, and that mental activity reflected itself throughout his administration in the White House.

When the mind says, "go forward," the physical body responds to its command, thus proving the truth of Andrew Carnegie's statement that "our only limitations are those which we set up in our own minds!"

A French Expedition had tried to build the Panama Canal, but failed.

Theodore Roosevelt said, "the anal shall be built" and he went to work then and there to express his faith in terms of action. The canal was built!

Personal power is wrapped up in the will to win!

But it can be released for action only by self-discipline, and by no other means.

Robert Louis Stevenson was a delicate youth from the day of his birth. His health prevented him from doing any steady work at his studies until he was past seventeen. At twenty-three his health became so bad that his physicians sent him to the South.

There he met the woman of his choice and fell in love.

His love for her was so great that it gave him a new lease on life, a new motive for action, and he began to write, although his physical body was scarcely strong enough to carry him around. He kept on writing until he had greatly enriched the world by his writings, now universally accepted as masterpieces.

The same motive, love, has given the wings of thought to many another who, like Robert Louis Stevenson, has made this a richer and a better world. Without the motive of love

Stevenson doubtlessly would have died without having made his contributions to mankind. He transmuted his love for the woman of his choice into literary works, through habits of self-discipline which placed the six departments of his mind under his control.

In a similar manner Charles Dickens converted a love tragedy into literary works which have enriched the world.

Instead of going down under the blow of his disappointment in his first love affair, he drowned his sorrow through the intensity of his action in writing. In that manner he closed the door behind an experience which many another might have used as a door of escape from his duty—an alibi for his failure.

Through self-discipline he converted his greatest sorrow into his greatest asset, for it revealed to him the presence of that "other self" wherein consisted the power of genius which he reflected in his literary works.

There is one unbeatable rule for the mastery of sorrows and disappointments, and that is transmutation of those emotional frustrations, through definitely planned work. It is a rule which has no equal.

And the secret of its power is self-discipline.

Freedom of body and mind, independence, and economic security are the results of personal initiative expressed through self-discipline. By no other means may these universal desires be assured.

We Near the End of Our Journey

Our journey on the road to Happy Valley is about ended.

You must travel the remainder of the distance alone. If you have followed the instructions I have given you, in the right kind of mental attitude, you are now in possession of the great Master Key which will unlock the gate to Happy Valley.

Now I shall reveal to you a great truth of the utmost importance: The Master Key to Riches consists entirely in the greatest power known to man; the power of thought!

You may take full possession of the Master Key by taking possession of your own mind, through the strictest of self-discipline.

Through self-discipline you may think yourself into or out of any circumstance of life!

Self-discipline will help you to control your mental attitude. Your mental attitude may help you to master every circumstance of your life, and to convert every adversity, every defeat, every failure into an asset of equivalent scope. That is why a Positive Mental Attitude heads the entire list of the Twelve Riches of Life.

Therefore, it should be obvious to you that the great Master Key to Riches is nothing more nor less than the self-discipline necessary to help you take full and complete possession of your own mind!

Start right where you stand, and become the master of yourself. Start now! Be done forever with that old self which has kept you in misery and want. Recognize and embrace that "other self" which can give you everything your heart craves, including entrance into the great estate of Happy Valley.

We have come to the end of our journey!

In departing may I wish you a happy and pleasant voyage into the new life you shall enjoy in Happy Valley?

*   *   *

The lights were dimmed. The masked rich man from Happy Valley disappeared into the darkness as mysteriously as he had come, but he had given every member of that huge audience a new birth of hope and faith and courage.

And we sincerely hope that the reading of his story has helped you to share these blessings. We hope that from this moment forward you will be always in full possession of your own mental attitude; that you may attune it to whatever station in life you demand of yourself.

Remember it is profoundly significant that the only thing over which you have complete control is your own mental attitude!

If the rich man from Happy Valley has brought you nothing but this great truth he has provided you with a source to riches of incomparable value; for this is the Master Key to Riches!

Napoleon Hill's Clubs Being Formed

Experience has proved that students of this philosophy who combine their forces, in group study-clubs, get more from the philosophy in the shortest time. These clubs meet once a week, analyze the lessons one by one, and cooperate in practical ways in helping one another to apply the philosophy, thereby applying the Master Mind principle to which Andrew Carnegie gave credit for his stupendous achievements in the steel industry.

The motto of the clubs is "All for one and one for all" and they make a literal application of the motto. Most of the clubs have in their membership men with a great variety of talent, business and professional experience, all of which is available, without cost, to every member, in the solution of his personal problems ranging all the way from domestic inharmonies to financing of businesses and ideas created by the members.

The first club was organized at Athens, Georgia. Before it had covered the fifth lesson every member of the club reported definite and substantial improvements in his financial and personal affairs, some of them having more than doubled their incomes.

Perhaps the greatest benefit growing out of these study clubs is the spirit of co-operation the members develop toward one another. This spirit does not stop with the members, but it extends to the community in which they live, and to the enterprises in which they make their living. Without a single exception every member of a study club has gone back to the principles of Americanism which have been responsible for the American way of life, and has begun to take his Americanism seriously. Thus these study clubs are making a tangible contribution to the support of the American way of life.

The Clubs Have "Women's Night" Sessions

Once a month the club members are permitted to bring their wives or prospective wives, for participation in the program. This plan has worked so satisfactorily that it has created a better domestic relationship in many families. One member brought his son to the club and the lad was so impressed that he became determined to lead his class in high school, and thereafter he made such rapid progress that the principal of the school made an investigation to learn what had happened to improve the boy so quickly.

Study Clubs Help Employees to Gain Promotions

Study clubs are being formed among employees consisting of those who wish to get ahead more rapidly. These clubs are showing such a definite improvement in the "mental attitude" of all employees of the organizations in which they are operating that they have met with the hearty approval of the management.

If You Wish to Attain to Leadership in the "New Order" of This Country

No matter what we may think of it, we are beginning an era in this country which marks a "new order" in human relationships. What course this change in the American way of life will take no one can say, hut this much we may prophesy safely: There will be new opportunities for leadership in all walks of life, in every trade, profession, business, industry; and in education, politics and religion.

The leadership in these fields in the future will go to those who understand the rules of leadership and know how to apply them!

These rules are covered, in terms anyone can understand, in the Philosophy.

These rules enabled Frank W. Woolworth to create a great fortune by injecting a new idea into the sale of merchandise.

They enabled Thomas A. Edison to become the greatest

inventor this country has produced, and at the same time manage, as the active leader, his vast industries and business enterprises—an accomplishment attained by very few inventors. Mr. Edison's philosophy of success is well in evidence throughout this course.

And they enabled Martin W. Littleton, an unknown young lawyer from a small town in Texas, to become one of the greatest and most successful lawyers of New York City.

They helped Andrew Carnegie, the poor immigrant lad from Scotland, to lift himself step by step until he climaxed his colorful career by the organization of the great United States Steel Corporation. Mr. Carnegie's contribution to this philosophy is found in every lesson. He tells, in his own language, how he raised one workman after another to a position of wealth and affluence, through his principles of leadership, among them Charles M. Schwab, who began with Mr. Carnegie as a stake driver and promoted himself to the presidency of the United States Steel Corporation.

Mr. Carnegie has gone; Mr. Schwab has gone; and many of the others whom he helped to become successful have gone; but the philosophy on which they climbed to the top is not gone! Mr. Carnegie bequeathed that to the American people. It has been preserved, without modification, for the benefit of any person who has the earnest desire to know how to make life pay on his own terms. Moreover, it has been presented in a reading course that requires but little effort to understand and apply.

So, Here the Story Ends!

No one is sitting in front of you with a stop watch, timing your reaction to opportunity, as Mr. Carnegie timed Napoleon Hill when he was given the job of organizing the world's first practical philosophy of individual achievement; but you who have read this book are now face to face with an opportunity which may be as great, from your point of view, as the one which Mr. Carnegie gave the unknown young newspaper man to whom he assigned the responsibility of taking to the world the "better portion of the Carnegie fortune."

THE MAGIC LADDER
TO SUCCESS

CONTENTS

The eight basic motivating forces which underlie all human action. The relationship between sexual urge and genius. The value of transmutation of sex energy. The ten major sources of mind stimulation. Power—what it is and how to organize and use it. Co-operation—the psychology of co-operative effort. Henry Ford, Thomas A. Edison, and Harvey Firestone—how they acquired power through the Master Mind principle. The big six—how they made the Master Mind principle yield them more than $25,000,000 a year.

How to stimulate the imaginative faculty. Telepathy— how thought vibrations pass from one mind to another, through the agency of the ether. How salesmen and public speakers may "tune in" on the thoughts of their audiences. Vibration—described by Dr. Alexander Graham Bell, inventor of the long-distance telephone.

Air and ether—how they carry vibrations. How and why ideas flash into the mind. Andrew Carnegie responsible for organization of Law of Success. Elbert H. Gary approves the Law of Success philosophy. One million dollars earned by students of Law of Success.

Spiritualism—what it is and how it works. Why some people antagonize others at sight, without knowing it. Why Henry Ford is the most powerful man living.

What we have learned from "Nature's Bible." Chemistry of the mind—how it will make or destroy you. What is meant by the Psychological moment in salesmanship.

The mind becomes devitalized—how to "recharge" it. The value and meaning of harmony in all co-operative efforts. Of what does Henry Ford's assets consist? The answer.

Education—what it is and what it is not! The secret of all financial success, as gathered from the study of 100 successful men and 20,000 failures. The relationship between vibration (or energy) and matter.

This lesson teaches how to accumulate power through singleness of purpose.

This lesson describes the six basic fears and explains how they may be eliminated.

How to save money. How the "habit" of saving develops power and character.

INTRODUCTORY STATEMENT

by the Author

For almost a quarter of a century I have been engaged in writing this book.

The task could not have been completed in less time for several reasons, not the least important of which is the fact that I had to inform myself, through years of research, as to what other men had discovered in connection with the causes of failure and success.

Another important reason why my labors have covered nearly a quarter of a century is the fact that I felt it necessary to prove that I could make the Law of Success philosophy work for myself before offering it to others.

I was born in the mountains of the South, in the midst of poverty and illiteracy. For three generations preceding me my ancestors, on both sides of the house, were contented to live in poverty and ignorance, and I would have followed in their footsteps had not my stepmother planted in my mind the seed of *desire* to whip poverty and illiteracy.

Nearly thirty years ago my stepmother made a remark which found a permanent lodging place in my mind, and to that remark may be traced the cause of my labors which have resulted in the completion of the Law of Success philosophy described in this book.

My stepmother was a woman of education, and came from a family with a long cultural record. Poverty and illiteracy irritated her, and she was not backward about saying so. She voluntarily assumed the task of planting ambition in our family, starting with my father, whom she sent away to college at the age of forty, while she managed what passed for a "farm" and a little country store that we owned, not to mention the support of five children, three of her own and my brother and myself.

Her example made a deep and lasting impression upon my mind!

From her I got my first impression of the value of a *definite major aim,* and later that impression became so obviously essential as one of the factors of success that I gave it second place in the list of seventeen principles outlined in this book.

When I began organizing the material for the Law of Success, I had no intention of creating a philosophy such as that described in this volume. My purpose, in the beginning, was to inform myself as to how other people had acquired wealth, so that I might follow their example.

But as the years passed I found myself becoming more eager for knowledge than for wealth, until my thirst for knowledge became so great that I practically lost sight of the original motive of financial gain which started me in search of knowledge.

In addition to the influence of my stepmother, I was fortunate enough to meet Dr. Alexander Graham Bell and Andrew Carnegie, who not only further influenced me to continue my research, but supplied me with much of the important scientific data which went into the building of the Law of Success philosophy.

Later I met Dr. Elmer Gates and many of the other men of recognized ability whom I have mentioned on another page, who not only encouraged me to continue my labor of building a philosophy of success, but gave me full benefit of their own rich experiences as their personal contribution to my task.

I have mentioned these details for what I believe to be a very important reason, namely, the fact that the difference between success and failure is often (if not, in fact, always) determined by definite environmental influences which may be usually traced to *one person.*

In my case this person was my stepmother.

Except for her influence in planting the seed of ambition in my mind, I never would have written a philosophy of success that is now rendering useful service to tens of thousands of people in every civilized country on earth.

Unfortunately, I shall never be able to ascertain the exact number of people who will receive from my work the inspiration that will lead to great achievement, but I do know, from what I have already seen in this direction, that the number will be stupendous. Perhaps it would be no exaggeration to say that no less than ten thousand people have already found, through this philosophy, the road to success.

While the Law of Success was still in the experimental stage, and as a part of my plan for giving it a practical trial before publishing it in textbooks, I personally passed it on, through lectures, to no less than 100,000 people. Many whom I know to have received their first impulse of ambition from these lectures have since become wealthy, although some of them may have lost sight of the cause of their prosperity, while others perhaps would not be generous enough to admit that my labor had marked important turning points in their lives.

My belief that this philosophy of success is destined to bring prosperity to almost countless thousands of people throughout the world is based upon what I have seen happen in the past, and upon very definite plans which I have formulated for teaching it.

I hope to have, very soon, able teachers in every city in America who will conduct schools of instruction for the purpose of teaching the Law of Success. I am engaged at this time in training teachers, and it is my aim to continue this work. For this purpose I have acquired a beautiful, six-hundred-acre estate in the Catskill Mountains, one hundred miles from New York City, where my school and headquarters will eventually be located. My teachers will be recruited from students of this philosophy who show, by their records, unusual aptitude for this sort of work.

The Law of Success will be translated into many foreign languages and taught in other countries. One of my most prominent students, who is a moving picture producer of more than ordinary ability, is planning the production of a series of talking pictures based upon the Law of Success textbooks. Through these pictures he will plant the seed of this philosophy in millions of minds.

Quite aside from my own program for the distribution of the Law of Success textbooks throughout the world, there is another, and, I believe, a more vital reason why this philosophy is destined to play an important part in the lives of great numbers of people. I have reference to the state of unrest which is manifesting itself, not only here in America, but throughout the world.

Since the World War, millions of people have been fired with ambition to whip poverty and to gain for themselves better stations in life. Moreover, this is most decidedly an age of scientific discovery, which has put sound legs under the seventeen principles of the Law of Success, thus giving it a standing that it did not enjoy fifteen years ago.

On account of the world unrest which is so prevalent to-day, there is a very definite demand for an "evangelism" of success that will inspire people with higher hopes and ambitions for personal achievement.

For the reasons here stated, I have arrived at last at an altitude on the mountain of life from which I may look backward into the valleys of struggle and hardship, poverty, and failure through which I have passed, with a feeling that I have not altogether lived in vain; that the punishment I have undergone has been more than offset by the joy and prosperity I have helped others to obtain.

Turning in the other direction, I can see that the summit of the mountain of success is still far in the distance and far from being finished and that my work is barely more than begun.

Not long ago I received a letter from a former president of the United States, who congratulated me upon sticking to my job for a quarter of a century, and suggested that I must feel very proud to have "arrived" at the top of the mountain of success in time to enjoy the fruits of my labors. His letter brought to my mind the thought that one never "arrives," if one continues to search for knowledge, because we no sooner reach the top of one peak than we discover that there are still higher mountains yet to be scaled in the distance.

No, I have not "arrived," but I have found happiness in abundance and financial prosperity sufficient for my needs, *solely through having lost myself in service to others who were earnestly struggling to find themselves.* It seems worthy of mention that I did not prosper greatly until I became more concerned about spreading the Law of Success philosophy where it would help others than I was about accumulating money.

In this manner, with apologies for the personal references, would I acquaint you with the motive and the influence which started me on the work of organizing the philosophy described in this book.

ACKNOWLEDGMENT OF HELP RENDERED IN THE PREPARATION OF THE MATERIAL THAT HAS GONE INTO THIS BOOK

This volume is the result of an analysis of the life work of over one hundred men and women who have attained outstanding success in their respective callings and of over twenty thousand men and women who were classed as failures.

In his labors of research and analysis the author received valuable assistance, either in person or by studying their life work, from the following men:

Henry Ford
John Burroughs
Luther Burbank
Thomas A. Edison
Harvey S. Firestone
John D. Rockefeller
Charles M. Schwab

Woodrow Wilson
Darwin P. Kingsley
Wm. Wrigley, Jr.
A. D. Lasker
E. A. Filene
James J. Hill
Dr. Glenn Frank
Capt. Geo. M. Alexander
Hugh Chalmers
John Wanamaker
Marshall Field
Edward W. Bok
Cyrus H. K. Curtis
George W. Perkins
Henry L. Doherty
George S. Parker
Gen. Rufus A. Ayers
Judge Elbert H. Gary
William Howard Taft
John W. Davis
Samuel Insull
Judge Daniel T. Wright
F. W. Woolworth
Elbert Hubbard
O. H. Harriman
Edwin C. Barnes
E. H. Harriman
Gov. Robt. L. Taylor
Wilbur Wright
George Eastman
William H. French
Charles P. Stienmetz
John H. Patterson

E. M. Statler
Don R. Mellett
Theodore Roosevelt
Dr. E. W. Strickler
Stuart Austin Wier
Harris F. Williams
Dr. Alexander Graham Bell

Of the men named, perhaps Henry Ford and Andrew Carnegie should be acknowledged as having contributed most to the building of this philosophy, for the reason that it was Mr. Carnegie who first suggested writing it and Henry Ford whose life work has supplied much of the material that has gone into its organization and served, in other ways, to prove the soundness of the entire philosophy.

Many of the men who supplied the author of the Law of Success with the most valuable portion of the data which have gone into the building of this philosophy have died before it was completed. To those who are still living, the author here makes grateful acknowledgment of the service they have rendered him, without which cooperation this philosophy never could have been completed.

The Author

HOW TO READ THIS BOOK FOR PROFIT

Experience with many tens of thousands of people who have attended lectures by the author of the Law of Success and with the thousands of people who have read the eight textbooks in which this philosophy has been presented has brought to light the fact that the philosophy stimulates the mind and causes the birth of scores of ideas.

As you read this book you will observe, as thousands of others have done, that ideas will begin to "flash" into your mind. Capture these ideas, with the aid of a notebook and pencil, as they may lead you to the attainment of your coveted goal in life. Many students of this philosophy have created valuable inventions while reading the Law of Success textbooks. Clergymen have been inspired by this philosophy to write sermons which lifted them to great heights of eloquence. The Law of Success philosophy is a mind fertilizer. It will cause the mind to function as a magnet that will attract brilliant ideas.

The value of this book is not in its own pages, but it lies in your own reaction to that which you read on these pages. Any brain that can create new ideas in abundance is capable, also, of organizing great power! The main purpose of the Law of Success philosophy is to stimulate the *imaginative* faculties of the brain so they will readily create new and usable ideas for any emergency in life.

Read this book with pencil in hand, and as you read, underscore all statements which cause new ideas to "flash" into your mind. This method will serve to fix such ideas in your mind permanently. You cannot assimilate the entire subject matter of this philosophy at one reading of this book. Read it many times, and at each reading follow the habit of marking the lines which inspire new ideas.

This procedure will reveal to you one of the great mysteries of the human mind by introducing you to a source of knowledge which cannot be described adequately to any except those who have discovered this source for themselves. *In this statement lies a hint of the nature of the secret of success which the Law of Success philosophy has handed over to so many of its students throughout the world!* No one may ever come into possession of this secret except by the method of procedure here described.

THE SEVENTEEN FACTORS OF WHICH THE LAW OF SUCCESS IS COMPOSED

This basic Reading Course presents the principles through which success may be attained. At the outset let us define success as:

> "The power *with which to acquire whatever one wants without violating the rights of others."*

The factors through which power may be acquired and used in harmony with the above definition are seventeen in number, viz:

1. The Master Mind
2. A Definite Chief Aim
3. Self-Confidence
4. The Habit of Saving
5. Imagination
6. Initiative and Leadership
7. Enthusiasm
8. Self-Control

9. Doing More than Paid For
10. A Pleasing Personality
11. Accurate Thinking
12. Co-operation
13. Concentration
14. Profiting by Failures
15. Tolerance
16. The Golden Rule
17. The Habit of Health

The purpose of this Reading Course is to describe how one may apply these seventeen factors so as to acquire personal power for use in any calling and for the solution of all of one's economic problems. Let us begin this description by a complete analysis of each of these seventeen factors.

LESSON 1
THE MASTER MIND

The Master Mind principle may be defined as "A composite mind, consisting of two or more individual minds working in perfect harmony, with a definite aim in view."

Keep in mind the definition of success, which is attainable through the application of *power*, and you will more quickly grasp the meaning of the term "Master Mind," as it will be immediately obvious that a group of two or more minds, working in harmony, and perfectly coordinated, will create power in abundance.

All success is achieved through the application of *power*. The starting point, however, may be described as a *burning desire* for the achievement of some specific, definite objective.

Just as the oak tree, in the embryo, sleeps within the acorn, *success* begins in the form of an intense *desire*. Out of strong desires grow the motivating forces which cause men to cherish hopes, build plans, develop courage, and stimulate their minds to a highly intensified degree of *action* in pursuit of some *definite* plan or purpose.

Desire, then, is the starting point of all human achievement. There is nothing back of desire except the stimuli through which *strong desire* is fanned into a hot flame of *action.* These stimuli are known and have been included as a part of the Law of Success philosophy described in this book.

It has been said, and not without reason, that one may have anything one wants, within reasonable limitations, providing one *wants it badly enough!* Anyone who is capable of stimulating the mind to an intense state of *desire* is capable also of more than average achievement in the pursuit of that desire. It must be remembered that *wishing* for a thing is not the same as *desiring* it with such intensity that out of this desire grow impelling forces of action which drive one to build plans and put those plans to work. A wish is merely a passive form of desire. Most people never advance beyond the "wishing" stage.

THE BASIC MOTIVATING FORCES WHICH UNDERLIE ALL HUMAN ACTION

There are eight basic motivating forces, one or more of which is the starting point of all noteworthy human achievement. These motivating forces are:

1. The urge of self-preservation
2. The desire for sexual contact
3. The desire for financial gain
4. The desire for life after death
5. The desire for fame; to possess *power*
6. The urge of *love* (separate and distinct from sex urge)
7. The desire for revenge (prevalent in the more undeveloped minds)
8. The desire to indulge one's egotism

Men make use of great power only when urged by one or more of these eight basic motives. The imaginative forces of the human mind become active only when spurred on by the stimulation of well-defined *motive!* Master salesmen have discovered that all salesmanship is based upon an appeal to one or more of these eight basic motives which impel men and women to action. Without this discovery no one could become a master salesman.

What is salesmanship? It is the presentation of an idea, plan, or suggestion which gives the prospective purchaser a strong motive for making a purchase. The able salesman never asks a purchaser to buy without presenting a *well-defined motive* as to why the purchase should be made.

Knowledge of merchandise or service offered by the salesman, of itself, is not sufficient to make a master salesman. The offering must be accompanied by a thorough description of the motive which should prompt the purchaser to buy. The most effective sales plan is one which appeals to the prospective purchaser through the greatest number of the eight basic motives and crystallizes these motives into a *burning desire* for the object offered for sale.

*   *   *

The eight basic motives serve not only as the basis of appeal to other minds, where co-operative action from other people is sought, but they serve also as the starting point of *action* in one's own mind. Men of ordinary ability become supermen when aroused by some outward or inner stimulant which harnesses one or more of the eight basic motives for action.

Bring a man face to face with the possibility of death, in a sudden emergency, and he will develop physical strength and imaginative strategy of which he would not be capable under the influence of a less urgent motive for action.

When driven by the natural desire for sexual contact, men will build plans, use strategy, develop imagination, and indulge in action in a thousand different ways of which they are not capable without the urge of this desire.

The desire for financial gain often lifts men of mediocre ability into positions of great power because this desire causes them to build plans, develop imagination, and indulge in forms of action in which they would not engage without this motive of gain. The desire for fame and for personal power over others is easily discernible as the chief motivating force in the lives of leaders in every walk of life.

The animalistic desire for revenge often drives men to build the most intricate and ingenious plans for carrying out their objective.

Love for the opposite sex (and sometimes for the same sex) serves as a mind stimulant that drives men to almost unbelievable heights of achievement.

The desire for life after death is such a strong motivating force that it not only drives men to both constructive and destructive extremes in their search for a plan by which this perpetuation may be brought about, but it also develops highly effective leadership ability, evidence of which may be found in the life work of practically all the founders of religion.

If you would achieve great success, plant in your mind a strong motive!

Millions of people struggle all the days of their lives with no stronger motive than that of being able to acquire the necessities of life, such as food, shelter, and clothing. Now and then a man will step out of the ranks of this great army and *demand* of himself and of the world more than a mere living. He will motivate himself with the strong *desire* for fortune, and presto! as if by the hand of magic, his financial status changes and he begins to turn his action into cash.

Power and success are synonomous terms. Success is not attained through honesty alone, as some would have us believe. The poor-houses are filled with people who, perhaps, were honest enough. They failed to accumulate money because they lacked the knowledge of how to acquire and use *power!*

The Master Mind principle described in this lesson is the medium through which all personal power is applied. For this reason, every known mind stimulant, and every basic motive which inspires action in all human endeavor, has been mentioned in this chapter.

THE TWO FORMS OF POWER

There are two forms of power which we shall analyze in this lesson. One is mental power, and it is acquired through the process of thought. It is expressed through definite plans of action, as the result of organized knowledge. The ability to think, plan, and act through well-organized procedure is the starting point of all mental power.

The other form of power is physical. It is expressed through natural laws, in the form of electrical energy, gravitation, steam pressure, etc. In this lesson we shall analyze both mental and physical power, and explain the relationship between the two.

Knowledge, alone, is not power. *Great personal power* is acquired only through the harmonious co-operation of a number of people who concentrate their efforts upon some definite plan.

THE NATURE OF PHYSICAL POWER

The state of advancement known as "civilization" is but the measure of knowledge which the race has accumulated. Among the useful knowledge organized by man, he has discovered and catalogued the eighty-odd physical elements of which all material forms in the universe consist.

By study, and analysis, and accurate measurements man

has discovered the "bigness" of the material side of the universe as represented by planets, suns, and stars, some of which are known to be over one million times as large as the little earth on which he lives.

On the other hand, man has discovered the "littleness" of the physical forms which constitute the universe by reducing the eighty-odd physical elements to molecules, atoms, and finally to the smallest particle, the electron. An electron cannot be seen; it is but a center of force consisting of a positive or a negative. The electron is the beginning of everything of a physical nature.

MOLECULES, ATOMS, AND ELECTRONS

To understand the process through which knowledge is gathered, organized and classified, it seems essential for the student to begin with the smallest and simplest particles of physical matter, because these are the ABCs with which Nature has constructed the entire physical portion of the universe.

The molecule consists of atoms, which are said to be invisible particles of matter revolving continuously with the speed of lightning, on exactly the same principle that the earth revolves on its axis.

These little particles of matter known as atoms, which revolve in one continuous circuit, in the molecule, are said to be made up of electrons, the smallest particles of physical matter. As already stated, the electron is nothing but two forms of force. The electron is uniform, of but one class, size, and nature. Thus in a grain of sand or a drop of water is duplicated the entire principle upon which the whole universe operates.

How stupendous! You may gather some slight idea of the magnitude of it all the next time you eat a meal by remembering that every article of food you eat, the plate on which you eat it, the tableware and the table itself, are, in final analysis, but a collection of *electrons*.

In the world of physical matter, whether one is looking at the largest star that floats through the heavens or the smallest grain of sand to be found on earth, the object under observation is but an organized collection of molecules, atoms, and electrons revolving at inconceivable speed.

Every particle of physical matter is in a continuous state of highly agitated motion. Nothing is ever still, although nearly all physical matter may appear, to the physical eye, to be motionless. There is no "solid" physical matter. The hardest piece of steel is but an organized mass of revolving molecules, atoms, and electrons. Moreover, the electrons in a piece of steel are of the same nature, and move at the same rate of speed, as the electrons in gold, silver, brass, or pewter.

The eighty-odd forms of physical matter appear to be different from one another, and they are different, because they are made up of different combinations of atoms (although the electrons in those atoms are always the same, except that some electrons are positive and some are negative, meaning that some carry a positive charge of electrification while others carry a negative charge).

Through the science of chemistry, matter may be broken up into atoms which are, within themselves, unchangeable. The eighty-odd elements are created through, and by reason of, combining and changing the positions of the atoms. To illustrate the modus operandi of chemistry through which this change of atomic position is wrought, in terms of modern science:

"Add four electrons (two positive and two negative) to the hydrogen atom, and you have the element lithium; knock out of the lithium atom (composed of three positive and three negative electrons) one positive and one negative electron, and you have one atom of helium (composed of two positive and two negative electrons)."

Thus it may be seen that the eighty-odd physical elements of the universe differ from one another only in the number of electrons composing their atoms, and the number and arrangement of those atoms in the molecules of each element.

As an illustration, an atom of mercury contains eighty positive charges (electrons) on its nucleus, and eighty negative outlying charges (electrons). If the chemist were to expel two of its positive electrons, it would instantly become the metal known as platinum. If the chemist then could go a step further and take from it a negative ("planetary") electron, the mercury atom would then have lost two positive electrons and one negative; that is, one positive charge on the whole; hence it would retain seventy-nine positive charges on the nucleus and seventy-nine outlying negative electrons, thereby becoming *gold!*

The formula through which this electronic change might be produced has been the object of diligent search by the alchemists all back down the ages, and of the modern chemists of to-day.

It is a fact known to every chemist that literally tens of thousands of synthetic substances may be composed out of only four kinds of atoms, viz., hydrogen, oxygen, nitrogen, and carbon.

The electron is the universal particle with which Nature builds all material forms, from a grain of sand to the largest star that floats through space. The electron is Nature's "building block" out of which she erects an oak tree or a pine, a rock of sandstone or granite, a mouse or an elephant.

Some of the ablest thinkers have reasoned that the earth on which we live, and every material particle of the earth, began with two atoms which attached themselves to each other, and through hundreds of millions of years of flight through space, kept contracting and accumulating other atoms until, step by step, the earth was formed. This, they point out, would account for the various and differing stratums of the earth's substances, such as the coal beds, the iron ore deposits, the gold and silver deposits, the copper deposits, etc.

They reason that, as the earth whirled through space, it contracted groups of various kinds of nebulae, which it promptly appropriated through the law of magnetic attraction. There is much to be seen, in the earth's surface composition, to support this theory, although there may be no positive evidence of its soundness.

These facts concerning the smallest analyzable particles of matter have been briefly referred to as a starting point from which we shall undertake to ascertain how to develop and apply the laws of *power*.

It has been noticed that all matter is in a constant state of vibration or motion; that the molecule is made up of rapidly moving particles called atoms, which, in turn, are made up of rapidly moving particles called electrons.

THE VIBRATING PRINCIPLE OF MATTER

In every particle of matter there is an invisible force which causes the atoms to move around one another at an inconceivable rate of speed.

This is a form of energy which has never been analyzed. Thus far it has baffled the entire scientific world. By many scientists it is believed to be the same energy as that which we call electricity. Others prefer to call it vibration. It is believed by some investigators that the rate of speed with which this force (call it whatever you will) moves determines the nature of the physical objects of the universe.

One rate of vibration causes what is known as sound. The human ear can detect only the sound which is produced through from thirty-two to thirty-eight thousand vibrations per second.

As the rate of vibrations per second increases above that which we call sound, they begin to manifest themselves in the form of heat. Heat begins with about one million and a half vibrations per second.

Still higher up the scale, vibrations begin to register in the form of light. Three million vibrations per second create violet light. Above this number vibration sheds ultra-violet rays (which are invisible to the naked eye) and other invisible radiations.

And still higher up the scale, just how high no one at present seems to know, vibrations create the power with which man *thinks*.

It is the belief of this author that the portion of vibration out of which grows all known forms of energy is universal in nature; that the "fluid" portion of sound is the same as the "fluid" portion of light, the difference in effect between sound and light being only a difference in rate of vibration; also that the "fluid" portion of thought is exactly the same as that in sound, heat, and light, excepting the number of vibrations per second.

Just as there is but one form of physical matter of which the earth and all the other planets, suns, and stars are composed—the electron—so is there but one form of "fluid" energy which causes all matter to remain in a constant state of rapid motion.

AIR AND ETHER

The vast space between the suns, moons, stars, and other planets of the universe is filled with a form of energy known as ether. It is this author's belief that the "fluid" energy, which keeps all the particles of matter in motion, is the same as the universal "fluid" known as ether, which fills all the space of the universe. Within a certain distance of the earth's surface, estimated by some to be about fifty miles, there exists what is called air, which is a gaseous substance composed of oxygen and nitrogen. Air is a conductor of sound vibrations, but a nonconductor of light and the higher vibrations, which are carried by the ether. The ether is a conductor of all vibrations from sound to thought.

Air is a localized substance which performs, in the main, the service of feeding all animal and plant life with oxygen and nitrogen, without which neither could exist. Nitrogen is one of the chief necessities of plant life, and oxygen one of the mainstays of animal life. Near the top of very high mountains the air becomes very light, because it contains but little nitrogen, which is the reason why plant life cannot exist there. On the other hand, the "light" air found in the high altitude consists largely of oxygen which is the chief reason why tubercular patients are sent to high altitudes.

*   *   *

Even this brief statement concerning molecules, atoms, electrons, air, ether, and the like may be heavy reading, but, as will be seen shortly, this introduction plays an essential part as the foundation of this philosophy of success.

Do not become discouraged if the description of this foundation appears to have none of the thrilling effects of a modern tale of fiction. You are seriously engaged in finding out what are your available powers and how to organize and apply these powers. To successfully complete this discovery you must combine determination, persistency, and a well-defined *desire* to gather and organize knowledge.

THE NATURE OF MENTAL POWER

The late Dr. Alexander Graham Bell, inventor of the long-distance telephone and one of the accepted authorities on the subject of vibration, is here introduced in support of the statements in this volume concerning the subject of vibration, which is the basis of all mental power, and of all thought.

"Suppose you have the power to make an iron rod vibrate with any desired frequency in a dark room. At first, when vibrating slowly, its movement will be indicated by only one sense, that of touch. As soon as the vibrations increase, a low sound will emanate from it and it will appeal to two senses.

"At about thirty-two thousand vibrations to the second the sound will be loud and shrill; but at forty thousand vibrations it will be silent and the movements of the rod will not be perceived by touch. Its movements will be perceived by no ordinary human sense.

"From this point up to about one million and a half vibrations per second, we have no sense that can appreciate any effect of the intervening vibrations. After that stage is reached, movement is indicated first by the sense of temperature and then, when the rod becomes red hot, by the sense of sight. At three million vibrations it sheds violet light. Above that it sheds ultraviolet rays and other invisible radiations, some of which can be perceived by instruments and employed by us.

"Now it has occurred to me that there must be a great deal to be learned about the effect of those vibrations in the great gap where ordinary human senses are unable to hear, see or feel the movement. The power to send wireless messages by ether vibrations lies in that gap, but the gap is so great that it seems there must be much more. You must make machines practically to supply new senses, as the wireless instruments do.

"Can it be said, when you think of that great gap, that there are not many forms of vibrations that may give us results as wonderful as, or even more wonderful than, the wireless waves? It seems to me that in this gap lie the vibrations which we have assumed to be given off by our brain and nerve cells when we think. But then, again, they may be higher up in the scale beyond the vibrations that produce the ultraviolet rays. (Author's note: The last sentence suggests the theory held by this author.)

"Do we need a wire to carry these vibrations? Will they not pass through the ether without a wire, just as the wireless waves do? How will they be perceived by the recipient? Will he hear a series of signals, or will he find that another man's thoughts have entered into his brain?

"We may indulge in some speculations based on what we know of the wireless waves, which, as I have said, are all we can recognize of a vast series of vibrations which theoretically must exist. If the thought waves are similar to the wireless waves, they must pass from the brain and flow endlessly around the world and the universe. The body and the skull and other solid obstacles would form no obstruction to their passage, as they pass through the ether which surrounds the molecules of every substance, no matter how solid and dense.

"You ask if there would not be constant interference and confusion if other people's thought were flowing through our brains and setting up thoughts in them that did not originate with ourselves?

"How do you know that other men's thoughts are not interfering with yours now? I have noticed a good many phenomena of mind disturbances that I have never been able to explain. For instance, there is the inspiration or the discouragement that a speaker feels in addressing an audience. I have experienced this many times in my life and have never been able to define exactly the physical causes of it.

"Many recent scientific discoveries, in my opinion, point to a day, not far distant perhaps, when men will read one another's thoughts, when thoughts will be conveyed directly from brain to brain without the intervention of speech, writing or any of the present known methods of communication.

"It is not unreasonable to look forward to a time when we shall see without eyes, hear without ears, and talk without tongues.

"Briefly, the hypothesis that mind can communicate directly with mind rests on the theory that thought or vital force is a form of electrical disturbance, that it can be taken up by induction and transmitted to a distance either through a wire or simply through the all-pervading ether, as in the case of wireless telegraph waves.

"There are many analogies which suggest that thought is of the nature of an electrical disturbance. A nerve which is of the same substance as the brain is an excellent conductor of the electric current. When we first passed an electrical current through the nerves of a dead man, we were shocked and amazed to see him sit up and move. The electrified nerves produced contraction of the muscles very much as in life.

> Putting ideas to work is a profitable business, but it makes a slight difference whether the ideas were created by you or by someone else.

"The nerves appear to act upon the muscles very much as the electric current acts upon an electromagnet. The current magnetizes a bar of iron placed at right angles to it, and the nerves produce, through the intangible current of vital force that flows through them, contraction of the muscular fibers that are arranged at right angles to them.

"It would be possible to cite many reasons why thought and vital force may be regarded as of the same nature as electricity. The electric current is held to be a wave motion of the ether—the hypothetical substance that fills all space and pervades all substances. We believe that there must be ether, because without it the electric current could not pass through a vacuum, or sunlight through space. It is reasonable to believe that only a wave motion of a similar character can produce the phenomena of thought and vital force. We may assume that the brain cells act as a battery and that the current produced flows along the nerves.

"But does it end there? Does it not pass out of the body in waves which flow around the world unperceived by our senses, just as the wireless waves passed unperceived before Hertz and others discovered their existence?"

EVERY MIND BOTH A BROADCASTING AND A RECEIVING STATION

This author has proved, to his own satisfaction at least, that every human brain is both a broadcasting and a receiving station for vibrations of thought frequency.

If this theory should turn out to be a fact, and methods of reasonable control should be established, imagine the part it would play in the gathering, classifying, and organizing of knowledge. The possibility, much less the probability of such a reality, staggers the mind of man!

Thomas Paine was one of the great minds of the American Revolutionary period. To him more, perhaps, than to any other one person, we owe both the beginning and the happy ending of the Revolution, for it was his keen mind that both helped in drawing up the Declaration of Independence and in persuading the signers of that document to translate it into terms of reality.

In speaking of the source of his great storehouse of knowledge, Paine thus described it:

"Any person who has made observations on the state of progress of the human mind, by observing his own, cannot but have observed that there are two distinct classes of what are called thoughts: Those that we produce in ourselves by reflection and the act of thinking, and those that bolt into the mind of their own accord. I have always made it a rule to treat these voluntary visitors with civility, taking care to examine, as well as I was able, if they were worth entertaining; and it is from them I have acquired almost all the knowledge that I have. As to the learning that any person gains from school education, it serves only like a small capital, to put him in the way of beginning learning for himself afterwards. Every person of learning is finally his own teacher, the reason for which is, that principles, being of a distinct quality to circumstances, cannot be impressed upon the memory; their place of mental residence is the understanding, and they are never so lasting as when they begin by conception."

In the foregoing words Paine, the great American patriot and philosopher, described a phenomenon which at one time or another is the experience of every person. Who is so unfortunate as not to have received positive evidence that thoughts and even complete ideas will "pop" into the mind from the outside sources?

What means of conveyance is there for such visitors except the ether? Ether fills the boundless space of the universe. It is the medium of conveyance for all known forms of vibration such as sound, light, and heat. Why would it not be, also, the medium of conveyance of the vibration of thought?

Every mind, or brain, is directly connected with every other brain by means of the ether. Every thought released by any brain may be instantly picked up and interpreted by all other brains that are en rapport with the sending brain. This author is as sure of this fact as he is that the chemical formula H_2O will produce water.

Nor is the probability of ether being a conveyer of thought from mind to mind the most astounding of its performances. It is the belief of this author that every thought vibration released by any brain is picked up by the ether and kept in motion in circuitous wave lengths corresponding in length to the intensity of the energy used in its release; that these vibrations remain in motion forever; that they are one of the two sources from which thoughts which "pop" into one's mind emanate, the other source being direct and immediate contact through the ether with the brain releasing the thought vibration.

Thus it will be seen that if this theory is a fact, the boundless space of the whole universe is now and will continue to become literally a library wherein may be found all the thoughts released by mankind.

The author is here laying the foundation for one of the most important hypotheses enumerated in this chapter.

According to men of science, most of the useful knowledge to which the human race has become heir has been preserved and accurately recorded in Nature's Bible. By turning back the pages of this unalterable Bible, man has read the story of the terrific struggle through and out of which the present civilization has grown. The pages of this Bible are made up of the physical elements of which this earth and the other planets consist, and of the ether which fills all space.

By turning back the pages written on stone and covered near the surface of this earth on which he lives, man has uncovered the bones, skeletons, footprints, and other unmistakable evidence of the history of animal life on this earth, planted there for his enlightenment and guidance by the hand of Mother Nature throughout unbelievable periods of time. The evidence is plain and unmistakable. The great stone pages of Nature's Bible found on this earth, and the endless pages of that Bible represented by the ether wherein all past human thought has been recorded, constitute an authentic source of communication between the Creator and man. This Bible was begun before man had reached the thinking stage; indeed, before man had reached the amœba (one-cell animal) stage of development.

This Bible is above and beyond the power of man to alter. Moreover, it tells its story in universal language which all who have eyes may read. Nature's Bible, from whence we have derived all the knowledge that is worth knowing, is one that no man may alter or in any manner tamper with.

The most marvelous discovery yet made by man is the recently discovered radio principle, which operates through the aid of ether; an important portion of Nature's Bible. Imagine the ether picking up the ordinary vibration of sound, and transforming (stepping up the rate of vibration) that vibration from audio-frequency into radio-frequency, carrying it to a properly attuned receiving station and there transforming it back into its original form of audio-frequency, all in the flash of a second. It should surprise no one that such a force could gather up the vibration of thought and keep that vibration in motion forever.

The established and known fact of instantaneous transmission of sound, through the agency of the ether, by means of the modern radio apparatus, removes the theory of transmission of thought vibrations from mind to mind from the possible to the probable.

THE MASTER MIND

We come now to the next step in the description of the ways and means by which one may gather, classify, and organize useful knowledge, through harmonious alliance of two or more minds, out of which grows a Master Mind.

The term "Master Mind" is abstract, and has no counterpart in the field of known facts, except to a small number of people who have made a careful study of the effect of one mind upon other minds.

This author has searched in vain through all the textbooks and essays available on the subject of the human mind, but nowhere has been found even the slightest reference to the principle here described as the "Master Mind." The term first came to the attention of the author through an interview with Andrew Carnegie, in the manner described in another chapter.

CHEMISTRY OF THE MIND

It is this author's belief that the mind is made up of the same energy as that which constitutes the ether which fills the universe. It is a fact, as well known to the layman as to the man of scientific investigation, that some minds clash the moment they come in contact with each other. Between the two extremes of natural antagonism and natural affinity growing out of the meeting or contacting of minds, there is a wide range of possibility for varying reactions of mind upon mind.

Some minds are so naturally adapted to each other that "love at first sight" is the inevitable outcome of the contact. Who has not known of such an experience? In other cases minds are so antagonistic that violent mutual dislike shows itself at first meeting. These results occur without a word being spoken, and without the slightest signs of any of the usual causes for love and hate acting as a stimulus.

It is quite probable that the "mind" is made up of a substance or energy, call it what you will, similar to (if not, in fact, the same substance) the ether. When two minds come close enough to each other to form a contact, the mixing of the units of this "mind stuff" (let us call it the electrons of the ether) sets up a chemical reaction and starts vibrations which affect the two individuals pleasantly or unpleasantly.

The effect of the meeting of two minds is obvious to even the most casual observer. Every effect must have a cause! What could be more reasonable than to suspect that the cause of the change in mental attitude between the two minds, which have just come in contact, is none other than the disturbance of the electrons or units of each mind in the process of rearranging themselves in the new field created by the contact?

For the purpose of establishing this philosophy upon a sound foundation, we have gone a long way toward success by admitting that the meeting or coming in close contact of two minds sets up in each of those minds a certain noticeable "effect" or state of mind quite different from the one existing immediately prior to the contact. While it is desirable, it is not essential to know what is the "cause" of this reaction of mind upon mind.

That the reaction takes place in every instance is a known fact, which gives us a starting point from which we may show what is meant by the term "Master Mind."

A Master Mind may be created through the bringing together or blending, in a spirit of perfect harmony, of two or more minds. Out of this harmonious blending, the chemistry of the mind creates a third mind which may be appropriated and used by one or all of the individual minds. This Master Mind will remain available as long as the friendly, harmonious alliance between the individual minds exists. It will disintegrate and all evidence of its existence disappear the moment the friendly alliance is broken.

This principle of mind chemistry is the basis and cause of practically all the so-called "soul mate" and "eternal triangle" cases, so many of which unfortunately find their way into the divorce courts and meet with popular ridicule from ignorant and uneducated people who manufacture vulgarity and scandal out of one of the greatest of Nature's laws.

The entire civilized world knows that the first two or three years of association after marriage are often marked by much disagreement of a more or less petty nature. These are the years of "adjustment." If the marriage survives them, it is more than apt to become a permanent alliance. These facts no experienced married person will deny. Again we see the "effect" without understanding the "cause."

While there are other contributing causes, yet, in the main, lack of harmony during these early years of marriage is due to the slowness of the chemistry of the minds in blending harmoniously. Stated differently, the electrons or units of the energy called the mind are often neither extremely friendly nor antagonistic upon first contact; but through constant association they gradually adapt themselves in harmony, except in rare cases where association has the opposite effect of leading eventually to open hostility between these units.

It is a well-known fact that after a man and a woman have lived together for ten to fifteen years, they become practically indispensable to each other, even though there may not be the slightest evidence of the state of mind called love. Moreover, this association and relationship sexually not only develops a natural affinity between the two minds, but it actually causes the two people to take on a similar facial expression and to closely re-semble each other in many other marked ways. Any competent analyst of human nature can easily go into a crowd of strange people and pick out the wife after having been introduced to her husband. The expression of the eyes, the contour of the faces, and the tone of the voices of the people who have long been associ-ated in marriage become similar to a marked degree.

So marked is the effect of the chemistry of the human mind that any experienced public speaker may quickly interpret the manner in which his statements are accepted by his audience. Antagonism in the mind of but one person in an audience of one thousand may be readily detected by the speaker who has learned how to "feel" and register the effects of antagonism. Moreover, the public speaker can make these interpretations without observing or in any manner being influenced by the expression on the faces of those in his audience. On account of this fact, an audience may cause a speaker to rise to great heights of oratory, or heckle him into failure, without making a sound or denoting a single expres-sion of satisfaction or dissatisfaction through the features of the face.

All "Master Salesmen" know the moment the "psychological time for closing" has arrived; not by what the prospective buyer says, but from the effect of the chemistry of his mind as inter-preted or "felt" by the salesman. Words often belie the intentions of those speaking them, but a correct interpretation of the chem-istry of the mind leaves no loophole for such a possibility. Every able salesman knows that the majority of buyers have a habit of affecting a negative attitude almost to the very climax of a sale.

Every able lawyer has developed a sixth sense with which he is enabled to "feel" his way through the most artfully selected words of the clever witness who is lying, and correctly interpret that which is in the mind of the witness through the chemistry of the mind. Many lawyers have developed this ability without knowing the real source of it; they possess the technique without the scientific understanding upon which it is based. Many salesmen have done the same thing.

One who is gifted in the art of correctly interpreting the chemistry of the minds of others may, figuratively speaking, walk in at the front door of the mansion of a given mind and leisurely explore the entire building, denoting all its details, walking out again with a complete picture of the interior of the building without the owner of the building so much as knowing that he has entertained a visitor. It will be observed, in the chapter on Accurate Thinking, that this principle may be put to a very practical use (having reference to the principle of the chemistry of the mind).

Enough has already been stated to introduce the principle of mind chemistry, and to prove, with the aid of the reader's own everyday experiences and casual observations that the moment two minds come within close range of each other, a noticeable mental change takes place in both, sometimes registering in the nature of antagonism and at other times registering in the nature of friendliness. Every mind has what might be termed an electric field. The nature of this field varies, depending upon the "mood" of the individual mind back of it, and upon the nature of the chemistry of the mind creating the "field."

It is believed by this author that the normal or natural condition of the chemistry of any individual mind is the result of his physical heredity, plus the nature of thoughts which have dominated that mind; that every mind is continuously changing to the extent that the individual's philosophy and general habits of thought change the chemistry of his or her mind. These principles the author *believes* to be true. That any individual may voluntarily change the chemistry of his or her mind so that it will either attract or repel all with whom it comes in contact is a *known fact!* Stated in another manner, any person may assume a mental attitude which will attract and please others or repel and antagonize them, and this without the aid of words, or facial expression, or other form of bodily movement or demeanor.

Go back, now, to the definition of a "Master Mind"—a mind which grows out of the blending and co-ordination of two or more minds, *in a spirit of perfect harmony,* and you will catch the full significance of the word "harmony" as it is here used. Two minds will not blend nor can they be co-ordinated unless the element of perfect harmony is present, wherein lies the secret of success or failure of practically all business and social partnerships.

Every sales manager and every military commander and every leader in any other walk of life understands the necessity of an "esprit de corps"—a spirit of common understanding and co-operation—in the attainment of success. This mass spirit of harmony of purpose is obtained through discipline, voluntary or forced, of such a nature that the individual minds become blended into a "Master Mind," by which is meant that the chemistry of the individual minds is modified in such a manner that these minds blend and function as one.

The methods through which this "blending" process takes place are as numerous as are the individuals engaged in the various forms of leadership. Every leader has his or her own method of co-ordinating the minds of the followers. One will use force. Another uses persuasion. One will play upon the fear of penalties, while another plays upon rewards, in order to reduce the individual minds of given groups of people to where they may be blended into a mass mind. The student will not have to search deeply into history of statesmanship, politics, business, or finance, to discover the technique employed by the leaders in these fields in the process of blending the minds of individuals into a mass mind.

The really great leaders of the world, however, have been provided by nature with a combination of mind chemistry favorable as a nucleus of attraction for other minds. Napoleon was a notable example of a man possessing the magnetic type of mind which had a very decided tendency to attract all minds with which it came in contact. Soldiers followed Napoleon to certain death without flinching, because of the impelling or attracting nature of his personality, and that personality was nothing more nor less than the chemistry of his mind.

No group of minds can be blended into a "Master Mind" if one of the individuals of that group possesses an extremely negative, repellent mind. The negative and positive minds will not blend in the sense here described as a "Master Mind." Lack of knowledge of this fact has brought many an otherwise able leader to defeat.

Any leader who understands this principle of mind chemistry may temporarily blend the minds of practically any group of people, so that it will represent a mass mind, but the composition will disintegrate almost the very moment the leader's presence is removed from the group. The most successful life insurance sales organizations and other sales forces meet once a week, or more often, *for the purpose of merging the individual minds into a Master Mind which will, for a limited number of days, serve as a stimulus to the individual minds!*

It may be, and generally is, true that the leaders of these groups do not understand what actually takes place in these meetings, which are usually given over to talks by the leader and other members of the group; meanwhile the minds of the individuals are "contacting" and recharging one another.

The brain of a human being may be compared to an electric battery in that it will become exhausted or run down, causing the owner of it to feel despondent, discouraged and lacking in "pep." Who is so fortunate as never to have had such a feeling? The human brain, when in this depleted condition, must be recharged, and the manner in which this is done is through contact with a more vital mind or minds. The great leaders understand the necessity of this "recharging" process, and moreover, they understand how to accomplish this result. *This knowledge is the main feature which distinguishes a leader from a follower!*

Fortunate is the person who understands this principle sufficiently well to keep his or her brain vitalized or "recharged" by periodically contacting it with a more vital mind. Sexual contact is one of the most effective of the stimuli through which a mind may be recharged, providing the contact is intelligently made between man and woman who have genuine affection for each other. Any other sort of sexual relationship is a devitalizer of the mind.

Before passing away from the brief reference made to sexual contact as a means of revitalizing a depleted mind, it seems appropriate to call attention to the fact that all of the great leaders, in whatever walks of life they have arisen, have been and are people of highly sexed natures. (The word "sex" is a decent word. You'll find it in all the dictionaries.)

There is a growing tendency upon the part of the best-informed physicians and other health practitioners to accept the theory that all diseases begin when the brain of the individual is in a depleted or devitalized state. Stated in another way, it is a known fact that a person who has a perfectly vitalized brain is practically, if not entirely, immune from all manner of disease.

Every intelligent health practitioner, of whatever school or type, knows that "Nature," or the mind, cures disease in every instance where a cure is affected. Medicines, faith, laying on of hands, chiropractic, osteopathy, and all other forms of outside stimulant are nothing more than artificial aids to Nature, or, to state it correctly, mere methods of setting the chemistry of the mind into motion to the end that it readjusts the cells and tissues of the body, revitalizes the brain, and otherwise causes the human machine to function normally.

The most orthodox practitioner should admit the truth of this statement.

What, then, may be the possibilities of the future in the field of mind chemistry?

Through the principle of harmonious blending of minds, perfect health may be enjoyed. Through the aid of this same principle, sufficient power may be developed to solve the problems of economic necessity which constantly press upon every individual.

We may judge the future possibilities of mind chemistry by taking inventory of its past achievements, keeping in mind the fact that these achievements have been largely the result of accidental discovery and of chance groupings of minds. We are approaching the time when the professorate of the universities will teach mind chemistry the same as other subjects are now taught. Meanwhile, study and experimentation in connection with this subject open vistas of possibility for the individual student.

MIND CHEMISTRY AND ECONOMIC POWER

That mind chemistry may be appropriately applied to the work-a-day affairs of the economic and commercial world is a demonstrable fact.

Through the blending of two or more minds, in a spirit of *perfect harmony*, the principle of mind chemistry may be made to develop sufficient power to enable the individuals whose minds have been thus blended to perform seemingly superhuman feats. Power is the force with which men achieve success in any undertaking. Power, in unlimited quantities, may be enjoyed by any group of men, or men and women, who possess the wisdom with which to submerge their own personalities and their own immediate individual interests, through the blending of their minds in a spirit of perfect harmony.

Observe the frequency with which the word "harmony" appears throughout this introduction! There can be no development of a "Master Mind" where this element of *perfect harmony* does not exist. The individual units of one mind will not blend with the individual units of another mind *until the two minds have been aroused and warmed, as it were, with a spirit of perfect harmony of purpose*. The moment two minds begin to take divergent roads of interest, the individual units of each mind separate, and the third element, known as a "Master Mind" which grew out of the friendly or harmonious alliance, will disintegrate.

> Is it not strange that nowhere in history
> do we find a record of one great man
> who attained his greatness through deceit,
> trickery, and by double-crossing his
> business associates?

We come, now, to the study of some well-known men who have accumulated great power (also great fortunes) through the application of the Master Mind.

Let us begin with three great men who are known to be men of great achievement in their respective fields of business and professional endeavor.

Their names are Henry Ford, Thomas A. Edison, and Harvey Firestone.

Of the three Henry Ford is by far the most *powerful*, having reference to economic and financial power. Mr. Ford is the most powerful man now living on earth. Many who have studied Mr. Ford believe him to be the most powerful man who ever lived. As far as is known Mr. Ford is the only man now living, or who ever lived, with sufficient power to outwit the money trust of the United States. Mr. Ford gathers millions of dollars with as great ease as a child fills its bucket with sand when playing on the beach. It has been said by those who were in position to know that Mr. Ford, if he needed it, could send out the call for money and gather in a billion dollars (a thousand million dollars) and have it available for use within one week. No one who knows of Ford's achievements doubts this. Those who know him well know that he could do it with no more effort than the average man expends in raising the money with which to pay a month's house rent.

Mr. Edison, as everyone knows, is a philosopher, scientist, and inventor. He is, perhaps, the keenest Bible student on earth; a student of Nature's Bible, however. Mr. Edison has such a keen insight into Mother Nature's Bible that he has harnessed and combined for the good of mankind, more of Nature's Laws than any person now living or who ever lived. It was he who brought together the point of a needle and a piece of revolving wax in such a way that the vibration of the human voice may be recorded and reproduced through the modern talking machine.

And it may be Edison or a man of his type, who will eventually enable man to pick up and correctly interpret the vibrations of thought which are now recorded in the boundless universe of ether, just as he has enabled man to record and reproduce the spoken word.

It was Edison who first harnessed the lightning and made it serve as a light for man's use, through the aid of the incandescent electric light bulb.

It was Edison who gave the world the modern moving picture.

These are but a few of his outstanding achievements. These modern "miracles," which he has performed in the very midst of the bright light of science, transcend all of the "miracles" described by Jules Verne and others in books of fiction.

Mr. Firestone is the moving spirit in the great Firestone Tire industry in Akron, Ohio. His industrial achievements are so well known wherever automobiles are used that no special comment on them seems necessary.

All three men began their careers, business and professional, without capital and with but little schooling of that type usually referred to as "education."

All three men are now well educated. All three are wealthy. All three are powerful. Now let us inquire into the source of their wealth and power. Thus far we have been dealing only with effect; the true philosopher wishes to understand the "cause" of a given effect.

It is a matter of general knowledge that Mr. Ford, Mr. Edison, and Mr. Firestone are close personal friends, and have been so for many years; that in former years they were in the habit of going away to the woods once a year for a period of rest, meditation, and recuperation.

But it is not generally known—it is a grave doubt if these three men, themselves, know it—that there exists between the three men a bond of harmony which has caused their minds to become blended into a "Master Mind" which is the real source of the power of each. This mass mind, growing out of the coordination of the individual minds of Ford, Edison, and Firestone, has

enabled these men to "tune in" on forces and sources of knowledge with which most men are to no extent familiar.

If the student doubts either the principle or the effects here
described, let him remember that more than half the theory here
set forth is a known fact. For example, it is known that these
three men have great power. It is known that they are wealthy.
It is known that they began without capital and with but little
schooling. It is known that they form periodic mind contacts. It
is known that they are harmonious and friendly. It is known that
their achievements are so outstanding as to make it impossible
to compare these achievements with those of other men in their
respective fields of activity.

All these "effects" are known to practically every schoolboy
in the civilized world, therefore there can be no dispute as far as
effects are concerned.

Of one fact connected with the "cause" of the achievements
of Edison, Ford, and Firestone we may be sure, namely, that these
achievements are in no way based upon trickery, deceit, or any
other form of unnatural law. These men do not possess a stock
of legerdemain. They work with natural laws which, for the most
part, are well known to all economists and leaders in the field
of science, with the possible exception of the law upon which
chemistry of the mind is based. As yet chemistry of the mind
is not sufficiently developed to be classed, by scientific men, in
their catalogue of known laws.

A "Master Mind" may be created by any group of people
who will co-ordinate their minds in a spirit of perfect harmony.
The group may consist of any number from two upward. Best
results appear available from the blending of six or seven minds.

It has been suggested that Jesus Christ discovered how
to make use of the principle of mind chemistry, and that His
seemingly miraculous performances grew out of the power He

developed through the blending of the minds of His twelve
disciples. It has been pointed out that when one of the disciples
broke faith (Judas Iscariot) the "Master Mind" immediately
disintegrated and Jesus met with the supreme catastrophe of
His life.

When two or more people harmonize their minds and produce the effect known as a "Master Mind," each person in the
group becomes vested with the power to contact with and gather
knowledge through the "subconscious" minds of all the other
members of the group. This power becomes immediately noticeable, having the effect of stimulating the mind to a higher rate of
vibration, and otherwise evidencing itself in the form of a more
vivid imagination and the consciousness of what appears to be
a sixth sense. It is through this sixth sense that new ideas will
"flash" into the mind. These ideas take on the nature and form
of the subject dominating the mind of the individual. If the entire group has met for the purpose of discussing a given subject,
ideas concerning that subject will come pouring into the minds
of all present, as if an outside influence were dictating them. The
minds of those participating in the "Master Mind" become as
magnets, attracting ideas and thought stimuli of the most highly
organized and practical nature, from—no one knows where!

The process of mind blending here described as a "Master
Mind" may be likened to the act of one who connects many electric batteries to a single transmission wire, thereby "stepping up"
the power passing over that line by the amount of energy the
batteries carry. Just so in the case of blending individual minds
into a "Master Mind." Each mind, through the principle of mind
chemistry, stimulates all the other minds in the group, until the
mind energy thus becomes so great that it penetrates and connects with the universal energy known as ether, which, in turn,
touches every atom of matter in the universe.

Every public speaker has felt the influence of mind chemistry, for it is a well-known fact that as soon as the individual minds of an audience become en rapport (attuned to the rate of vibration of the mind of the speaker) with the speaker, there is a noticeable increase of enthusiasm in the speaker's mind, and he often rises to heights of oratory which surprise all, including himself.

The first five to ten minutes of the average speech are devoted to what is known as "warming up." By this is meant the process through which the minds of the speaker and his audience are becoming blended in a spirit of *perfect harmony*.

Every speaker knows what happens when this state of "perfect harmony" fails to materialize upon the part of his audience.

The seemingly supernatural phenomena occurring in spiritualistic meetings are the result of the reaction, upon one another, of the minds in the group. These phenomena seldom begin to manifest themselves under ten to twenty minutes after the group is formed, for the reason that this is about the time required for the minds in the group to become harmonized or blended.

The "messages" received by members of a spiritualistic group probably come from one of two sources, or from both, namely:

First: From the vast storehouse of the subconscious mind of some member of the group, or,

Second: From the universal storehouse of the ether, in which, it is more than probable, all thought vibration is preserved.

Neither any known natural law nor human reason support the theory of communication with individuals who have died.

It is a known fact that any individual may explore the store of knowledge in another's mind, through this principle of mind chemistry, and it seems reasonable to suppose that this power may be extended to include contact with whatever vibrations are available in the ether, if there are any.

The theory that all the higher and more refined vibrations, such as thought, are preserved in the ether, grows out of the known fact that neither matter nor energy (the two known elements of the universe) may be either created or destroyed. It is reasonable to suppose that all vibrations, which have been "stepped up" suffi- ciently to be picked up and absorbed in the ether, will go on for- ever. The lower vibrations, which do not blend with or otherwise contact the ether, probably exist a natural life and die out.

All the so-called geniuses probably gained their reputations because, by mere chance or otherwise, they formed alliances with other minds which enabled them to "step up" their own mind vibrations to where they were enabled to contact the vast Temple of Knowledge recorded and filed in the ether of the uni- verse. All of the great geniuses, as far as this author has been enabled to gather the facts, were highly sexed people. The fact that sexual contact is the greatest known mind stimulant lends color to the theory herein described.

Enquiring further into the source of economic power, as manifested by the achievements of men in the field of business, let us study the case of the Chicago group known as the Big Six, consisting of Wm. Wrigley, Jr., who owns the chewing gum busi- ness bearing his name, and whose individual income is said to be more than fifteen million dollars a year; John R. Thomp- son, who operates the chain of lunch rooms bearing his name; Mr. A. D. Lasker, who owns the Lord & Thomas Advertising Agency; Mr. McCullough, who owns the Parmalee Express Company, the largest transfer business in America; and, Mr. Ritchie and Mr. Hertz, who own the Yellow Taxicab business.

A reliable financial reporting company has estimated the yearly income of these six men at upward of twenty-five million dollars, or an average of more than four million dollars a year per man.

Analysis of the entire group of six men discloses the fact that not one of them had any special educational advantages; that all began without capital or extensive credit; that their financial achievement has been due to their own individual plans and not to any fortunate turn of the wheel of chance.

Many years ago these six men formed a friendly alliance, meeting at stated periods for the purpose of assisting one another with ideas and suggestions in their various and sundry lines of business endeavor.

With the exception of Hertz and Ritchie, none of the six men were in any manner associated in a legal partnership. These meetings were strictly for the purpose of co-operating on the give-and-take basis of assisting one another with ideas and suggestions.

It is said that each of the individuals belonging to this Big Six group is a millionaire many times over. As a rule there is nothing worthy of special comment on behalf of a man who does nothing more than accumulate a few million dollars. However, there is something connected with the financial success of this particular group of men that is well worth comment, study, analysis, and even emulation, and that "something" is the fact that they have learned how to coordinate their individual minds by blending them in a spirit of perfect harmony, thereby creating a "Master Mind" that unlocks, to each individual of the group, doors which are closed to most of the human race.

The United States Steel Corporation is one of the strongest and most powerful industrial organizations in the world. The idea out of which this great industrial giant grew was born in the mind of Elbert H. Gary, a more or less commonplace lawyer, who was born and reared in a small Illinois town near Chicago.

Mr. Gary surrounded himself with a group of men whose minds he successfully blended in a spirit of perfect harmony, thereby creating the "Master Mind" which is the moving spirit of the great United States Steel Corporation.

Search where you will and wherever you find an outstanding success in business, finance, industry, or in any of the professions, you may be sure that back of the success is some individual who has applied the principle of mind chemistry through which a "Master Mind" has been created. These outstanding successes often appear to be the handiwork of but one person, but search closely and the other individuals whose minds have been co-ordinated with his own may be found. Remember that two or more persons may operate the principle of mind chemistry so as to create a "Master Mind."

Power (man power) is *organized knowledge, expressed through intelligent action!*

No effort can be said to be *organized* unless the individuals engaged in the effort co-ordinate their knowledge and energy in a spirit of perfect harmony. Lack of such harmonious co-ordination of effort is the main cause of practically every business failure.

An interesting experiment was conducted by this author in collaboration with the students of a well-known college. Each student was requested to write an essay on "How and Why Henry Ford Became Wealthy."

Each student was required to describe, as a part of his or her essay, what was believed to be the nature of Ford's real assets, of what these assets consisted in detail.

The majority of the students gathered financial statements and inventories of the Ford assets and used these as the basis of their estimates of Ford's wealth.

Included in these "sources of Ford's wealth" were such items as cash in banks, raw and finished materials in stock, real estate and buildings, good will, estimated at from ten to twenty-five per cent of the value of the material assets.

One student out of the entire group of several hundred, answered as follows:

"Henry Ford's assets consist, in the main, of two items, viz: (1) Working capital and raw and finished materials; (2) The knowledge, gained from experience, by Henry Ford himself, and the co-operation of a well-trained organization which understands how to apply this knowledge to best advantage from the Ford viewpoint. It is impossible to estimate, with anything approximating correctness, the actual dollars and cents value of either of these two groups of assets, but it is my opinion that their relative values are:

The organized knowledge of the Ford Organization	75%
The value of cash and physical assets of every nature, including raw and finished materials	25%

This author is of the opinion that this statement was not compiled by the young man whose name was signed to it, without the assistance of some very analytical and experienced mind or minds.

Unquestionably the biggest asset that Henry Ford has is his own brain. Next to this would come the brains of his immediate circle of associates, for it has been through co-ordination of these that the physical assets which he controls were accumulated.

Destroy every plant the Ford Motor Company owns; every piece of machinery; every ton of raw or finished material; every finished automobile, and every dollar on deposit in any bank, and Ford would still be the most powerful man, economically, on earth. His brains which have built the Ford business could duplicate it again in short order. Capital is always available in unlimited quantities, to such brains as Ford's.

Economically, Ford is the most powerful man on earth, because he has the keenest and most practical conception of the principle of *organized knowledge* of any man on earth, as far as this author has the means of knowing.

Despite Ford's great power and financial success, it may be that he has blundered often in the application of the principles through which he accumulated this power. There is but little doubt that Ford's methods of mind co-ordination have often been crude; they must needs have been in the earlier days of this experience, before he gained the wisdom of application that would naturally go with maturity of years.

Neither can there be but little doubt that Ford's application of the principle of mind chemistry was, at least at the start, the result of a chance alliance with other minds; particularly the mind of Edison. It is more than probable that Mr. Ford's remarkable insight into the law of nature was first begun as the result of his friendly alliance with his own wife long before he ever met either Mr. Edison or Mr. Firestone. Many a man is made by his wife, through application of the "Master Mind" principle, who never knows the real source of his success. Mrs. Ford is a most remarkably intelligent woman, and this author has reason to believe that it was her mind, blended with Mr. Ford's, which gave him his first real start toward power.

It may be mentioned, without in any way depriving Ford of any honor or glory, that in his earlier days he had to combat the powerful enemies of illiteracy and ignorance to a greater extent than did either Edison or Firestone, both of whom were gifted by natural heredity with a most fortunate aptitude for acquiring and applying knowledge. Ford had to hew his talent out of the rough, raw timbers of his none too favorable hereditary estate.

Within an inconceivably short period of time Ford has mastered three of the most stubborn enemies of mankind and transformed them into assets constituting the very foundation of his success.

These enemies are: ignorance, illiteracy, and poverty!

Any man who can stay the hand of these three savage forces, much less harness and use them to good account, is well worth close study by the less fortunate individuals.

*   *   *

This is an age of *industrial power* in which we are living!

The source of all this *power* is *organized effort*. Not only has the management of industrial enterprises efficiently organized individual workers, but in many instances mergers of industry have been affected in such a manner and to the end that these combinations (as in the case of the United States Steel Corporation, for example) have accumulated practically unlimited power.

One may hardly glance at the news of a day's events without seeing a report of some business, industrial, or financial merger, bringing under one management enormous resources and thus creating great power.

One day it is a group of banks; another day it is a chain of railroads; the next day it is a combination of steel plants, all merging, for the purpose of developing power through highly organized and coordinated effort.

Knowledge, general in nature and unorganized, is not *power*; it is only potential power—the material out of which real power may be developed. Any modern library contains an unorganized record of all the knowledge of value to which the present civilization is heir, but this knowledge is not power because it is not organized.

Every form of energy and every specie of animal or plant life, to survive, must be organized. The oversized animals whose bones have filled Nature's bone yard through extinction have left mute, but certain evidence that nonorganization means annihilation.

From the electron—the smallest particle of matter—to the largest star in the universe, these and every material thing in between these two extremes, offer proof positive that one of Nature's first laws is that of *organization*. Fortunate is the individual who recognizes the importance of this law and makes it his business to familiarize himself with the various ways in which the law may be applied to advantage.

The astute business man has not only recognized the importance of the law of organized effort, but he has made this law the warp and woof of his *power*.

Without any knowledge whatsover of the principle of mind chemistry, or that such a principle exists, many men have accumulated great power by merely organizing the knowledge they possessed. The majority of all who have discovered the principle of mind chemistry and developed that principle into a "Master Mind" have stumbled upon this knowledge by the merest of accidents; often failing to recognize the real nature of their discovery or understand the source of their power.

This author is of the opinion that all living persons, who, at the present time, are consciously making use of the principle of mind chemistry in developing power through the blending of minds, may be counted on the fingers of the two hands, with, perhaps, several fingers left to spare.

If this estimate is even approximately true, the student will readily see that there is but slight danger of the field of mind chemistry practice becoming overcrowded.

The man who has a DEFINITE AIM in mind, and a definite plan for attaining it, has already gone nine-tenths of the way toward success.

It is a well-known fact that one of the most difficult tasks that any businessman must perform is that of inducing those who are associated with him to co-ordinate their efforts in a spirit of harmony. To induce continuous co-operation between a group of workers in any undertaking is next to impossible. Only the most efficient leaders can accomplish this highly desired object, but once in a great while such a leader will rise above the horizon in the field of industry, business, or finance, and then the world hears of a Henry Ford, Thomas A. Edison, John D. Rockefeller, Sr., E. H. Harriman, or James J. Hill.

Power and success are synonymous terms!

One grows out of the other; therefore, any person who has the knowledge and the ability to develop power, through the principle of harmonious co-ordination of effort between individual minds, or in any other manner, may be successful in any reasonable undertaking that is possible of successful termination.

*   *   *

It must not be presumed that a "Master Mind" will immediately spring, mushroom fashion, out of every group of minds which make a pretense of co-ordination in a spirit of *harmony!*

Harmony, in the real sense of meaning of the word, is as rare among groups of people as is genuine Christianity among those who proclaim themselves Christians.

Harmony is the nucleus around which the state of mind known as the "Master Mind" must be developed. Without this element of harmony there can be no "Master Mind," a truth which cannot be repeated too often.

Woodrow Wilson had in mind the development of a "Master Mind," to be composed of minds representing the civilized nations of the world, in his proposal of the League of Nations.

Wilson's conception was the most far-reaching humanitarian idea ever created in the mind of man, because it dealt with a principle which embraces sufficient power to establish a real Brotherhood of Man on earth. The League of Nations, or some similar blending of international minds, in a spirit of harmony, is sure to become a reality.

The time when such unity of minds will take place will be measured largely by the time required for the great universities and *nonsectarian* institutions of learning to supplant ignorance and superstition with understanding and wisdom. This time is rapidly approaching.

THE PSYCHOLOGY OF THE REVIVAL MEETING

The old religious orgy known as the "revival" offers a favorable opportunity to study the principle of mind chemistry known as "Master Mind."

It will be observed that music plays no small part in bringing about the harmony essential to the blending of a group of minds in a revival meeting. Without music the revival meeting would be a tame affair.

During revival services the leader of the meeting has no difficulty in creating harmony in the minds of his devotees, but it is a well-known fact that this state of harmony lasts no longer than the presence of the leader, after which the "Master Mind" he has temporarily created, disintegrates.

By arousing the emotional nature of his followers, the revivalist has no difficulty, under the proper stage setting and with the embellishment of the right sort of music, in creating a "Master Mind" which becomes noticeable to all who come in contact with it. The very air becomes charged with a positive, pleasing influence which changes the entire chemistry of all minds present.

The revivalist calls this energy the "Spirit of the Lord."

This author, through experiments conducted with a group of scientific investigators and laymen, who were unaware of the nature of the experiment, has created the same state of mind and the same positive atmosphere without calling it the "Spirit of the Lord."

On many occasions this author has witnessed the creation of the same positive atmosphere in a group of men and women engaged in the business of salesmanship, without calling it the "Spirit of the Lord."

The author helped conduct a school of salesmanship for Harrison Parker, founder of the Co-operative Society, of Chicago, and, by the use of the same principle of mind chemistry, which the revivalist calls the "Spirit of the Lord," so transformed the nature of a group of three thousand men and women (all of them were without former sales experience) that they sold more than ten million dollars worth of securities in less than nine months, and earned more than one million dollars for themselves.

It was found that the average person who joined this school would reach the zenith of his or her selling power within one week, after which it was necessary to revitalize the individual's brain through a group sales meeting. These sales meetings were conducted on very much the same order as are the modern revival meetings of the religionist, with much the same stage equipment, including music and "high-powered" speakers, who exhorted the sales people in very much the same manner as does the modern religious revivalist.

Call it psychology, mind chemistry, or anything you please (they are all based upon the same principle), but there is nothing more certain than the fact that wherever a group of minds are brought into contact, in a spirit of *perfect harmony*, each mind in the group becomes immediately supplemented and re-enforced by a noticeable energy called a "Master Mind."

For all this writer professes to know, this uncharted energy may be the "Spirit of the Lord," but it operates just as favorably when called by any other name.

The human brain and nervous system constitute a piece of intricate machinery which but few, if any, understand. When controlled and properly directed, this piece of machinery can be made to perform wonders of achievement and, if not controlled, it will perform wonders fantastic and phantom-like in nature, as may be seen by examining the inmates of any insane asylum.

The human brain has direct connection with a continuous influx of energy from which man derives his power to think. The brain receives this energy, mixes it with the energy created by the food taken into the body, and distributes it to every portion of the body, through the aid of the blood and the nervous system. It thus becomes what we call life.

From what source this outside energy comes no one seems to know; all we know about it is that we must have it or die. It seems reasonable to presume that this energy is none other than that which we call ether, and, that it flows into the body along with the oxygen from the air, as we breathe.

Every normal human body possesses a first-class chemical laboratory and a stock of chemicals sufficient to carry on the business of breaking up, assimilating, and properly mixing and compounding the food we take into the body, preparatory to distributing it to wherever it is needed as a body builder.

Ample tests have been made, both with man and beast, to prove that the energy known as the mind plays an important part in this chemical operation of compounding and transforming of food into the required substances to build and keep the body in repair.

It is known that worry, excitement, or fear will interfere with the digestive process, and in extreme cases stop this process altogether, resulting in illness or death. It is obvious, then, that the mind enters into the chemistry of food digestion and distribution.

It is believed by many eminent authorities, although it may never have been scientifically proved, that the energy known as thought may become contaminated with negative or "unsociable" units to such an extent that the whole nervous system is thrown out of working order, digestion is interfered with, and various and sundry forms of disease will manifest themselves. Financial difficulties and unrequited love affairs head the list of causes of such mind disturbances.

A negative environment, such as that existing where some member of the family is constantly "nagging," will interfere with the chemistry of the mind to such an extent that the individual will lose ambition and gradually sink into oblivion. It is because of this fact that the old saying that a man's wife may either "make" or "break" him is literally true.

Any high school student knows that certain food combinations will, if taken into the stomach, result in indigestion, violent pain, and even death. Good health depends, in part at least, upon a food combination that "harmonizes." But harmony of food combination is not sufficient to insure good health; there must be harmony also between the units of energy known as the mind.

"Harmony" is one of Nature's laws, without which there can be no such thing as *organized energy*, or life in any form whatsoever.

The health of the body as well as the mind, is literally built upon the principle of *harmony!* The energy known as life begins to disintegrate and death approaches when the organs of the body stop working in harmony.

The moment harmony ceases at the source of any form of organized energy (power), units of that energy are thrown into a chaotic state of disorder and the power is rendered neutral or passive.

Harmony is also the nucleus around which the principle of mind chemistry known as a "Master Mind" develops power. Destroy this harmony and you destroy the power growing out of the co-ordinated effort of a group of individual minds.

This truth has been stated, restated, and presented in every manner which the author could conceive, with unending repetition, for the reason that unless the student grasps this principle and learns to apply it, this treatise on the Master Mind is useless.

Success in life, no matter what one may call success, is very largely a matter of adaptation to environment in such a manner that there is harmony between the individual and his environment. The palace of a king becomes as a hovel of a peasant if harmony does not abound within its walls. Conversely stated, the hut of a peasant may be made to yield more happiness than that of the mansion of the rich man, if harmony obtains in the former and not in the latter.

Without perfect harmony the science of astronomy would be as useless as the "bones of a saint," because the stars and planets would clash with one another, and all would be in a state of chaos and disorder.

Without the law of harmony the blood might deposit the food which grows finger nails, on the scalp where hair is supposed to grow, and thus create a horny growth which might easily be mistaken, by the superstitious, to signify man's relationship to a certain imaginary gentleman with horns often referred to by the more primitive type.

Without the law of harmony there can be no organization of knowledge, for what, may one ask, is organized knowledge except the harmony of facts and truths and natural laws?

The moment discord begins to creep in at the front door,

harmony edges out at the back door, so to speak, whether the application is made to a business partnership or the orderly movement of the planets of the heavens.

If the student gathers the impression that the author is laying undue stress upon the importance of *harmony*, let it be remembered that lack of harmony is the first, and often the last and only cause of *failure!*

There can be no poetry, nor music, nor oratory worthy of notice without the presence of harmony.

Good architecture is largely a matter of harmony. Without harmony a house is nothing but a mass of building material, more or less a monstrosity.

Sound business management plants the very sinews of its existence in harmony.

Every well-dressed man or woman is a living picture and a moving example of harmony.

With all these "work-a-day" illustrations of the important part which harmony plays in the affairs of the world, nay, in operation of the entire universe, how could any intelligent person leave harmony out of his "Definite Aim" in life? As well have no "Definite Aim" as to omit harmony as the chief stone of its foundation.

*   *   *

The human body is a complex organization of organs, glands, blood vessels, nerves, brain cells, muscles, etc. The mind energy which stimulates to action and co-ordinates the efforts of the component parts of the body is also a plurality of ever-varying and changing energies. From birth until death there is a continuous struggle, often assuming the nature of open combat, between the forces of the mind. For example, the lifelong struggle between the motivating forces and desires of the human mind, which take place between the impulses of right and wrong, are well known to everyone.

Every human being possesses at least two distinct mind powers or personalities, and as many as six distinct personalities have been discovered in one person. One of man's most delicate tasks is that of harmonizing these mind forces so that they may be organized and directed toward the orderly attainment of a given objective. Without this element of harmony no individual can become an accurate thinker.

It is no wonder that leaders in business and industrial enterprises, as well as those in other fields of endeavor, find it so difficult to organize groups of people so they will function without friction in the attainment of a given objective. Each individual human being possesses forces, within himself, which are hard to harmonize, even when he is placed in the environment most favorable to harmony. If the chemistry of the individual's mind is such that the units of his mind cannot be easily harmonized, think how much more difficult it must be to harmonize a group of minds so they will function as one, in an orderly manner, through what is known as a "Master Mind."

The leader who successfully develops and directs the energies of a "Master Mind" must possess tact, patience, persistence, self-confidence, intimate knowledge of mind chemistry, and the ability to adapt himself (in a state of perfect poise and harmony) to quickly changing circumstances without showing the least sign of annoyance.

How many are there who can measure up to this requirement?

The successful leader must possess the ability to change the color of his mind, Chameleon-like, to fit every circumstance that arises in connection with the object of his leadership. Moreover, he must possess the ability to change from one mood to another without showing the slightest signs of anger or lack of self-control. The successful leader must understand the Seventeen Laws of Success and be able to put into practice any combination of these laws whenever occasion demands.

Without this ability no leader can be powerful, and without power no leader can long endure.

THE MEANING OF EDUCATION

There has long been a general misconception of the meaning of the word "educate." The dictionaries have not aided in the elimination of this misunderstanding because they have defined the word "educate" as an act of imparting knowledge.

The word educate has its roots in the Latin word educo, which means to develop *from within;* to educe; to draw out; to grow through the law of *use.*

Nature hates idleness in all its forms. She gives continuous life only to those elements which are in use. Tie up an arm, or any other portion of the body, taking it out of use, and the idle part will soon atrophy and become lifeless. Reverse the order, give an arm more than normal use, such as that engaged in by the blacksmith who wields a heavy hammer all day long, and that arm (developed from within) grows strong.

Power grows out of *organized knowledge,* but, mind you, it "grows out of it" through application and use!

A man may become a walking encyclopedia of knowledge without possessing any power of value. This knowledge becomes power only to the extent that it is organized, classified and put into action. Some of the best educated men the world has known possessed much less general knowledge than some who have been known as fools, the difference between the two being that the former put what knowledge they possessed into use, while the latter made no such application.

An "educated" person is one who knows how to acquire

everything he needs in the attainment of his main purpose in life, without violating the rights of his fellow men. It might be a surprise to many so-called men of "learning" to know that they come nowhere near qualification as men of "education." It might also be a great surprise to many who believe they suffer from lack of "learning" to know that they are well "educated."

The successful lawyer is not necessarily the one who memorizes the greatest number of principles of law. On the contrary, the successful lawyer is the one who knows where to find a principle of law, plus a variety of opinions supporting that principle which fit the immediate needs of a given case.

In other words, the successful lawyer is he who knows where to find the law he wants when he needs it.

This principle applies, with equal force, to the affairs of industry and business.

Henry Ford had but little elementary schooling, yet he is one of the best "educated" men in the world because he has acquired the ability to so combine natural and economic laws, to say nothing of the minds of men, that he has the power to get anything of a material nature he wants.

Some years ago during the World War, Mr. Ford brought suit against the *Chicago Tribune,* charging that newspaper with libelous publication of statements concerning him, one of which was the statement that Ford was an "ignoramus," an ignorant pacifist, etc.

When the suit came up for trial, the attorneys for the *Tribune* undertook to prove, by Ford himself, that their statement was true; that he was ignorant, and with this object in view they catechized and cross-examined him on all manner of subjects.

One question they asked was:

"How many soldiers did the British send over to subdue the rebellion in the Colonies in 1776?"

With a dry grin on his face Ford nonchalantly replied:

"I do not know just how many, but I have heard that it was a lot more than ever went back."

Loud laughter from Court, jury, court room spectators, and even from the frustrated lawyer who had asked the question.

This line of interrogation was continued for an hour or more, Ford remaining perfectly calm the meanwhile. Finally, however, he had permitted the "smart Aleck" lawyers to play with him until he was tired of it, and in reply to a question which was particularly obnoxious and insulting, Ford straightened himself up, pointed his finger at the questioning lawyer and replied:

"If I should really wish to answer the foolish questions you have just asked, or any of the others you have been asking, let me remind you that I have a row of electric push buttons hanging over my desk and, by placing my finger on the right button, I could call in men who could give me the correct answer to all the questions you have asked and to many that you have not the intelligence to either ask or answer. Now, will you kindly tell me why I should bother about filling my mind with a lot of useless details in order to answer every fool question that anyone may ask, when I have able men all about me who can supply me with all the facts I want when I call for them?"

This answer is quoted from memory, but it substantially relates Ford's answer.

There was silence in the court room. The questioning attorney's underjaw dropped down, his eyes opened widely; the judge leaned forward from the bench and gazed in Mr. Ford's direction; many of the jury awoke and looked around as if they had heard an explosion, which they actually had.

A prominent clergyman, who was present in the court room at the time, said later that the scene reminded him of that which must have existed when Jesus Christ was on trial before Pontius Pilate, just after he had given his famous reply to Pilate's question, "What is truth?"

In the vernacular of the day, Ford's reply knocked the questioner cold.

Up to the time of that reply the lawyer had been enjoying considerable fun at what he believed to be Ford's expense, by adroitly displaying his (the lawyer's) sample case of general knowledge and comparing it with what he inferred to be Ford's ignorance as to many events and subjects.

But that answer spoiled the lawyer's fun!

It also proved once more (to all who had the intelligence to accept the proof) that true education means mind development; not merely the gathering and classifying of knowledge.

Ford could not, in all probability, have named the capitals of all the States of the United States, but he could have, and in fact had, gathered the "capital" with which to "turn many wheels" within every state in the Union.

Education—let us not forget this—consists of the power with which to get everything one needs without violating the rights of his fellow men. Ford comes well within that definition, for the reason which the author has here tried to make plain, by relating the foregoing incident connected with the simple Ford philosophy.

There are many men of "learning" who could easily entangle Ford, theoretically, with a maze of questions none of which he, personally, could answer. But Ford could wage a battle in industry or finance that would exterminate those same men with all of their abstract knowledge and wisdom.

Ford probably could not go into his chemical laboratory and separate water into its component atoms of hydrogen and oxygen and then recombine these atoms in their former order, but he knows how to surround himself with chemists who can do this for him if he wants it done. *The man who can intelligently use the knowledge possessed by another is as much or more a man of education as the person who merely has the knowledge but does not know what to do with it.*

Education consists of doing— not merely of KNOWING!

THE RELATIONSHIP BETWEEN SEXUAL URGE AND GENIUS

The urge of sex is, by far, the most powerful of the eight basic motivating forces which stimulate the mind to *action*. Because of the importance of this subject it has been reserved as the closing chapter of the first of the seventeen factors constituting the Law of Success.

The part which sexual urge plays in the achievement of outstanding success was first discovered by the author in his studies of the biographies of great leaders, and in his analysis of men and women of the present age who have risen high in their chosen fields of endeavor.

The subject of sex is one in connection with which most people are unpardonably ignorant. Sexual urge has been slandered and burlesqued by the ignorant and the vulgar-minded for so long that the very word sex is seldom mentioned in polite society. Men and women who are known to be blessed with highly sexed natures are usually looked upon as people who will bear watching, and, instead of being called "blessed," they are usually called "cursed."

During the early years of research, when this philosophy was in the embryonic stage, the author made the discovery that every great leader in art and music, and literary work and statesmanship, and in practically every other walk of life, was a highly sexed person. Among the group whose biographies were carefully studied let us mention, for the purpose of refreshing the reader's memory on the subject, the following:

Napoleon Bonaparte
Shakespeare
George Washington
Abraham Lincoln
Ralph Waldo Emerson
Robert Burns
Thomas Jefferson

Let us recall, also, a few names of highly sexed gentlemen of a later age who are known to have been men of great achievement in their respective callings:

Elbert Hubbard
Elbert H. Gary
Oscar Wilde
Woodrow Wilson
John H. Patterson
Stanford White
Enrico Caruso

For ethical reasons it would hardly be appropriate to mention the names of men who are still living, but the reader may easily supply these names by taking inventory of *all* men who enjoy the reputation of great leadership in their respective callings.

Sexual urge is the highest and most refined form of human emotion. It "steps up" the rate of vibration of the mind as no other emotion can, and causes the imaginative faculties of the brain to function in the form of *genius*. Far from being something of which one should be ashamed, a highly sexed nature is a blessing of which one should feel proud, and for which no apologies should be offered.

THE VALUE OF TRANSMUTATION OF SEXUAL URGE

To be highly sexed is not sufficient, of itself, to produce a genius. Only those who understand the nature of sexual urge, and who know how to transmute this powerful emotion into other channels of action than that of sexual contact, rise to the status of a genius. The urge of sex is a driving force compared to which all other motivating forces must take second place at best. A mind that has been aroused through intense sexual desire becomes receptive to the impulse of ideas which "flash" into the mind from outside sources through what is ordinarily known as *inspiration*.

It is the belief of this author—a belief not without considerable evidence to back it—that all so-called "revelations," of whatever nature, from religion to art, are superinduced by intense desire for sexual contact. All so-called "magnetic" people are highly sexed. People who are brilliant, charming, versatile, and accomplished are generally highly sexed. Prove this for yourself by analyzing those whom you know to be highly sexed.

Destroy the capacity for strong sexual desire and you have removed all that is powerful about a human being. If you wish proof of this, observe what happens to the "spirited" stallion or any other male animal, such as a bull or a hog, after it has been altered sexually; the moment sexual urge has been destroyed in any animal, from man on down to the lowest forms of animal life, the capacity for dominating *action* goes with it. This is a statement of biological fact too well known to be disputed. Moreover, it is a fact that is significant, and important.

SEX ENERGY HAS THERAPEUTIC VALUE

It is a fact well known to scientists, although not generally known to the layman, that sexual contact has a therapeutic value unknown in connection with any other human emotion. This fact may be easily verified, however, by even the most casual study of the subject, by observing the physical state of the body following sexual contact between two people who are properly mated or affinitized. What mind is so vulgar and ignorant as not to have observed that following sexual contact, between two people who are properly "balanced," or mated, the physical body becomes relaxed and calm? Relaxation, superinduced in this manner, provides the nervous system with a most favorable opportunity to balance and distribute the nervous energy of the body to all the organs of the body. *Properly distributed nervous energy is the force which maintains a healthy body.* Also, nervous energy properly distributed, through relaxation, is the agency which eliminates the cause of all physical ailments.

These briefly stated facts are not mere opinions of the author of this philosophy. They have been gleaned from twenty-five years of careful research in connection with which the author has had the collaboration of some of the most eminent scientists known to the past and present generation, one of whom was a well-known physician who was bold enough to admit that he had often recommended a change in sexual consorts for patients who were suffering from hypochondriacal conditions (patients suffering with imaginary illness), and in that manner produced cures that would not have been possible in any other manner. This physician went even farther by predicting that the time was not far distant when this form of therapeutics would be more generally understood and used. The suggestion is here offered for what it may be worth, without comment from the author of this philosophy other than the statement that most of the human race is still woefully ignorant of the possibilities of the urge of sex, not only in connection with the maintenance of health, but also in connection with the creation of genius.

It seemed quite significant to this author, when he made

the discovery that practically every great leader, whom he has had the privilege of studying at close range, was a man whose achievements were largely inspired by a woman. In many instances, the "woman in the case" is a modest little wife of whom the public hears but little. In a few cases the source of inspiration has been traced to the "other woman." A great, enduring love is a sufficient motive to drive even a mediocre man to unbelievable heights of achievement, a statement of fact which should be kept in mind by all wives of men.

Sexual urge is the most effective known agency through which the mind may be "stepped up" to where it becomes a Master Mind!

THE TEN MAJOR SOURCES OF MIND STIMULATION

It may be helpful to here outline the major sources of mind stimulation, in view of the fact that all great achievements are the result of some form of stimuli which "step up" the mind to a high rate of vibration. These stimuli are listed in the order of what the author believes to be their importance, as follows:

1. *Sexual contact* between two people who are motivated by a genuine feeling of love.
2. *Love,* not necessarily accompanied by sexual contact.
3. *Burning desire* for fame, power, and financial gain.
4. *Music.* Acts as a mighty stimulant to a highly emotionalized person.
5. *Friendship,* between either those of the same sex or the opposite sex, accompanied by a desire to be mutually helpful in some definite undertaking or calling.
6. *Master Mind alliance,* between two or more people who ally themselves, mentally, for the purpose of mutual help, in a spirit of unselfishness.

7. *Mutual suffering*, such as that experienced by
    people who are unjustly persecuted, through
    racial, religious, and economic differences of
    opinion.
8. *Autosuggestion*, through which an individual may
    step up his or her own mind, through constant
    self-suggestion with a definite motive. (Perhaps
    this source of mind stimulation should have
    been placed nearer the top of the list.)
9. *Suggestion.* The influence of outside suggestion
    may lift one to great heights of achievement, or,
    if negatively used, dash one to the bottomless pit
    of failure and destruction.
10. *Narcotics and alcohol.* This source of mind stimula-
    tion is totally destructive, and leads, finally, to ne-
    gation of all the other nine sources of stimulation.

Mind stimulant is any influence which will, temporarily or
permanently, "step up" the rate of vibration of the brain. Here you
have a brief description of all the major sources of mind stimulation. Through these sources of stimulation one may commune,
temporarily, with Infinite Intelligence, a procedure which constitutes all there is of genius. *The forgeoing statement is definite and
plain. Take it or leave it, just as you please!* The statement is made as a
positive fact because this author has had the privilege of helping
to raise scores of mediocre men and women out of mediocrity
into states of mind which entitled them to rank as geniuses. Some
have been able to remain in this exalted state, while others have
relapsed to their former status, either temporarily or permanently.

The author personally interviews and analyzes an average
of a dozen men and women every day for the purpose of helping them discover the most suitable source of mind stimulation

and the most profitable outlet for their talent resulting from this stimulation.

On many scores of occasions the author has had the experience of seeing a client create some useful invention, or some unique plan of rendering useful service, right in the midst of the analysis.

Not two hours previous to the writing of these lines a client whose name is H. Gundelach came, with his wife, for analysis, and before the work had proceeded for more than thirty minutes, Mr. Gundelach conceived an idea for a new style of interlocking brick suitable for building public highways which has the possibility of rendering useful service all over America, to say nothing of making a huge fortune for himself. Perhaps it would be more correct to say that the three of us—he and his wife and the author—conceived the idea simultaneously.

INTEMPERANCE

The use of alcohol and narcotics as mind stimulants is condemned without exception, on the ground that such use eventually destroys the normal functioning power of the brain. While it is true that some of the greatest literary geniuses of the past used liquor as a mind stimulant, with temporary success, it is equally true that such use generally became an excess which destroyed them. Edgar Allan Poe and Robert Burns both used alcohol as a mind stimulant, with telling effects, but both were finally destroyed through *excessive* use of this form of stimulant. Of the ten stimulants described in this chapter, but nine are safe for use and even these cannot be used excessively.

Sexual contact is the most powerful of all the mind stimulants, but, this, too, may be used to excess with as damaging effects as the excessive use of alcohol or narcotics. Excessive eating may be just as damaging as any other form of excess, and in many thousands of cases this form of indulgence destroys all possibility of great achievement.

One of the seventeen factors of the Law of Success is that of self-control. As will be seen, when that subject is reached, self-control, in the sense that it is a part of this philosophy, is a balance wheel which guards the individual against excesses of every nature whatsoever. The three major excesses which are destroying people throughout the world to-day are: the excess of eating, the excess of sexual indulgence, and the excess of strong drinks and drugs. *One is just as fatal to success as either of the other two.*

WHY MEN DO NOT SUCCEED BEFORE FORTY

The major reason why the average man does not begin to strike his real stride in his chosen life work, before the age of forty, *is his tendency to dissipate his energy through overindulgence in sexual contact.* The average male does not learn that sexual urge has other possibilities than that of use in sexual contact, until he has reached the age of forty to forty-five years. Up to this age the life of the average male (in which classification the majority of all males may be properly placed) is just one long, continuous orgy of sexual intercourse, through which all his finer and more powerful emotions are sown wildly to the four winds. This is not merely the opinion of this author; it is a statement of fact based upon careful analysis of over twenty thousand people. Intelligent study and analysis of twenty thousand people gives a very accurate cross-section classification of the entire human race.

Between overeating and overindulgence in sexual contact, the average man has but little energy left for other uses, until he has passed the age of forty, and in altogether too many instances men never gain mastery of themselves with reference to these two forms of weakness. A sad statement of fact is the truth that the majority of men do not look upon overindulgence in eating and in sexual contact as being dangerous excesses which destroy their chances of success in life. There is no argument over the detrimental effects of excessive use of alcohol and narcotics, as everyone knows that such overindulgence is fatal to success, but not everyone knows that excesses in sexual contact and in eating can be just as ruinous.

The desire for sexual contact is the strongest, most powerful, and most impelling of all human desires, and for this very reason it may be harnessed and transmuted into channels other than that of sexual contact in a manner that will raise one to great heights of genius. On the other hand, this powerful urge, if not controlled and so transmuted, may and often does lower man to the level of an ordinary beast.

In closing this chapter, may the author not offer a word of reply to those who may feel that even the very brief reference here made to the subject of sex might be harmful to the young men and young women? The reply is this: *Ignorance of the subject of sex, due to lack of free discussion of the subject by those who really understand it, has resulted in destructive use of the emotion of sex all back down the ages.* Moreover, if anyone should feel that this brief reference might hurt the morals of the young people of this generation, let that person keep in mind the fact that most young people get their sex education from less commendable sources than a book of this nature, and such education is generally accompanied by interpretations of the power of sex which in no way relate the subjects of sex and genius, and in no manner even suggest that there is such a possibility as the transmutation of sex power into art and literary works of the most commendable order, and business leadership, and a multitude of other constructive forms of helpful service. This is an age of frank discussion of the great mysteries of life, among which the subject of sex may be properly classified. Finally, the urge of sex is biological in nature and *it cannot be suppressed through silence!* In truth, the emotion of sexual urge is the finest of all human emotions, and the sexual relationship the most beautiful of all relationships. Why, then, cast the slurring innuendo that the sexual relationship is something ugly and vulgar by trying to shroud the subject in a dark background of silence?

*   *   *

For lack of space the subject of the Master Mind must be ended here. We pass next to the discussion of the second of the seventeen factors of the Law of Success, with both apology and regret that this lack of space forbids us to discuss the remaining sixteen subjects as extensively as we have covered the subject of the Master Mind.

LESSON 2
A DEFINITE CHIEF AIM

To be successful in any sort of endeavor you must have a definite goal toward which to work. You must have definite plans for attaining this goal. Nothing is ever accomplished that is worthwhile without a definite plan of procedure that is systematically and continuously followed out day by day.

A definite chief aim is placed at the beginning of the Seventeen Laws of Success for the reason that without it the other Sixteen Laws would be useless, for how could one hope to succeed, or how could one know when he had succeeded, without first having determined what he wanted to accomplish?

During the past twenty odd years the author has analyzed more than twenty thousand people, in nearly all walks of life, and startling as it may seem, ninety-five per cent of these people were failures. By this is meant that they were barely making enough on which to exist, some of them not even doing this well. The other five per cent were successful, meaning by *"success"* that they were making enough for all their needs and laying something by for the sake of ultimate financial independence.

Now the significant thing about this discovery was that the five per cent who were succeeding had *a definite chief aim* and also a plan for attaining that aim. In other words, those who knew what they wanted, and had a plan for getting it, were succeeding while those who did not know what they wanted were *getting just that—nothing!*

If a man is engaged in the business of selling, or rendering service which calls for methods of handling his customers that will cause them to patronize him continuously, he must have a *definite plan* for bringing about this result. The plan may be one thing, or it may be something else, but in the main it should be distinctive and of such a nature that it will impress itself upon the minds of his patrons in a *favorable* manner. Anyone can hand out merchandise to those who come, voluntarily, and ask for it, but not everyone has acquired the art of delivering with the merchandise that unseen "something" which causes the customer to repeat and come back for more. Here is where the necessity of a *definite aim* and a definite plan for attaining it enters.

Within recent years gasoline filling stations have become so numerous that one may be found just around the corner, so to speak, in every community. The gas, oil, and other supplies sold at the majority of these service stations is good, there being but little difference between the quality received at one station and that received at another. Despite this fact, however, there are motorists who will drive miles out of their way, or delay the purchase of oil and gas until the very last minute, for the purpose of buying these supplies from some "favorite" service station.

Now, the question arises, *"What causes these people to do this?"*

And the answer is, *"People trade at service stations where they are served by men who cultivate them."*

What is meant by *"men who cultivate them?"* It means that a few filling station men have created *definite plans* for studying and catering to motorists in such a manner that these motorists will return again. Good oil and gas, alone, cannot compete with the filling station manager who makes it his business to know people and cater to them according to their mannerisms and characteristics. One filling station manager makes it his business to watch the tires on every automobile that drives up, and when he sees a tire that needs more inflation he promptly "gives it the air." If the windshield is dusty or dirty he wipes it with a wet cloth. If a car is covered with dust he gets busy with a duster. In these and scores of other ways, he impresses the motorist with the fact that he makes it his business to render service that is a bit different. All this does not "just happen." He has a *definite plan* and also a *definite purpose* in doing it, and that purpose is to bring motorists back to his station.

This is a brief statement of what is meant by *a definite chief aim*.

Let us now go a bit deeper into the study of the psychological principle upon which the law of *a definite chief aim* is based. Careful study of more than one hundred of the leading men in practically all walks of life has disclosed the fact that every one of these men worked with *a definite chief aim* and also a *definite plan* for its attainment.

The human mind is something like a magnet in that it will attract the counterparts of the dominating thoughts held in the mind, and especially those which constitute *a definite chief aim* or purpose. For example, if a man establishes, as his *definite chief aim*, and as his daily working purpose, the adding of say one hundred new customers who will regularly purchase the merchandise or service he is rendering, immediately that aim or purpose becomes a dominating influence in his mind, and this influence will drive him to do that which is necessary to secure these additional one hundred customers.

Manufacturers of automobiles and other lines of merchandise often establish what they call "quotas," covering the number of automobiles or the amount of merchandise that must be sold in each territory. These "quotas," when definitely established, constitute a *definite chief aim* toward which all who are engaged in the distribution of the automobiles or merchandise direct their efforts. Seldom does anyone fail to make the established quotas, but it is a well-known fact that had there been no "quotas" the actual sales would have been far less than they were with them. In other words, to achieve success in selling or in practically any other line of endeavor, one must set up a mark at which to shoot, so to speak, and without this target there will be but slim results.

Scientists have discovered in recent years, along with the other startling discoveries such as radio, television, mastery of the air, etc., that any man may achieve practically any end which he may set up in his own mind as *a definite chief aim*. It is literally true that the man with a definite purpose, and with full faith in his ability to realize that purpose, cannot be permanently defeated. He may meet with temporary defeat; perhaps many such defeats, but *failure*, never!

Your first step on the road to Success is to know where you are going, how you intend to travel, and when you intend to get there, which is only another way of saying that you must determine upon *a definite chief aim*. This aim, when decided upon, must be written out in clear language so it can be understood by any other person. If there is anything "hazy" about your aim, it is not *definite*. A man who knew what he was saying once stated that nine-tenths of success, in any undertaking, was in knowing what was wanted. This is true.

The moment you write out a statement of your *chief aim*, your action plants an image of that aim firmly in your subconscious mind, and, through some process which even the most enlightened scientists have not yet discovered, Nature causes your subconscious mind to use that *chief aim* as a pattern or blue print by which the major portion of your thoughts, ideas, and efforts are directed toward the attainment of the objective on which the *aim* is based.

> There is a sure way to avoid criticism;
> be nothing, do nothing! Get a job as
> street-sweeper and kill off ambition.
> The formula always works.

This is a strange, abstract truth—something that cannot be weighed, meditated upon—but it is a truth nevertheless!

You will be taken further into the mysteries of this strange law when you reach the law of *imagination*, further on, and also when you reach some of the other laws.

LESSON 3
SELF-CONFIDENCE

The third of the Seventeen Laws of Success is Self-Confidence. This term is self-explanatory—it means that to achieve success you must believe in yourself. However, this does not mean that you have no limitations; it means that you are to take inventory of yourself, find out what qualities you have that are strong and useful, and then organize these qualities into a definite plan *of action with which to attain the object of your* definite chief aim.

In all the languages of the world there is no one word that carries the same or even approximately the same meaning as the word *"faith."* If there are any such things as "miracles," they are performed only with the aid of super-faith. The doubting type of mind is not a creative mind. Search where and how you may, and you will not discover one single record of great achievement, in any line of endeavor, that was not conceived in *imagination* and brought into reality through *faith!*

To succeed, you must have *faith* in your own ability to do whatever you make up your mind to do. Also, you must cultivate the habit of *faith* in those who are associated with you, whether they are in position of authority over you, or you over them. The psychological reason for this will be covered thoroughly and plainly in the Law on *Co-operation*, further on.

Doubters are not builders! Had Columbus lacked Self-Confidence and *faith* in his own judgment, the richest and most glorious spot of ground on this earth might never have been discovered, and these lines might never have been written. Had George Washington and his compatriots of the 1776 historical fame not possessed Self-Confidence, Cornwallis' armies would have conquered and the United States of America would be ruled to-day from a little island lying three thousand miles away in the East.

A definite chief aim is the starting point of all noteworthy achievement, but Self-Confidence is the unseen force which coaxes, drives, or leads one on and on until the object of the *aim* is a reality. Without Self-Confidence man's achievements would never get beyond the "aim" stage, and mere aims, within themselves, are worth nothing. Many people have vague sorts of aims, but they get nowhere because they lack the Self-Confidence to create *definite plans* for attaining these aims.

Fear is the main enemy of Self-Confidence. Every person comes into this world cursed, to some extent, with Six Basic Fears, all of which must be mastered before one may develop sufficient Self-Confidence to attain outstanding success.

These six basic fears are:

1. The Fear of Criticism
2. The Fear of Ill Health
3. The Fear of Poverty
4. The Fear of Old Age
5. The Fear of Loss of Love of Someone (ordinarily called jealousy)
6. The Fear of Death

Space will not permit a lengthy description of how and where these Six Fears came from. In the main, however, they were acquired through early childhood environment, by teaching, the telling of ghost stories, discussion of "hell-fire," and in many other ways. Fear of Criticism is placed at the head of the list because it is, perhaps, the most common and one of the most destructive of the entire six fears. But for the Fear of Criticism men would not have bald heads, because baldness is the result of tight hatbands, and hats are worn only because most men are afraid of what "they will say" if hats are left off. Women seldom have bald heads because they wear loose hats, permitting the nervous energy to properly feed the roots of the hair.

Knowledge of this basic Fear of Criticism brings hundreds of millions of dollars to the manufacturers of clothing each year, and costs timid people the same amount, because most people lack the personality or the courage to wear clothes which are one season out of style. To some extent this basic Fear of Criticism is employed by the manufacturers of automobiles who change models every season, as not many men wish to drive a car whose lines and general appearance are a season or so behind the times.

Before you can develop Self-Confidence sufficient to master the obstacles which stand between you and success, you must take inventory of yourself and find out how many of these six basic fears are standing in your way. A few days of study, thought, and reflection will readily enable you to lay your fingers on the particular fear or fears which stand between you and Self-Confidence. Once you discover these enemies, you may easily eliminate them, through procedure which will be described later on.

The fears of Ill Health, Poverty, Old Age and Death are mainly the results of the hold-over effects of teachings of a bygone age, when men were taught to believe that death might bring with it a world and a life more horrible than the one on this earth; a life associated with fire and eternal torment. The effect of this teaching so shocked the sensibilities of the human mind that fear became imbedded in the subconscious mind and, in that manner, was transmitted from parent to child and thus kept alive from generation to generation. Scientists differ as to the extent that such fears can be transmitted from parent to child, through physical heredity, but they are all in accord on this point, that the discussion of such matters in the presence of a child is sufficient to plant the *"fear"* impulse in its subconscious mind, where nothing but strong resolution and great *faith* in a belief opposite to the thing feared can eliminate the damage done.

The Fear of Loss of Love of Someone (jealousy) is a hold over from the days of human savagery, when it was man's habit to steal his fellow man's mate by force. The practice of one man stealing another's mate still exists, to some extent, but the stealing is now done through allurements of one sort or another—fine clothes, motor cars, furs, jewels, and other trinkets—and not by the use of force. However, there is still enough of this element in the man animal to cause his fellow man to stand in awe of him, to some extent. Thus the Fear of Loss of Love (or jealousy) has a biological as well as an economic basis for its existence. Jealousy is a form of insanity, because it is often indulged in without the slightest reason for its existence. Despite this fact, this fear causes untold suffering, annoyance, and failure in this world. To understand the nature of this fear and how one comes by it is a step in the direction of its mastery.

Every student of this philosophy should do a certain amount of collateral reading, selecting biographies of men who have attained outstanding success, because this is sure to disclose the fact that these men met with practically every conceivable sort of temporary defeat, yet, despite these discouraging experiences, they developed Self-Confidence sufficient to enable them to master every obstacle that stood in their way. Among the books recommended by the author of the Law of Success are:

The Man From Maine, by Edward W. Bok
Compensation, by Ralph Waldo Emerson
The Age of Reason, by Thomas Paine
The Ascent of Man, by Henry Drummond
The Science of Power, by Benjamin Kidd

These five subjects will give you the complete story of the stupendously interesting evolutionary process through which the mind of man has reached its present stage of development. Incidentally, after reading these books, you will have a better basis on which to build Self-Confidence, for you will then understand why there are but few "impossibilities" known to man, if, in fact, there are any. By all means read the last two books if you cannot or do not wish to read the entire list. To do so, and to understand that which you read, will give you the equivalent of the best sort of college education from many viewpoints.

LESSON 4
THE HABIT OF SAVING

It is an embarrassing admission, but it is true, that a poverty-stricken person is less than the dust of the earth as far as the achievement of noteworthy success is concerned. It may be, and perhaps is true, that money is not success, *but unless you have it or can command its use, you will not get far, no matter what may be your* definite chief aim. *As business is conducted to-day—as civilization stands to-day— money is an absolute essential for success, and there is no known formula for financial independence except that which is connected, in one way or another, with systematic saving.*

The amount saved from week to week or from month to month is not of great consequence so long as the saving is regular and systematic. This is true because the *habit* of saving adds something to the other qualities essential for success which can be had in no other way.

It is doubtful if any person can develop Self-Confidence to the highest possible point without the protection and independence which belong to those who have saved and are saving money. There is something about the knowledge that one has some money ahead which gives faith and self-reliance such as can be had in no other way.

Without money a person is at the mercy of every person who wishes to exploit or prey upon him. If the man who does not save and has no money offers his personal services for sale he must accept what the purchaser offers; there is no alternative.

If opportunity to profit by trade or otherwise comes along, it is of no avail to the man who has neither money nor credit, and it must be kept in mind that credit is generally based upon the money one has or its equivalent.

When the Law of Success philosophy was first created, the Law of Saving was not included as one of the Seventeen Laws, with the result that thousands of people who experimented with this philosophy found that it carried them almost within reach of their goal of success, only to dash their hopes to pieces on the rocks of—what? For years the author of the course and the creator of the philosophy searched for the reason why the philosophy fell just barely short of its intended purpose. Through many years of experimentation and research it was finally discovered that one Law was lacking, and that was the law of *the habit of saving.*

When this Law was added the students of the Law of Success philosophy began to prosper without exception, and now, barely three years since the discovery was made, thousands of people have used the philosophy for the attainment of success and not one single case of failure has been reported.

The amount of your income is of but little importance if you do not systematically save a portion of it. Ten thousand dollars a year income is no better than two thousand dollars unless a part of it is saved. As a matter of fact a ten-thousand-dollar-a-year income may be far worse for the man who received it than would be a two-thousand-dollar income, if the entire amount is spent and dissipated, because the act of dissipation may undermine the health and in other ways destroy the chances of success.

Millions of people have read stories by great writers of Henry Ford's stupendous achievements, and of his great wealth, but it is safe to say that not one out of every thousand of these people have taken the trouble or done enough thinking to determine the real basis of Ford's success. Through a test made by the author of the Law of Success philosophy, five hundred people were given an outline of the twelve fundamentals which have been largely responsible for Ford's success. In this outline it was pointed out that the amount of cash received each year from the floor sweepings and trash taken from the Ford plants amounts to nearly $600,000. Not one of the entire five hundred placed any significance upon this fact. Not one of the five hundred discovered, or if they did they failed to mention it, the fact that Ford has always been a systematic saver of resources.

The Spending *habit* is highly developed in most Americans, but we know little of the more important *habit* of saving. Woolworth built the highest skyscraper in the world and accumulated a fortune of over one hundred million dollars by *saving* the dimes which millions of Americans threw away for trash which they did not really need. The habit of spending money is a mania with most people, and this habit keeps their noses to the grindstone all the days of their lives.

Tests have been made which show, conclusively, that the majority of business men will not place their resources or even positions involving responsibilities in other directions in the hands of those who have not formed the habit of saving money. The *savings habit* is the finest sort of recommendation of any man, no matter what position he may hold or what position he may seek to hold.

The late James J. Hill (who was well prepared to speak with authority on the subject) said that there is a rule by which any man may test himself and determine, well in advance, whether or not he would succeed in life, and that this rule was, "He must have formed the habit of systematic saving of money."

LESSON 5
INITIATIVE AND LEADERSHIP

All people may be placed in one or the other of two general classes. One is known as leaders and the other as followers. Not often do the "followers" achieve noteworthy success, and never succeed until they break away from the ranks of the "followers" and become "leaders."

There is a mistaken notion being broadcast in the world among a certain class of people, to the effect that a man is paid for that which he knows. This is only partly true, and, like all other half truths, it does more damage than an out-and-out falsehood.

The truth is that a man is paid not only for that which he *knows*, but more particularly for that which *he does* with what he knows, or, that which he *gets others to do.*

Without *initiative* no man will achieve success, no matter what he may consider success, because he will do nothing out of the ordinary run of mediocre work such as nearly all men are forced to do in order to have a place to sleep, something to eat, and clothes to wear. These three necessities may be had, of a certain kind, without the aid of *initiative* and *leadership*, but the moment a man makes up his mind to acquire more than the bare necessities of life, he must either cultivate the habits of *initiative* and *leadership* or else find himself hedged in behind a stone wall.

The first step essential in the development of *initiative* and *leadership* is that of forming the habit of prompt and firm *decision*. All successful people have a certain amount of *decision*. The man who wavers between two or more half-baked and more or less vague notions of what he wants to do generally ends by doing nothing.

There had been "talk" about building the Panama Canal for many generations, but the actual work of building the canal never got much beyond the "talk" stage until the late Theodore Roosevelt became President of the United States. With the firmness of *decision* which was the very warp and woof of his achievements and the real basis of his reputation as a leader, Roosevelt took the *initiative*, had a bill framed for Congress to pass, providing the money, went to work with a spirit of *self-confidence*, plus a *definite chief aim* and a *definite plan* for its attainment, and lo! the much-talked-of Panama Canal became a splendid reality.

It is not enough to have a *definite chief aim* and a *definite plan* for its achievement, even though the plan may be perfectly practical and you may have all the necessary ability to carry it through successfully—you must have more than these—you must actually take the *initiative* and put the wheels of your plan into motion and keep them turning until your goal has been reached.

Study those whom you know to be failures (you'll find them all around you) and observe that, without a single exception, they lack the firmness of *decision*, even in matters of the smallest importance. Such people usually "talk" a great deal, but they are very short on performance. "Deeds, not words" should be the motto of the man who intends to succeed in life, no matter what may be his calling, or what he has selected as his *definite chief aim*.

Lack of *decision* has often resulted in insanity. Nothing is very bad or dreadful, once one has reached a decision to face the consequences. This truth was demonstrated quite effectively by a man who was condemned to die in the electric chair. When asked how it felt to know that he was to die in another half hour he replied, "Well, it does not bother me in the least. I made up my mind that I had to go sometime, and it might as well be now as a few years later, because my life has been nothing but a sad failure and a constant source of trouble anyway. Just think, it will soon all be over!"

The man was actually relieved to know that the responsibilities of life to which he had been subjected, and which had brought him to such an ignoble ending, were about to cease.

Prominent and successful leaders are always people who reach decisions quickly, yet it is not to be assumed that quick decisions are always advisable. There are circumstances calling for deliberation, the study of *facts* connected with the intended *decision*, etc. However, after all available facts have been gathered and organized, there is no excuse for delaying *decision*, and the person who practices the habit of such delay cannot become an effective leader until he masters this shortcoming.

Julius Cæsar had long wanted to conquer the armies of another country, but he faltered because he was not sure of the loyalty of his own armies. Finally he decided upon a plan which would insure this loyalty. Loading his soldiers on boats he set sail for the shores of his enemy, unloaded the soldiers and implements of war, and then gave the order for all the boats to be burned. Turning to his generals he said, "Now it is win or perish! We have no choice! Pass the word to your men and let them know that it is the lives of our enemies or our own." They went

into battle and won—won because all his soldiers had reached
a *decision to win!*

> There is a mistaken idea floating around
> that a man should be paid for that which
> he knows. In reality a man is paid for that
> which he does with what he knows, or that
> which he can get others to do with it.

Grant said, "We will fight it out along these lines if it takes
all summer," and despite his deficiencies he stood by that *decision* and won!

When asked by one of his sailors what he would do if they
saw no signs of land by the following day, Columbus replied, "If
we see no land to-morrow we will sail on and on." He, too, had
a *definite chief aim,* a *definite plan* for its attainment, and he had
reached a *decision* not to turn back.

It is a known fact that many men cannot do their best until
they are actually fighting with their backs to the wall, under
the stress of the most urgent necessity. Impending danger will
enable a man to develop superhuman courage and strength of
both body and mind far out of proportion to that normally used.

Napoleon, when surprised by the enemy, having discovered
that there was a deep camouflaged ditch just ahead of the line of
march of his armies, gave the order for his cavalry to charge. He
waited until the dead bodies of men and horses filled the ditch,
then marched his soldiers across and whipped the enemy. That
required *decision;* moreover, it required *instantaneous decision.*
One minute of faltering or hesitation and he would have been
flanked by the enemy and captured. He did the unexpected, the
"impossible," and got away with it.

In the field of selling nearly all salesmen are met with the stereotyped alibi, "I will think it over and let you know later," which really means that "I do not wish to buy, but I lack the courage to reach a definite *decision* and frankly say so." Being a leader, and understanding the value of *initiative*, the real sales-man does not take such alibis for an answer. The real salesman begins, immediately, to assist the prospective purchaser in the process of "thinking it over" and in short order the job is com-pleted and the sale has been made.

LESSON 6
IMAGINATION

No man ever accomplished anything, never created anything, never built any plan or developed a definite chief aim *without the use of his* imagination!

Everything that any man ever created or built was first visioned, in his own mind, through *imagination!*

Years before it became a reality the late John Wanamaker saw, in his own *imagination*, in practically all of its details, the gigantic business which now bears his name, and despite the fact that he was then without the capital to create such a business, he managed to get it and lived to see the business he had dreamed of in his mind become a splendid reality.

In the workshop of the *imagination* one may take old, well-known ideas or concepts, or parts of ideas, and combine them with still other old ideas or parts of ideas, and out of this combination create that which seems to be new. This process is the major principle of all invention.

One may have a *definite chief aim* and a plan for achieving it;

may possess *self-confidence* in abundance; may have a highly developed *habit of saving,* and both *initiative* and *leadership* in abundance, but if the element of *imagination* is missing these other
qualities will be held useless, because there will be no driving
force to shape the use of these qualities. In the workshop of the
imagination all plans are created, and without plans, no achievement is possible except by mere accident.

Witness the manner in which the *imagination* can be used
as both the beginning and the end of successful plans: Clarence
Saunders, who created the well-known chain of Piggly-Wiggly
self-help grocery stores, conceived the idea on which the stores
were based, or rather borrowed it, from the cafeteria restaurant
system. While working as a grocer's helper Mr. Saunders went
into a cafeteria for lunch. Standing in line, waiting for his turn
at the food counters, the wheels of his *imagination* began to turn,
and he reasoned, to himself, something like this:

"People seem to like to stand in line and help themselves.
Moreover, I see that more people can be served this way, with
fewer salespeople. Why would it not be a good idea to introduce
this plan in the grocery business, so people could come in, wander
around with a basket, pick up what they wanted, and pay on the
way out?"

Then and there, with that bit of elementary *"imagining,"* Mr.
Saunders sowed the seed of an idea which later became the Piggly-
Wiggly stores system and made him a multimillionaire in the
bargain.

"Ideas" are the most profitable products of the human mind,
and they are all created in the *imagination.* The five and ten cent
store system is the result of *imagination.* The system was created
by F. W. Woolworth, and it "happened" in this way: Woolworth
was working as a salesman in a retail store. The owner of the
store complained that he had a considerable amount of old,

unsalable merchandise on hand that was in the way, and was about to throw some of it into the trash box to be consigned to the furnace, when Woolworth's *imagination* began to function.

"I have an idea," said he, "how to make this merchandise sell. Let's put it all on a table and place a big sign on the table saying that all articles will be sold at ten cents each."

The "idea" seemed feasible; it was tried, worked satisfactorily, and then began further development which resulted, finally, in the big chain of Woolworth stores which belted the entire country and made the man who used his *imagination* a multimillionaire.

Ideas are valuable in any business, and the man who makes it his business to cultivate the power of *imagination*, out of which ideas are born, will sooner or later find himself headed toward financial success with tremendous power back of him.

Thomas A. Edison invented the incandescent electric light bulb by the use of his *imagination*, when he assembled two old and well-known principles in a combination in which they had never before been associated. A brief description of just how this was accomplished will help you to vision the manner in which the *imagination* may be made to solve problems, overcome obstacles and lay the foundation for great achievements in any undertaking.

Mr. Edison discovered, as other experimenters had before him, that a light could be created by applying electrical energy to a wire, thus heating the wire to a white heat. The trouble, however, came because of the fact that no one had found a way to control the heat. The wire soon burned out when heated sufficiently to give a clear light.

After many years of experimentation Mr. Edison happened to think of the old, well-known method of burning charcoal, and saw, instantly, that this principle held the secret to the needed control of heat essential in creating a light by applying electrical power to a wire.

Charcoal is made by placing a pile of wood on the ground, setting the wood on fire, and then covering it over with dirt, thereby cutting off most of the oxygen from the fire, which enables the wood to burn slowly, but it cannot blaze and the stick cannot burn up entirely. This because there can be no combustion where there is no oxygen, and but little combustion where there is but little oxygen. With this knowledge in mind Edison went into his laboratory, placed the wire, with which he had been experimenting, inside a vacuum tube, thus cutting off *all* the oxygen, applied the electrical power, and lo! he had a perfect incandescent light bulb. The wire inside the bulb could not burn up because there was no oxygen inside to create combustion sufficient to burn it up.

Thus it happened that one of the most useful of modern inventions was created by combining two principles in a new way.

There is nothing absolutely new!

That which seems to be new is but a combination of ideas or elements of something old. This is literally true in the creation of business plans, invention, the manufacture of metals, and everything else created by man.

What is known as a "basic" patent is rarely offered for record at the Patent Office, meaning a patent that embraces really new and heretofore undiscovered principles. Most of the hundreds of thousands of patents applied for and granted every year, many of which are of a most useful nature, involve nothing more than a new arrangement or combination of old and well-known principles which have been used many times before in other ways and for other purposes.

When Mr. Saunders created his famous Piggly-Wiggly stores system, he did not even combine two ideas; he merely took an old idea that he saw in use *and gave it a new setting,* or in other words, put it to a new use, but this required *imagination.*

To cultivate the *imagination* so it will eventually suggest ideas on its own initiative, you should make it your business to keep a record of all the useful, ingenious and practical ideas you see in use in other lines of work outside of your own occupation, as well as in connection with your own work. Start with an ordinary, pocket-size notebook, and catalogue every idea, or concept, or thought that occurs to you which is capable of practical use, and then take these ideas and work them into new plans. By and by the time will come when the powers of your own *imagination* will go into the storehouse of your own subconscious mind, where all the knowledge you have ever gathered is stored, assemble this knowledge into new combinations, and hand over to you the results in the shape of *brand new ideas,* or what appear to be new ideas.

This procedure is practical because it has been followed successfully by some of the best-known leaders, inventors, and business men.

Let us here define the word *imagination* as "The workshop of the mind wherein may be assembled, in new and varying combinations, all ideas, thoughts, plans, facts, principles, and theories known to man."

A single combination of ideas, which may be merely parts of old and well-known ideas, may be worth anywhere from a few cents to a few millions of dollars. Imagination is the one faculty on which there is no set price or value. It is the most important of the faculties of the mind, for it is here that all of man's motives are given the impulse necessary to turn them into *action.*

The dreamer, who does nothing more than dream, uses imagination, but he falls short of utilizing this great faculty efficiently because he does not add to it the impulse to put his thoughts into *action.* Here is where *initiative* enters and goes to work for him, providing he is familiar with the Laws of Success and understands that ideas, of themselves, are worthless until put into action.

The dreamer who creates practical ideas must place back of these ideas three of the laws which have preceded this one, on *imagination*, namely:

1. The Law of a Definite Chief Aim
2. The Law of Self-Confidence
3. The Law of Initiative and Leadership

Without the influence of these three laws no man may put into action his thoughts and ideas, although the power to dream, imagine, and create may be highly developed.

It is your business to succeed in life! How? That is something you must answer for yourself, but, in the main, you must proceed something after this order:

1. Adopt a definite purpose and create a definite
   plan for its attainment.
2. Take the initiative and begin putting your plan
   into action.
3. Back your initiative with belief in yourself and in
   your ability to successfully complete your plan.

No matter who you are, what you are doing, how much your income is, how little money you have, if you have a sound mind and if you are capable of using your *imagination*, you can gradually make a place for yourself that will command for you respect and give you all the worldly goods that you need. There is no trick connected with this. The procedure is simple, as you may start with a very simple, elementary idea, plan, or purpose, and gradually develop it into something more pretentious.

Your *imagination* may not be sufficiently developed, at this time, to enable you to create some useful invention, but you can begin exercising this faculty by using it to create ways and means of improving the methods of performing your present work, whatever it may be. Your *imagination* will grow strong in proportion to the extent that you command it and direct it into use. Look about you and you will find plenty of opportunities to exercise your *imagination*. Do not wait for someone to show you what to do, but use vision and let your *imagination* suggest what to do. Do not wait for someone to pay you for using your *imagination*, because your real pay will come from the fact that every time you use it constructively, in creating new combinations of ideas, it will grow stronger, and if you keep up this practice the time will come, very soon, when your services will be sought eagerly, at any price within reason.

If a man works in a gasoline filling station, for example, it may seem to him that he has but little range of opportunity to use his *imagination*. Nothing could be further from the real facts, for as a matter of fact, any man holding such a position may give his *imagination* the very finest sort of exercise by making it his business to cultivate every motorist whom he serves in such a manner that the motorist will come back for more service. Moreover, he may go a step further and work out ways and means of adding one new customer each day, or even one a week, or one a month, and in that manner very materially and quickly add to his income. Sooner or later, through this sort of exercise of his *imagination*, backed up by *self-confidence* and *initiative*, plus a *definite chief aim*, the man who follows this practice will be sure to create some new plan that will draw customers to his filling station from far and near, and he will then be on the great Highway to Success.

A complete analysis of occupations shows that the most profitable occupation on earth, taken as a whole, is that of salesmanship. The man whose fertile mind and *imagination* create a new and useful invention may not have sufficient ability to market his invention, and may therefore have to dispose of it for a mere pittance, as is, in fact, so often the case; but the man who has the ability to market that invention may (and generally does) make a fortune out of it.

Any man who can create plans and ideas that will cause the number of patrons of any business to constantly increase, and who is able to send all the patrons away satisfied, is well on the way toward *success*, regardless of the commodity, service, or wares he may be selling.

It is not the purpose of this brief outline of the Law of Success philosophy to show the student what to do and how to do it, but the general rules of procedure which apply in all successful undertakings have been here enumerated so anyone may understand them. These rules are simple and easily adopted by anyone.

LESSON 7
ENTHUSIASM

It seems more than a mere coincidence that the most successful people, in all walks of life—and particularly is this true in selling—are of the enthusiastic type.

Enthusiasm is a driving force which not only gives greater power to the man who has it, but it is contagious and affects all whom it reaches. Enthusiasm over the work in which one is engaged takes the drudgery out of that work. It has been observed that laborers, engaged in the toilsome job of ditch digging, can take the drabness out of their work by singing as they work.

When the "Yanks" went into action, during the World War, they went in singing and full of enthusiasm. This was too much for the war-worn soldiers who had been in the field long enough to wear off their enthusiasm, and they made poor match indeed for the "Yanks."

The Filene Department Store, in Boston, is opened with music furnished by the store band every morning during the summer months. The sales people dance to the music, catch the rhythm of the tunes, and when the doors are finally opened for business the patrons of the store meet a jolly crowd of enthusiastic, cheerful, smiling sales people, many of whom are still softly humming the tune to which they had been dancing but a few minutes before. This spirit of enthusiasm remains with the sales people throughout the day. It lightens their work and creates an "atmosphere" in the store which is pleasing to the customers.

During the World War, it was discovered that, by introducing music, with the aid of bands and orchestras, etc., into the plants where war materials were being made, production was stimulated, in some instances as much as fifty per cent above normal production without the music. Moreover, it was discovered that the workers not only turned out much more work during the day, but they came to the end of the day without fatigue, many of them whistling or singing on their way home. Enthusiasm gives greater power to one's efforts, no matter what sort of work one may be engaged in.

The starting point of enthusiasm is "motive," or well-defined desire. Enthusiasm is simply a high rate of vibration of the mind. Elsewhere in this book may be found a complete list of the mind stimulants which will superinduce the state of mind known as enthusiasm. The urge of sexual desire is the greatest known mind stimulant. People who do not feel a strong desire for sexual contact are seldom, if ever, capable of becoming highly enthusiastic over anything. Transmutation of the great driving force of sex desire is the basis of practically all the works of genius. (By "transmutation" is meant the switching of thought from sexual contact to any other form of physical action.)

The importance of enthusiasm, as one of the seventeen essentials of the Law of Success, is explained in the chapter on the Master Mind. The strange phenomenon felt by those who co-ordinate their efforts, in a spirit of harmony, for the purpose of availing themselves of the Master Mind principle, is merely a high rate of vibration of their minds known as enthusiasm.

It is a well-known fact that men succeed most readily when engaged in an occupation which they like best, and this for the reason that they readily become enthusiastic over that which they like best. Enthusiasm is also the basis of creative imagination. When the mind is vibrating at a high rate, it is receptive to similar high rates of vibration, from outside sources, thus providing a favorable condition for creative imagination. It will be observed that enthusiasm plays an important part in four of the other principles constituting the Law of Success philosophy, namely, the Master Mind, Imagination, Accurate Thought, and Pleasing Personality.

Enthusiasm, to be of value, must be controlled and directed to definite ends. Uncontrolled enthusiasm may be, and generally is, destructive. The acts of so-called "bad boys" are nothing more nor less than uncontrolled enthusiasm. The wasted energy of uncontrolled enthusiasm expressed through promiscuous sexual contact, and sex desire not expressed through contact, by the majority of young men, is sufficient to lift them to high achievement if this urge were harnessed and transformed into some other form of physical action.

The next chapter, on Self-Control, appropriately follows the subject of Enthusiasm, as much self-control is necessary in the mastery of enthusiasm.

LESSON 8
SELF-CONTROL

Lack of Self-Control has brought grief to more people than any other one shortcoming known to the human race. This evil shows itself, at one time or another, in every person's life.

Every successful person must have some sort of a balance wheel for his or her emotions. When a person "loses his temper," something takes place in his brain which should be better understood. When a person becomes extremely angry, the suprarenal glands begin to empty their contents into the blood, and if this is kept up for any great length of time the amount will be sufficient to do serious damage to the entire system, sometimes resulting in death.

Suprarenal is Nature's "repair kit" with which she causes the blood to coagulate and stop the flow, in the event of injury. Anger immediately excites the suprarenal glands and their contents begin to pour into the blood. This accounts for one turning white and red in the face, alternately, as the flow of blood throughout the body is temporarily checked. No doubt Nature created this system for man's protection during the savage stage of his development, when anger usually preceded a terrific fight with some other savage, which might mean opening of the veins and loss of blood.

Scientists have found, by experiment, that a dog will, when tormented until it becomes angry, throw off enough poison with each exhalation of breath to kill a guinea pig. An angry man will do the same.

But there are other reasons why one should develop Self-Control. For example, the man who lacks Self-Control may be easily mastered by one who has such control, and tricked into saying or doing that which may later be embarrassing to him.

Success in life is very largely a matter of harmonious negotiation with other people, and this requires Self-Control in abundance.

The author of the Law of Success philosophy once observed a long line of angry women in front of the "Complaint Desk" of a large Chicago department store. Watching at a distance, it was seen that the young woman, who was hearing the complaints, kept sweetly cool and smiled all the while, notwithstanding the fact that some of the women were very abusive. One by one this young woman directed the women to the right department, and she did it with such poise that it caused the author to walk up closer where he could see just what was happening. Standing just back of the young woman at the Complaint Desk was another young woman who was also listening to the conversations, and making notes and passing them over the shoulder of the young woman who was actually handling the Desk.

If you wish to sell me something be sure to create for me a plan through which I can harness that which you wish to sell me so

it will help pull my load and I will be more
eager to buy than you are to sell.

These notes contained the gist of each complaint, minus the vitriol and abuse of the person making the complaint. *The woman at the desk was stone deaf!* She was getting all the facts that she needed through her assistant, at her back.

The manager of the store said that this was the only system he had found that enabled him to handle the Complaint Desk properly, as human nerves were not strong enough to listen all day long, day in and day out, to abusive language without causing the person doing the listening to become angry, lose Self-Control, and "strike back."

An angry man is suffering with a degree of temporary insanity, and therefore he is hardly capable of diplomatic negotiation with others. For this reason the angry man, or the one who has no Self-Control, is an easy victim of the man who has such control. No man may become powerful without first gaining control of himself.

Self-Control is also a balance wheel for the person who is too optimistic and whose *enthusiasm* needs checking, for it is possible to become entirely too enthusiastic; so much so that one becomes a bore to all those near him.

LESSON 9
THE HABIT OF DOING MORE THAN PAID FOR

This law is a stumbling block on which many a promising career has been shattered. There is a general attitude among people to perform just as little service as they can get by with, but if you will study these people carefully, you will observe that while they may be actually "getting by" temporarily, they are not, however, getting anything else.

There are two major reasons why all successful people must practice this Law, as follows:

1. Just as an arm or a limb of the body grows strong in exact proportion to its use, so does the mind grow strong through use. By rendering the greatest possible amount of service the faculties through which the service is rendered are put into use and, eventually, become strong and accurate.

2. By rendering more service than that for which you are paid, you will be turning the spotlight

of *favorable* attention upon yourself, and it will
not be long before you will be sought with fancy
offers for your services, and there will be a continuous market for those services.

"Do the thing and you shall have the power," was the admonition of Emerson, the great modern philosopher.

That is literally true! Practice makes perfect. The better you
do your work, the more adept you become at doing it, and this,
in time, will lead to such perfection that you will have but few, if
any, equals in your field of endeavor.

By rendering more service and better service than that for
which you are paid, you thereby take advantage of the Law of Increasing Returns through the operation of which you will eventually be paid, in one way or another, for far more service than
you actually perform.

This is no mere finely spun theory. It actually works out in
the most practical tests. You must not imagine, however, that the
Law always works instantaneously. You may render more service and better service than you are supposed to render for a
few days, then discontinue the practice and go back to the old,
usual habit of doing as little as can be safely trusted to get you
by, and the results will in no way benefit you. But adopt the habit
as a part of your life's philosophy, and let it become known by
all who know you that you render such service out of choice, not
as a matter of accident, but by *deliberate intent,* and soon you will
see keen competition for your service.

You will not find very many people rendering such service,
which is all the better for you, because you will stand out in
bold contrast with practically all others who are engaged in work
similar to yours. Contrast is a powerful law, and you may, in this
manner, profit by contrast.

Some people set up the weak argument that it does not pay

to render more service and better service than one is paid to render because it is not appreciated, and that they work for people who are selfish and will not recognize such service.

Splendid! The more selfish an employer is the more apt he will be inclined to wish to hold the services of a person who makes it his business to render such unusual service, that is greater in quantity and better in quality than most people render. This very selfishness will "force" such an employer to recognize such services. However, if he should happen to be the proverbial exception who has not sufficient vision to analyze those who work for him, then it is only a matter of time until all who render such service will attract the attention of other employers who will gladly reward that sort of service.

Careful study of the lives of successful men has shown that faithfully practicing this one Law alone has brought the usual emoluments in which success is measured in plentiful quantities. If the author of this philosophy had to choose one of the Seventeen Laws of Success as being the most important, and had to discard all the others except the one chosen, he would, without a moment's hesitation, choose this Law of *Rendering More Service and Better Service than Paid for.*

LESSON 10
A PLEASING PERSONALITY

A Pleasing Personality, naturally, is a personality that does not antag-
onize. Personality cannot be defined in one word, nor with half a dozen
words, for it represents the sum total of all one's characteristics, good
and bad.

Your Personality is totally unlike any other personality. It
is the sum total of qualities, emotions, characteristics, appear-
ances, etc., which distinguish you from all other people on
earth.

Your clothes form an important part of your personality;
the way you wear them, the harmony of colors you select, the
quality and many other details all go to indicate much that belongs distinctly as a part of your personality. The psychologists
claim that they can accurately analyze any person, in many
important respects, by turning that person loose in a clothing
store where there is a great variety of clothing, with instructions to select whatever may be wanted and dress in the clothes
selected.

Your facial expression, as shown by the lines of your face, or the lack of lines, forms an important part of your personality. Your voice, its pitch, tone, volume, and the language you use form important parts of your personality, because they mark you instantly, once you have spoken, as a person of refinement or the opposite.

The manner in which you shake hands constitutes an important part of your Personality. If, when shaking hands, you merely hold out a cold "hunk" of flesh and bones that is limp and lifeless, you are displaying a sign of a Personality that is not mixed with *enthusiasm* or *initiative*.

A Pleasing Personality usually may be found in the person who speaks gently and kindly, selecting refined words that do not offend, in a modest tone of voice; who selects clothing of appropriate style and colors which harmonize; who is unselfish and not only willing, but desirous of serving others; who is a friend of all humanity, the rich and the poor alike, regardless of politics, religion, or occupation; who refrains from speaking unkindly of others, either with or without cause; who manages to converse without being drawn into vulgar conversations or useless arguments on such debatable subjects as religion and politics; who sees both the good and the bad in people, but makes due allowance for the latter; who seeks neither to reform nor to reprimand others; who smiles frequently and deeply; who loves music and little children; who sympathizes with all who are in trouble and forgives acts of unkindness; who willingly grants others the right to do as they please as long as no one's rights are interfered with; who earnestly strives to be constructive in every thought and deed indulged in; who encourages others and spurs them on to greater and better achievement in their chosen line of work.

A Pleasing Personality is something that can be acquired

by anyone who has the determination to learn how to negotiate his or her way through life without friction, with the object of getting along peacefully and quietly with others.

One of the best-known and most successful men in America once said that he would prefer a Pleasing Personality, as it is defined in this course, to the college degree that was awarded him, more than fifty years ago, by Harvard University. It was his opinion that a man could accomplish more with a Pleasing Personality than he could with a college degree, minus the personality.

The development of a Pleasing Personality calls for exercise of Self-Control, because there will be many incidents and many people to try your patience and destroy your good resolutions to become pleasing. The reward is worthy of the effort, however, because one who possesses a Pleasing Personality stands out so boldly in contrast with the majority of people around him, that his pleasing qualities become all the more pronounced.

When Abraham Lincoln was a young man, he heard that a great lawyer, who was known to be an impressive orator, was to defend a client charged with murder, some forty miles from Lincoln's home. He walked the entire distance to hear this man, who was one of the spellbinders of the South. After he had heard the man's speech, and the orator was on his way out of the court room, Lincoln stepped into the aisle, held out his rough hand, and said, "I walked forty miles to hear you, and if I were to do it over, I would walk a hundred."

The lawyer looked young Lincoln over, turned up his nose, and, in a supercilious manner, walked out without speaking to Lincoln.

Years later these two met once again, this time in the White House, where this selfsame lawyer had come to petition the

"President of the United States" in behalf of a man who had been condemned to death.

Lincoln listened patiently to all the lawyer had to say, and, when he had finished speaking, said, "I see you have lost none of your eloquence since I first heard you defend a murderer years ago, but you have changed considerably in other ways, because you now seem to be a polite gentleman of refinement, which was not the impression I got of you at our first meeting. I did you an injustice, perhaps, for which I now ask your pardon. Meanwhile, I shall sign a pardon for your client and we will call accounts square."

The lawyer's face turned white and red as he stammered a brief apology!

By his lack of a Pleasing Personality, at his first meeting with Lincoln, he was guilty of conduct which would have been costly to him, had the incident happened with one less charitable than the great Lincoln.

It has been said, and perhaps correctly, that "courtesy" represents the most valuable characteristic known to the human race. Courtesy costs nothing, yet it returns dividends that are stupendous if it is practiced as a matter of habit, in a spirit of sincerity.

A young friend of the author of this philosophy was employed as a service man in one of the gasoline filling stations belonging to a large corporation. One day a big car drove up to his station, and the man on the inside stepped out while the chauffeur purchased gas. While the gas was being delivered, this man entered into conversation with my young friend—or, perhaps I should more truthfully say—my young "acquaintance."

"Do you like your job?" the man inquired.

"Like it, hell!" replied the young bravo. "I like it just as much as a dog loves a tomcat."

"Well," said the stranger, "if you do not like your job, why do you work here?"

"Because I am just waiting for something better to turn up," was the quick rejoinder.

"How long do you think you will have to wait?" the man inquired.

"I dunno how long, but I hope I soon get out of here, because there is no opportunity here for a bright fellow like myself. Why, I'm a high school graduate and I can hold a better position if I had it."

"Yes?" said the stranger. "*If!* Now if I offered you a better position than the one you now have, would you be any better off than you are now?"

"I can't say," replied the service station man.

"Well," replied the stranger, "may I not offer the suggestion that better positions usually come to those who are prepared to fill them, but I do not believe you are ready for a better position; at least not while you are in your present frame of mind. Perhaps there is a big opportunity for you right where you stand. Let me recommend that you buy a copy of Russell Conwell's book, *Acres of Diamonds*, as it may give you an idea that will be useful to you all through life."

The stranger got into his automobile and drove away. He was the president of the company that owned the filling station. The young man was talking to his employer, without knowing it, but every word he uttered spoiled his chances of attracting *favorable* attention.

Later this same filling station was placed in charge of another young man, and it is one of the most profitable service stations operated by the company which owns it. The station is the same as it was before it was turned over to new management. The supplies sold are exactly the same. The prices charged are the same, *but* the Personality of the man who meets and impresses favorably or unfavorably those who drive up to this station for service is *not the same*.

Practically all success in life hinges, in the final analysis, on *personality*.

A nasty disposition can spoil the chances of the best educated man, and such dispositions do spoil not a few such men.

GOOD SHOWMANSHIP A PART OF PERSONALITY

Life may be properly called a great drama in which good showmanship is of the utmost importance. Successful people, in all callings, are generally good showmen; meaning, by this, that they practice the habit of catering or playing to the crowd. Let us compare some well-known men on the subject of their ability as showmen. The following men have enjoyed outstanding success in their respective callings, because of good showmanship:

Henry L. Doherty
Bernarr Macfadden
Theodore Roosevelt
Henry Ford
Thomas A. Edison
Billy Sunday
E. M. Statler
John H. Patterson
Wm. Randolph Hearst
Wm. C. Durant
Geo. Bernard Shaw
Arthur Brisbane

Following is a list of some well-known men, each a man of great ability, but falling short by comparison with the foregoing list, on the score of good showmanship:

Woodrow Wilson
Calvin Coolidge
Herbert Hoover
Abraham Lincoln
Dr. Elmer Gates

A good showman is one who understands how to cater to the masses. Success is not a matter of chance or luck. It is the result of careful planning and careful staging and able acting of parts by the players in the game.

What is to be done about his defect by the man who is not blessed with a personality which lends itself to able showmanship? Is such a person to be doomed to failure all his life because of Nature's oversight in not blessing him with such a personality?

Not at all! Here is where the principle of the Master Mind comes to the rescue. Those who do not have pleasing personalities may surround themselves with men and women who supply this defect. The late J. P. Morgan had a rather pugnacious attitude toward people which prevented him from being a good showman. However, he associated with himself others who supplied all that he lacked in this respect.

Henry Ford was not blessed, by Nature, with native ability as a good showman, and his personality is not one hundred per cent perfect by a long way, but, knowing how to make use of the Master Mind principle, he bridged this defect by surrounding himself with men who do have such ability.

What are the most essential characteristics of good showmanship?

First, the ability to appeal to the imagination of the public, and to keep people interested and curious concerning one's activities. Second, a keen sense of appreciation of the value of psychological appeal through advertising. Third, sufficient alertness of mind to enable one to capture and make use of the prejudices, likes, and dislikes of the public, at the psychological moment.

SUMMARY OF FACTORS WHICH CONSTITUTE A PLEASING PERSONALITY

Following is a condensed description of the major factors which serve as the basis of a Pleasing Personality:

1. Manner of shaking hands
2. Clothing and posture of the body
3. Voice, its tone, volume, and quality
4. Tactfulness
5. Sincerity of purpose
6. Choice of words, and their appropriateness
7. Poise
8. Unselfishness
9. Facial expression
10. Dominating thoughts (Which register in the minds of other people)
11. Enthusiasm
12. Honesty (Intellectual, moral, and economic)
13. Magnetism (High rate of vibration due to well-defined sexual urge)

If you wish to try an interesting and perhaps a beneficial experiment, analyze yourself and give yourself a grading on each of these thirteen factors of a Pleasing Personality. An accurate check-up on these thirteen points might easily bring to one's notice facts which would enable one to eliminate faults which make success impossible.

It will also be an interesting experiment if you form the habit of analyzing those whom you know intimately, measuring them by the thirteen points here described. Such a habit will, in time, help you to find in other people the causes of both success and failure.

LESSON 11
ACCURATE THINKING

The art of Accurate Thinking is not difficult to acquire, although certain definite rules must be followed. To think accurately one must follow at least two basic principles, as follows:

1. Accurate Thinking calls for the separation of *facts* from mere *information*.
2. *Facts*, when ascertained, must be separated into two classes; one is known as *important* and the other as *unimportant*, or irrelevant.

The question naturally arises, "What is an *important fact?*" and the answer is, "An *important fact* is any fact essential for the attainment of one's *definite chief aim* or purpose, or which may be useful or necessary in connection with one's daily occupation. All other facts, while they may be useful and interesting, are comparatively unimportant as far as the individual is concerned."

No man has the right to have an opinion on any subject,

unless he has arrived at that opinion by a process of reasoning that is based upon all the available *facts* connected with the subject of the opinion. Despite this fact, however, nearly everyone has opinions on nearly every subject, whether they are familiar with those subjects or have any *facts* connected with them or not.

Snap judgments and opinions that are not opinions at all, but mere wild conjectures or guesses, are valueless; "there's not an *idea* in a carload" of them. Any man may become an Accurate Thinker by making it his business to insist upon getting the Facts, all that are available with reasonable effort, before reaching decisions or creating opinions on any subject.

When you hear a man begin a discourse with such generalities as "I hear that so and so is the case," or, "I see by the papers that so and so did so and so," you may put that man down as one who is *not* an Accurate Thinker, and his opinions, guesses, statements, and conjectures should be accepted, if at all, with a good big handful of the proverbial salt of caution.

TIME is a master worker which heals
the wounds of failure and disappointment
and equalizes the inequalities and rights
the wrongs of the world.
Nothing is IMPOSSIBLE with TIME.

Be careful, also, that *you* do not indulge in wild, speculative language that is not based upon *known facts*.

It often requires considerable effort to *know facts* on any subject, which is perhaps the main reason why so few people take the time or go to the trouble to gather *facts* as the basis of their opinions.

You are presumably following this philosophy for the purpose of learning how you may become more successful, and if that is true then *you* must break away from the common practices of the masses who do not think and take the time to gather *facts* as the basis of your thoughts. That this requires effort is freely admitted, but it must be kept in mind that *success* is not something that one may come along and pluck from a tree, where it has grown of its own accord. Success is something that represents perseverance, self-sacrifice, determination, and strong character.

Everything has its price, and nothing may be obtained without paying this price; or, if something of value is obtained, it cannot be retained for long. The price of Accurate Thought is the effort required to gather and organize the *facts* on which to base the *thought*.

"How many automobiles pass this filling station each day," the manager of a chain of filling stations asked a new service man. "And on what days is traffic the heaviest?"

"I am of the opinion . . ." the young man began.

"Never mind your *opinion*," the manager interrupted. "What I asked you calls for an answer based upon *facts*. Opinions are worth nothing when the actual *facts* are obtainable."

With the aid of a pocket adder this young man began to count the automobiles that passed his station each day. He went a step further and recorded the number that actually stopped and purchased supplies, giving the figures day by day for two weeks, including Sundays.

Nor was this all! He estimated the number of automobiles that should have stopped at his station for supplies, day by day, for two weeks. Going still further, he created a plan that cost only a one-cent postal card per motorist, that actually increased the number of automobiles that stopped at his station for service the following two weeks. This was not a part of his required duties, but the question asked him by his manager had put him to *thinking*, and he made up his mind to profit by the incident.

The young man in question is now a half owner in a chain of filling stations of his own, and a moderately wealthy man, thanks to his ability to become an Accurate Thinker.

LESSON 12
CONCENTRATION

The jack-of-all-trades seldom accomplishes much at any trade. Life is so complex, and there are so many ways of dissipating energy unprofitably, that the habit of concentrated effort *must be formed and adhered to by all who succeed.*

Power is based upon organized effort or energy. Energy cannot be organized without the habit of *concentration* of all the faculties on one thing at a time. An ordinary reading glass may be used to so focus the rays of the sun that they will burn a hole in a board in a few minutes. Those same rays will not even heat the board until they are *concentrated* on one spot.

The human mind is something like the reading glass, because it is the medium through which all the faculties of the brain may be brought together and made to function, in co-ordinated formation, just as the rays of the sun may be focused on one spot with the aid of a reading glass.

It is worthy of serious consideration to remember that all the outstanding men of success, in all walks of life, concentrated the major portion of their thoughts and efforts upon some one *definite purpose,* objective, or *chief aim.*

Witness the impressive list of men whose success is due to their having acquired and practiced the habit of *concentration:*

Woolworth concentrated upon the single idea of five and ten cent stores and the result made of him a multimillionaire.

Henry Ford concentrated all his energies upon the single aim of creating a cheap but practical automobile, and that idea made of him the most powerful and the richest man who ever lived on this earth.

Marshall Field concentrated his efforts upon building "The World's Greatest Store" and was rewarded by tens of millions of dollars. The great Field Store, in Chicago, is a living monument to the soundness of the practice of *concentration.*

Van Heusen concentrated years of efforts on the production of a soft collar, and the idea made him wealthy in a comparatively short time.

Wrigley concentrated his efforts upon the production and sale of a humble five-cent package of chewing gum and was rewarded by millions of dollars for his perseverance.

Edison concentrated his mind upon the production of the talking machine, the electric light, the moving picture, and scores of other useful inventions, and they all became realities and made of Edison a wealthy man.

Edwin C. Barnes concentrated his mind upon becoming a business associate of Thomas A. Edison, and not only accomplished the desired end, but made several million dollars for himself and has now retired from active business, while still a comparatively young man.

Bessemer concentrated his thoughts upon a better way to produce steel and the now-famous Bessemer process is evidence that his efforts were not without reward.

George Eastman concentrated his energy upon producing the best kodak, and this one idea has made of him a multimillionaire.

Andrew Carnegie visioned a great steel industry, concentrated his mind upon that purpose, and made tens of millions of dollars.

James J. Hill, while still working as a telegrapher at forty dollars a month, concentrated upon a great transcontinental railway system and kept on thinking about it (*and acting on his thought as well*) until it became a splendid reality and made him one of the wealthy men of his time.

Cyrus H. K. Curtis concentrated his efforts upon one idea of producing the best and most popular magazine on earth, and the splendid *Saturday Evening Post* was but one of the results. He not only created a great magazine, but his concentration of thought brought him millions as well.

Orville Wright concentrated upon the one purpose of mastering the air with a heavier-than-air machine, and accomplished it within the memory of all now living.

Edward W. Bok could not speak English when he first came to this country, but very soon determined to become a great magazine editor, and his concentrated efforts made the *Ladies' Home Journal* a great periodical, and himself a wealthy man.

Marconi concentrated his mind upon the one thought of sending wireless messages, and now the sound of the human voice may be sent around the earth, without trouble.

Truly, whatever man can *imagine*, man can create, providing he *concentrates* his mind upon it with determination not to stop short of victory.

Dr. Gunsaulus was a young preacher who had an idea that required a million dollars for its development. He concentrated his mind upon the task and wrote one sermon which got him the million dollars the first time he delivered it.

Great and powerful is the human mind when functioning through the aid of *concentrated thought*.

Woodrow Wilson determined to become President of the United States twenty-five years before he actually occupied the President's chair in the White House, but he kept his mind concentrated upon this one purpose and eventually achieved it.

Henry L. Doherty concentrated on the organization and management of public utilities and became one of the most extensive and wealthy operators in this field.

Ingersoll concentrated on the production of a good, practical watch that could be sold for one dollar and his idea, plus his concentrated efforts, made of him a multimillionaire.

E. M. Statler concentrated on the building of hotels that render home-like service, without the annoyance of tips, and has made himself the leading hotel man of the world, to say nothing of many millions of dollars in wealth.

Martin W. Littleton heard a speech, when he was a small boy, which caused him to concentrate his mind upon the one idea of becoming the best lawyer in the United States, and it is said that he now accepts no fee under $25,000, yet he is kept busy all the time.

Rockefeller concentrated his efforts upon the refining and distribution of oil, and his efforts brought him tens of millions of dollars.

Russell Conwell concentrated a lifetime of effort on the delivery of his famous lecture, *Acres of Diamonds,* and that one lecture brought in more than six million dollars, and rendered the world a service the extent of which can never be estimated in mere money.

Lincoln concentrated his mind upon freedom for mankind, and saw his task through to an unfortunate end.

Gillette concentrated upon producing a safety razor, and the idea made him a multimillionaire.

William Randolph Hearst concentrated on newspapers, and has made millions out of his idea.

Helen Keller was born deaf, dumb, and blind, but through concentration she has learned to "hear" and to speak.

John H. Patterson concentrated upon cash registers, and the world paid him tribute in terms of millions of dollars for his idea.

So the story might go on and on in one continuous chain, as evidence that *concentrated* effort is profitable.

Find out what you wish to do—adopt a *definite chief aim*—then concentrate all your energies back of this purpose until it has reached a happy climax.

Observe, in analyzing the next Law, on *co-operation*, the close connection between the principles outlined and those associated with the Law of *Concentration*.

Wherever a group of people ally themselves in an organized, cooperative spirit for the carrying out of some definite purpose, it will be observed that they are employing the Law of *Concentration*, and unless they do so their alliance will be without real power.

Raindrops, as they fall through the air, each one for itself, helter-skelter, represent a very great form of energy, but this energy cannot be called real power until those raindrops are collected, in a river or dam, and made to pour their energy over a wheel in organized fashion; or, until they are confined in a boiler and converted into steam.

Everywhere, regardless of the form in which it is found, *power* is developed through *concentrated* energy. Whatever you are doing as your daily occupation, do it with all of your attention, all your heart and soul focused on that one definite thing.

LESSON 13
CO-OPERATION

This is distinctly an age of co-operation *in which we are living. The outstanding achievements in business, industry, finance, transportation, and politics are all based upon the principle of Cooperative effort.*

You can hardly read a daily paper one week in succession without seeing notice of some consolidation or merger of business or industrial interests. These mergers and friendly alliances of business are based upon *co-operation*, because co-operation brings together in a spirit of harmony of purpose all the energies, whether human or mechanical, so that they function as one, without friction.

Marshal Foch, technically at least, won the final decision in the late World War. The turning point came, as all will remember, when all the Allied Armies were placed under the direction of Foch, thus insuring perfectly co-ordinated effort, and *co-operation* such as would not have been possible under many leaders, each exerting an equal or similar amount of authority over the various allied armies.

To succeed in a big way, in any undertaking, means that one must have the friendly co-operation of others. The winning football team is the one which is best coached in the art of *co-operation*. The spirit of perfect teamwork must prevail in business, or the business will not get very far.

You will observe that some of the preceding Laws of this course must be practiced as a matter of habit before one can get perfect cooperation from others. For example, other people will not co-operate with you unless you have mastered and apply the Law of a *Pleasing Personality*. You will also notice that *Enthusiasm* and *Self-Control* and *The Habit of Doing More than Paid For* must be practiced before you can hope to gain full co-operation from others.

These Laws overlap one another, and all of them must be merged into the Law of *Co-operation*, which means that one, to gain co-operation from others, must form the habit of practicing the Laws named.

No man is willing to co-operate with a person who has an offensive Personality. No man is willing to co-operate with one who is not Enthusiastic, or who lacks Self-Control. *Power* comes from organized, *co-operative* effort!

A dozen well trained soldiers, working with perfectly co-ordinated effort, can master a mob of a thousand people who lack leadership and organization.

Education, in all of its forms, is nothing but *organized knowledge*, or, as it might be stated—co-operative facts!

Andrew Carnegie had but little schooling, yet he was a well educated man because he formed the habit of organizing his knowledge and shaping it into a *definite chief aim*. He also made use of the Law of Co-operation, as a result of which he made himself a multimillionaire; moreover, he made millionaires of scores of other men who were allied with him in his application of the Law of *Co-operation* which he so well understood.

It was Andrew Carnegie who gave the author of the Law of Success philosophy the idea upon which the entire philosophy was founded. The event is worth describing, as it involves a newly discovered Law which is the real basis of all effective co-operation.

The author went to interview Carnegie for the purpose of writing a story about his industrial career. The first question asked was:

"Mr. Carnegie, to what do you attribute your great success?"

"You have asked me a big question," said Carnegie, "and before I answer I would like for you to define the word 'success.' Just what do you call success?"

Before the author had time to reply, Carnegie anticipated the reply by saying:

"By success I think you mean my money, do you not?"

The author said, "Yes, that seems to be the term that stands for success."

"Oh, well," replied Carnegie, "if you merely wish to know how I got my money—if that is what *you* call *success*—I can easily answer your question.

"To begin with, let me tell you that we have, here in this steel business, a *Master Mind*. This Master Mind is not the mind of any one person, but it is the sum total of ability, knowledge, and experience of nearly a score of men whose minds have been perfectly co-ordinated so they function as one, in a spirit of harmonious *co-operation*. These men are the ones who manage the various departments of this business. Some of them have been associated with me for many years, while others have not been here so long.

"You may be surprised to know," Carnegie continued, "that I have had to fit and try, and then fit and try over and over again while finding men whose personalities were such that they could subordinate their own interests for the benefit of the business. One of the most important places on our staff has been filled by more than a dozen men before one was finally found who could do the work required in that position and at the same time *co-operate* in a spirit of harmony, with the other members of our staff. *My one big problem has been, and always will continue to be,* the difficulty in securing the services of men who will *co-operate,* because without co-operation the Master Mind of which I speak could not exist."

In these words, or their equivalent, as I am quoting from memory, the greatest of all the steel magnates the industry has ever known laid bare the real secret of his stupendous achievements. His statement led this author to a line of research covering a period of over twenty years, which resulted in the discovery that this same principle of which Carnegie spoke is also the secret of the success of most of the other successful men of this type who are at the heads of our great industries, financial institutions, railroads, banks, department stores, etc.

It is a fact, although the scientific world may not have so endorsed it, that wherever two or more minds are allied, or associated in any undertaking, in a spirit of *perfect harmony and co-operative effort* there arises, out of this alliance, an unseen power that gives greater energy to the efforts of those associated in the alliance.

You may test this out, in your own way, by watching the reaction of your own mind when you are in the presence of those with whom you are friendly as compared with what happens when you are in the presence of those whom you do not like. Friendly association inspires one with a mysterious energy not otherwise experienced, and this great truth is the very foundation stone of the Law of *Co-operation.*

An army that is forced to fight because the soldiers are afraid they will be shot down by their own leaders may be a very effective army, but such an army never has been a match for the army that goes into action of its own accord, with every man determined to win because he believes his side ought to win.

At the beginning of the World War the Germans were sweeping everything before them. The German soldiers, at that time, went into action singing. They had been thoroughly "sold" on the idea of "kultur." Their leaders had made them think they were bound to win because they ought to win.

However, as the war went along these same soldiers became "wised up" a bit, to use a slang term. It began to dawn upon their minds that the killing off of millions of men was a serious business. Next, the thought began to creep in that, after all, perhaps their kaiser was not the ordained agent of God, and that they might be fighting an unjust war.

From this point on the tide began to turn. They no longer went into battle singing. They no longer "felt proud to die for kultur," and the end of them was then but a short distance away.

So it is in every walk of life, in every human endeavor. The man who can subordinate his own personality, subdue his own self-interests and co-ordinate all his efforts, physical and mental, with those of other men, back of a common cause, believing that what he is doing is right and should be successful, has already gone nearly the entire distance toward success.

*   *   *

A few years ago the president of a well-known real estate company addressed the following letter to the author:

Dear Mr. Hill:

Our firm will give you a check for $10,000.00 if you will show us how to get the confidence of the public as effectively as you do in connection with the work in which you are engaged.

Very cordially,

To this letter the following reply was sent:

Dear Mr. J—:

May I not thank you for the compliment, and while I could use your check for $10,000, I am perfectly willing to give you, gratis, what information I have on the subject. If I have unusual ability to gain co-operation from other people, it is because of the following reasons:

1. *I render more service than I ask people to pay for.*
2. *I engage in no transaction, intentionally, which does not benefit all whom it affects.*
3. *I make no statements which I do not believe to be true.*
4. *I have a sincere desire in my heart to be of useful service to the greatest possible number of people.*
5. *I like people better than I like money.*
6. *I am doing my best to live as well as to teach my own philosophy of success.*
7. *I accept no favors, from anyone, without giving favors in return.*
8. *I ask nothing of any person without having a right to that for which I ask.*
9. *I enter into no arguments with people over trivial matters.*
10. *I spread the sunshine of optimism and good cheer wherever and whenever I can.*

11. *I never flatter people for the purpose of gaining their confidence.*

12. *I sell counsel and advice to other people, at a modest price, but* never offer free advice.

13. *While teaching others how to achieve success, I have demonstrated that I can make my philosophy work for myself, as well, thus "practicing that which I preach."*

14. *I am so thoroughly sold on the work in which I am engaged that my enthusiasm over it becomes "contagious" and others are influenced by it.*

Adversity is to the human being what the kiln is to the brick—it tempers the man so he can carry responsibilities and overcome obstacles without crumbling before them.

If there are any other elements entering into what you believe to be my ability to get the confidence of others, I do not know what they are. Incidentally, your letter raised an interesting question, and caused me to analyze myself as I had never done before. For this reason I refuse to accept your check, on the ground that you have caused me to do something which may be worth many times ten thousand dollars.

Very cordially,
Napoleon Hill

In these fourteen points may be found the elements which form the basis of all confidence-building relationships.

Co-operative effort brings power to those who can gain and permanently hold the confidence of great numbers of people. This author knows of no method of inducing others to co-operate, except that which is based upon the fourteen points here described.

LESSON 14
PROFITING BY FAILURE

*A wealthy philosopher, by the name of Croesus, was the official coun-
selor to his majesty, King Cyrus. He said some very wise things, in his
capacity as court philosopher, among them this:*

"I am reminded, O king, and take this lesson to heart, that
there is a wheel on which the affairs of men revolve, and its
mechanism is such that it prevents *any* man from being *always*
fortunate."

It is true; there is a sort of unseen Fate, or wheel, turning in
the lives of all of us, and sometimes it brings us good fortune
and sometimes ill fortune, despite anything that we as individual human beings, can do. However, this wheel obeys the law
of averages, thereby insuring us against continuous ill fortune.
If ill fortune comes to-day, there is hope in the thought that its
opposite will come in the next turn of the wheel, or the one following the next, etc.

Failure is one of the most beneficial parts of a human being's
experience, for the reason that there are many needed lessons

that must be learned before one commences to succeed which could be learned by no teacher other than *failure.*

Failure is always a blessing in disguise, providing it teaches us some useful lesson that we could not or would not have learned without it!

However, millions of people make the mistake of accepting *failure* as final, whereas it is, like most other events in life, but transitory, and for this reason should not be accepted as final.

Successful people must learn to distinguish between *failure* and *temporary defeat.* Every person experiences, at one time or another, some form of temporary defeat, and out of such experiences come some of the greatest and most beneficial lessons.

In truth, most of us are so constituted that if we never experienced temporary defeat (or, what some ignorantly call *failure*), we would soon become so egotistical and independent that we would imagine ourselves more important than Deity. There are a few such people in this world, and it is said of them that they refer to Deity, if at all, as *"Me* and God," with heavy emphasis on the *"Me"*!

Headaches are beneficial, despite the fact that they are very disagreeable, for the reason that they represent Nature's language in which she calls loudly for intelligent use of the human body; particularly of the stomach and tributary organs through which most of us create the majority of physical human ills.

It is the same regarding Temporary Defeat or Failure—these are Nature's symbols through which she signals us that we have been headed in the wrong direction, and if we are reasonably intelligent we heed these signals, steer a different course, and come, finally, to the objective of our *definite chief aim.*

The author of this philosophy has devoted more than a quarter of a century to research for the purpose of discovering what characteristics were possessed and employed by the successful men and women in the field of business, industry, politics, statesmanship, religion, finance, transportation, literature, science, etc. This research has involved the reading of more than one thousand books of a scientific, business, and biographical nature, or an average of more than one such book a week.

One of the most startling discoveries made by this enormous amount of research was the fact that all the outstanding successes, regardless of the field of endeavor in which they were engaged, were people who met with reverses, adversity, temporary defeat, and in some instances actual *permanent failure* (as far as they, as individuals, were concerned). Not one single successful person was discovered whose success was attained without the experience of what, in many instances, seemed like unbearable obstacles that had to be mastered.

It was discovered also *that in exact ratio to the extent that these successful people met squarely and did not budge from defeat they arose to the heights of success.* In other words, success is measured, always, by the extent to which any individual meets and squarely deals with the obstacles that arise in the course of his procedure in pursuit of his *definite chief aim.*

Let us recall a few of the great successes of the world who met with temporary defeat, and some of whom were permanent failures, as far as they, as individuals, were concerned.

Columbus started out to find a shorter passage to India, but discovered America instead. He died a prisoner, in chains, a victim of the ignorance of his times.

Thomas A. Edison met with defeat after defeat, more than ten thousand unsuccessful efforts in all, before he made a revolving piece of wax record and reproduce the sound of the human voice. He met with similar defeat before he created the modern incandescent electric light bulb.

Alexander Graham Bell met with years of defeat before he perfected the long distance telephone.

Woolworth's first Five and Ten Cent Store project was not a success, and he had to master the most trying obstacles before he finally got his true bearings and rode high on the road to success.

Fulton's steamboat was a fizzle, and people laughed at him so hard that he had to sneak out at night and conduct his experiments privately.

The Wright brothers smashed many airplanes and suffered much defeat before they created a heavier-than-air flying machine that was practical.

Henry Ford almost starved to death, figuratively if not literally, before he successfully completed his first working model of an automobile. Nor was this the end of his troubles; he spent years perfecting the famous Model T car which made his fame and fortune.

Do not think, for one moment, that these men rode to success on the wings of plenty, without opposition of the most heart-rending nature. We are too apt to look at men in the hour of their triumph without taking into consideration the setbacks, defeats, and adversities through which they had to pass before success came.

Napoleon met with defeat after defeat before he made himself the great power that he was, and even then he finally met with permanent *failure*. At many times, it is recorded in his biographies, he contemplated committing suicide, so great were his disappointments.

The Panama Canal was not built without defeat. Time after time many of the deep cuts fell in and the engineers had to go back and do their work all over again. It looked, on many occasions, to those on the outside, at least, as if some of the heavy cuts never could be made to stand up. But perseverance, plus *a definite chief aim,* finally delivered to the world the most marvelous artificial body of water in the world, viewed from the standpoint of usefulness.

There comes to mind what this author believes to be the finest poem ever written on the subject of *failure*. It so thoroughly and clearly states the benefits of defeat that it is here reprinted, as follows;

WHEN NATURE WANTS A MAN!
by Angela Morgan
Copyright, 1926, by Dodd, Mead and Company, Inc.

When Nature wants to drill a man,
And thrill a man,
And skill a man.
When Nature wants to mold a man
To play the noblest part;
When she yearns with all her heart
To create so great and bold a man
That all the world shall praise—
Watch her method, watch her ways!
How she ruthlessly perfects
Whom she royally elects;
How she hammers him and hurts him,
And with mighty blows converts him
Into trial shapes of clay which only Nature under-
stands—
While his tortured heart is crying and he lifts beseeching
hands!—
How she bends but never breaks,
When his good she undertakes . . .
How she uses whom she chooses
And with every purpose infuses him,

By every art induces him
To try his splendor out—
Nature knows what she's about.

When Nature wants to take a man,
And shake a man,
And wake a man;
When Nature wants to make a man
To do the Future's will;
When she tries with all her skill
And she yearns with all her soul
To create him large and whole . . .
With what cunning she prepares him!
How she goads and never spares him,
How she whets him, and she frets him,
And in poverty begets him . . .
How she often disappoints
Whom she sacredly anoints,
With what wisdom she will hide him,
Never minding what betide him
Though his genius sob with slighting, and his pride may
not forget!
Bids him struggle harder yet.
Makes him lonely
So that only
God's high messages shall reach him,
So that she may surely teach him
What the Hierarchy planned.
Though he may not understand
Gives him passions to command.
Now remorselessly she spurs him
With terrific ardor stirs him
When she poignantly prefers him!

When Nature wants to name a man
And fame a man
And tame a man;
When Nature wants to shame a man
To do his heavenly best . . .
When she tries the highest test
That the reckoning may bring—
When she wants a god or king!
How she reins him and restrains him
So his body scarce contains him
While she fires him
And inspires him!
Keeps him yearning, ever burning for a tantalizing goal—
Lures and lacerates his soul.
Sets a challenge for his spirit,
Draws it high when he's near it—
Makes a jungle that he clear it;
Makes a desert that he fear it
And subdue it if he can—
So doth Nature make a man.
Then, to test his spirit's wrath
Hurls a mountain in his path—
Puts a bitter choice before him
And relentless stands o'er him.
"Climb, or perish!" so she says . . .
Watch her purpose, watch her ways!

Nature's plan is wondrous kind
Could we understand her mind . . .
Fools are they who call her blind.
When his feet are torn and bleeding,
Yet his spirit mounts unheeding
All his higher powers speeding,

Blazing newer paths and fine;
When the force that is divine
Leaps to challenge every failure and his ardor still is sweet,
And love and hope are burning in the presence of defeat . . .
Lo, the crisis! Lo, the shout
That must call the leader out.
When the people need salvation
Doth he come to lead the nation . . .
Then doth Nature show her plan
When the world has found—a man!

Do not be afraid of temporary defeat, but make sure that you learn some lesson from every such defeat. That which we call "experience" consists, largely, of what we learn by mistakes—our own and those made by others—but take care not to ignore the knowledge that may be gained from mistakes.

LESSON 15
TOLERANCE

Intolerance has caused more grief than any other of man's many forms of ignorance. Practically all wars grow out of intolerance. Misunderstandings between so-called "capital" and "labor" are usually the outgrowth of intolerance.

It is impossible for any man to observe the Law on *Accurate Thought,* without having first acquired the habit of tolerance, for the reason that intolerance causes a man to fold the Book of Knowledge and write "Finis, I know it all!" on the cover.

The most damaging form of intolerance grows out of religious and racial differences of opinion. Civilization, as we know it to-day, bears the deep wounds of gross intolerance all back down the ages, mostly those of a religious nature.

This is the most democratic country on earth. We are the most cosmopolitan people on earth. We are made up of all nationalities and people of every religious belief. We live side by side with neighbors whose religion differs from our own. Whether we are good neighbors or bad depends largely on how tolerant we are with one another.

Intolerance is the result of ignorance, or, stated conversely, the lack of *knowledge*. Well-informed men are seldom intolerant, because they know that no man knows enough to entitle him to judge others by his standards.

Through the principle of social heredity we inherit, from our environment, and through our early religious teachings, our ideas of religion. Our teachers themselves may not be always right, and if we bear this thought in mind, we would not allow such teachings to influence us to believe that we have a corner on *truth*, and that people whose teachings on this subject have been different from our own are all wrong.

There are many reasons why one should be tolerant, the chief of them being the fact that tolerance permits cool reason to guide one in the direction of *facts*, and this, in turn, leads to *accurate thinking*.

The man whose mind has been closed by intolerance, no matter of what brand or nature, can never become an *accurate thinker*, which is sufficient reason to cause us to master *intolerance*.

It may not be your *duty* to be tolerant with other people whose ideas, religious views, politics, and racial tendencies are different from yours, but it is *your privilege!* You do not have to ask permission of anyone to be tolerant; this is something that you control, in your own mind; therefore, the responsibility that goes with the choice is also your own.

Intolerance is closely related to the *six basic fears* described in the Law of *Self-Confidence*, and it may be stated as a positive fact that intolerance is always the result of either *fear* or *ignorance*. There are no exceptions to this rule. The moment another person (providing he, himself, is not intolerant) discovers that you are cursed with intolerance he can easily and quickly mark you as being either the victim of *fear* and *superstition* or what is worse, *ignorance!*

Intolerance closes the doorway to opportunity in a thousand ways, and shuts out the light of intelligence.

The moment you open your mind to *facts*, and take the attitude that the last word is seldom said on any subject—that there always remains the chance that still more truth may be learned on every subject, you begin to cultivate the Law of *Tolerance*, and if you practice this habit for long you will soon become a thinker, with ability to solve the problems that confront you in your struggle to make a place for yourself in your chosen field of endeavor.

LESSON 16
PRACTICING THE GOLDEN RULE

This is, in some ways, the most important of the Seventeen Laws of Success. Despite the fact that the great philosophers for more than five thousand years back have all discovered the Law of the Golden Rule, and have made comment on it, the great majority of people of to-day look upon it as a sort of pretty text for preachers to build sermons on.

In truth the Golden Rule philosophy is based upon a powerful law which, when understood and faithfully practiced, will enable any man to get others to *co-operate* with him.

It is a well-known truth that most men follow the practice of returning good or evil, act for act. If you slander a man, he will slander you in return. If you praise a man, he will praise you in return. If you favor a man in business, he will favor you in return.

There are exceptions to this rule, to be sure, but by and large the law works out. Like attracts like. This is in accordance with a great natural law, and it works in every particle of matter and in every form of energy in the universe. Successful men attract successful men. Failures attract failures. The professional "bum" will make a bee line for the "flop" house, where he may associate with other "bums," even though he may be set down in a strange city, after dark.

The Law of the Golden Rule is closely related to the Law on *The Habit of Doing More than Paid For.* The very act of rendering more service than you are paid to render puts into operation this law through which "like attracts like," which is the selfsame law as that which forms the basis of the Golden Rule philosophy.

There is no escape from the fact that the man who renders more service than he is paid to render eventually will be eagerly sought by those who will be willing to pay him for more than he actually does. Compound interest on compound interest is Nature's rate, when she goes to pay the indebtedness incurred through application of this Law.

This law is so fundamental, so obvious, yet so simple. It is one of the great mysteries of human nature that it is not more generally understood and practiced. Back of its use lie possibilities that stagger the imagination of the most visionary person. Through its use may one learn the real secret—all the secret there is—about the art of *getting others to do that which we wish them to do.*

If you want a favor from someone, make it your business to seek out the person from whom you want the favor and, in an appropriate manner, render that person an equivalent of the favor you wish from him. If he does not respond at first, double the dose and render him another favor, and another, and another, and so on, until finally he will, out of shame if nothing more, come back and render you a favor.

You get others to co-operate with you by first co-operating with them!

The foregoing sentence is worth reading a hundred times, for it contains the gist of one of the most powerful laws available to the man who has the intention of attaining great success.

It may sometimes happen, and it will, that the particular

individual to whom you render useful service will never respond and render you a similar service, but *keep this important truth in mind*—that even though one person fails to respond, someone else will observe the transaction and, out of a sportsman's desire to see justice done, or perhaps with a more selfish motive in mind, will render you the service to which you are entitled.

"Whatsoever a man soweth that shall he also reap!"

This is more than a mere preachment; it is a great practical truth that may be made the foundation of every successful achievement. From winding pathways or straight, every thought you send out, every deed you perform, will gather a flock of other thoughts or deeds according to its own nature, and come back home to you in due time.

There is no escape from this truth. It is as eternal as the universe, as sure of operation as the law of gravitation. To ignore it is to mark yourself as ignorant, or indifferent, either of which will destroy your chances of success.

The Golden Rule philosophy is the real basis on which children should be governed. It is also the real basis on which "children grown tall" should be managed. Through force, or by taking advantage of unfair circumstances, a man may build a fortune without observing the Golden Rule, and many do this, but such fortunes cannot bring happiness, because ill-gotten gain is bound to destroy the peace of mind of all who get it. Wealth created or acquired by the Golden Rule philosophy does not bring with it a flock of regrets, nor does it disturb the conscience and destroy the peace of mind.

Ideas are the most valuable products of the human mind. If you can create usable ideas and put them to work you can take whatever you wish for your pay.

Fortunate is the man who makes the Golden Rule his business or professional slogan and then lives up to the slogan faithfully, both literally and figuratively, observing the spirit of it as well as the letter.

LESSON 17

THE HABIT OF HEALTH

We come now to the last of the seventeen factors of success. In previous chapters we have learned that success grows out of power; *that power is organized knowledge expressed in definite* action. *No one can remain intensely active very long without good health. The mind will not function properly unless it has a sound body in which to function. Practically all of the other sixteen factors which enter into the building of success depend, for their successful application, upon a healthy body.*

Good health is dependent, in the main, upon:

1. Proper food and air combinations
2. Proper elimination of waste fecal matter
3. Proper exercise
4. Right thinking

It is not the purpose of this chapter to present a treatise on how to remain healthy, as that is a task which belongs to the specialists in physical and mental therapeutics. However, no harm can be done by calling attention to the fact that poor health is usually superinduced by poor elimination. People who live in cities and eat the artificially prepared foods will find it necessary to constantly aid nature in the eliminative processes by flushing the intestinal tract with water at regular intervals of not more than one week each. Practically all headaches, sluggishness, loss of "pep" and similar feelings are mostly due to auto-intoxication, or intestinal poisoning through improper elimination.

Most people eat too much. Such people will find it helpful if they go on a ten-day fast about three times a year, during which time they will refrain from taking food of any nature whatsoever. During a fast the intestinal tract should be flushed with water daily. The experience of fasting will bring to all who have never tried it health-building values which can be attained in no other way. No one should experiment with fasting, dieting, or any other form of self-administered therapeutics, except under the direction of a physician of experience in such matters.

SEX ENERGY A HEALTH BUILDER

As a closing thought for this chapter the author has chosen to inject a very brief statement concerning the therapeutic value of sex energy. The foundation of fact which justifies the reference to sex, as a health builder, will be laid in the following manner:

It is a well-known fact that *thought* is the most powerful energy available to man.

It is equally as well known that negative thoughts of worry and envy and hatred and fear will destroy the digestive processes and bring about illness; this by reason of the fact that negative thought inhibits the flow of certain glandular contents which are essential in the digestive processes.

Negative thoughts cause "short circuits" in the nerve lines which carry nervous energy (or life force) from the central distributing station, the brain, to all parts of the body, where this energy performs its natural task of nourishment and of removal of worn-out cells and waste matter.

Sex energy is a highly vitalizing, positive force, when it is in a state of agitation, during the period of sexual contact, and because it is powerful it sweeps over the entire nervous system of the body and unties any "short circuits" which may exist in any of the nerve lines, thus insuring a complete flow of nervous energy to *all* parts of the body.

Sexual emotion is the most powerful of all the human emotions, and when it is actively engaged, it reaches and vitalizes every cell in every organ of the body, thereby causing the organs to function in a normal manner. Total abstinence, sexually, was not one of Nature's plans, and those who do not understand this truth usually pay for their ignorance out of a trust fund which Nature provided for the maintenance of health.

Thought controls all voluntary movements of the body. Are we in accord on this statement? Very well, if thought controls all voluntary movements of the body, may it not also be made to control, or at least materially influence, all involuntary movements of the body?

Thoughts of a negative nature, such as fear, worry, and anxiety, not only inhibit the flow of the digestive juices, but they also "tie knots" in the nerve lines which carry nervous energy to the various organs of the body.

Thoughts of a *positive* nature untie these knots in the nerve lines and permit the nervous energy to pass through. *Sex emotion is the most powerful form of positive thought.* Sex energy is Nature's own "medicine," proof of which is obvious if one will observe the state of mind and the perfectly relaxed condition of the body, following sexual contact.

Brief as it is, the foregoing statement should be made the starting point for some intelligent analysis of this subject by the reader of this book. Let us be open minded on this subject of sex.

No one knows the last word in connection with the subject; most of us do not even know the first word. Therefore, let us not pass judgment on a subject concerning which we know so very little until we have at least done some intelligent thinking on the subject. For all that most of us know, both poverty and ill health may be mastered through a complete understanding of the subject of sex energy, and this for the reason that sex energy is the most powerful mind stimulant known.

THE THIRTY MOST COMMON CAUSES OF FAILURE

Through the foregoing pages you have had a brief description of the seventeen factors through which success is attained. Now let us turn our attention to some of the factors which cause failure. Check the list and you will perhaps find here the cause of any failure, or temporary defeat, which you may have experienced. The list is based upon accurate analysis of over twenty thousand failures, and it covers men and women in every calling.

1. Unfavorable hereditary foundation (This cause of failure stands at the head of the list. Bad breeding is a handicap against which there is but little remedy, and it is one for which the individual, unfortunately, is not responsible.)
2. Lack of a well-defined purpose, or definite major aim toward which to strive.
3. Lack of ambition to aim above mediocrity
4. Insufficient education
5. Lack of self-discipline and tact, generally

    manifesting itself through all sorts of excesses;
    especially in sexual desires and eating

6. Ill health, usually due to preventable causes
7. Unfavorable environment during childhood, when character was being formed, resulting in vicious habits of body and mind
8. Procrastination
9. Lack of persistence and courage to blame one's self with one's failures
10. Negative personality
11. Lack of well-defined sexual urge
12. An uncontrollable desire to get *something* for *nothing* usually manifesting itself in habits of gambling
13. Lack of decision
14. One or more of the six basic fears described elsewhere in this book
15. Poor selection of a mate in marriage
16. Overcaution, destroying initiative and self-confidence
17. Poor selection of associates in business
18. Superstition and prejudice, generally traceable to lack of knowledge of natural laws
19. Wrong selection of occupation
20. Dissipation of energies, through lack of understanding of the law of concentration, resulting in what is commonly known as "jack-of-all-trades"
21. Lack of thrift
22. Lack of enthusiasm
23. Intolerance
24. Intemperance in eating, drinking, and sexual activities

25. Inability to co-operate with others in a spirit of harmony
26. Possession of power which was not acquired through self-effort, by slow, evolutionary pro-cesses of experience (as in the case of one who inherits wealth, or is placed in a position of power to which he is not entitled on merit)
27. Dishonesty
28. Egotism and vanity
29. Guessing instead of thinking
30. Lack of capital

Some may wonder why "lack of capital" was placed at the bottom of the list, and the answer is that anyone who can qualify with a reasonably high grade, on the other twenty-nine causes of failure, can always get all the capital needed for any purpose whatsoever.

The foregoing list does not include all the causes of failure, but it does represent the most common causes. Some may object that "unfavorable luck" should have been added to the list, but the answer to this complaint is that luck, or the law of chance, is subject to mastery by all who understand how to apply the sev-enteen factors of success. However, in fairness to those who may never have had the opportunity to master the seventeen factors of success, it must be admitted that luck, or an unfavorable turn of the wheel of chance, is sometimes the cause of failure.

Those who are inclined to attribute all their failures to "cir-cumstances" or luck, should remember the blunt injunction laid down by Napoleon, who said, "To hell with circumstances! I cre-ate circumstances." Most "circumstances" and unfavorable re-sults of luck are self-made, also. *Let us not forget this!*

Here is a statement of fact, and a confession, that is well-worth remembering. *The law of success philosophy, which is now rendering*

useful service to men and women all over this earth, is very largely the re-
sult of nearly twenty years of so-called failure upon the part of the author.
In the more extensive course on the Law of Success philosophy,
under the lesson on "Profiting by Failure," the student will observe
that the author met with failure and adversity and reverses so often
that he might have been justified in crying out, "Luck is against
me!" Seven major failures, and more scores of minor failures than
the author can, or cares to remember, laid the foundation for a philosophy which is now bringing success to tens of thousands of
people, *including the author!* "Bad luck" has been harnessed and put
to work, and the whole world is now paying substantial monetary
tribute to the man who ferreted out the happy thought that even
luck can be changed, and failures can be capitalized.

> *"There is a wheel on which the affairs of men revolve, and its*
> *mechanism is such that it prevents any man from being always*
> *fortunate."*

True enough! There is such a wheel of life, but it is rotating
continuously. If this wheel brings misfortune to-day, it can be
made to bring good fortune to-morrow. If this were not true, the
Law of Success philosophy would be a farce and a fake, offering
nothing but false hope.

The author was once told that he would always be a failure because he was born under an unfavorable star! Something
must have happened to antidote the bad influence of that star,
and something *has happened.* That "something" is the power to
master obstacles by first mastering self, which grew out of understanding and application of the Law of Success philosophy.
If the seventeen factors of success can offset the bad influence
of a star for this author, they can do the same for *you,* or for any
other person.

Laying our misfortunes to the influence of stars is just

another way of acknowledging our ignorance or our laziness. The only place that stars can bring you bad luck is in your own mind. You have possession of that mind, and it has the power to master all the bad influences which stand between you and success, including that of the stars.

If you really wish to see the cause of your bad luck and misfortunes, do not look up toward the stars; look in a mirror! You are the master of your fate! You are the captain of your soul. And this by reason of the fact that you have a mind which you, alone, control, and this mind can be stimulated and made to form a direct contact with all the power you need to solve any problem that may confront you. The person who blames his troubles upon stars thereby challenges the existence of Infinite Intelligence, or God, if you prefer that name.

THE MYSTERY OF THE POWER OF THOUGHT!

In front of the author's study, at Broadway and Forty-fourth Street, in New York City, stands the Paramount Building; a great tall, impressive building which serves as a daily reminder of the great power of *thought*.

Come, stand with me by the window of my study and let us analyze this modern skyscraper. Tell me, if you can, of what materials the building is constructed. Immediately you will say, "Why, it is built of brick and steel girders and plate glass and lumber," and you will be partly right, but you have not told the entire story.

The brick and steel and other materials which went into the *physical* portion of the building were necessary, but before any of those materials were laid into place the building, in its entirety, was constructed of another sort of material. It was first built, in the mind of Adolph Zukor, out of the intangible stuff known as *thought*.

Everything you have or ever will have, good or bad, was attracted to you by the nature of your *thoughts*. Positive thoughts attract positive, desirable objects; negative thoughts attract poverty and misery and a flock of other sorts of undesirable objects. Your brain is the magnet to which everything you possess clings, and make no mistake about this, your brain will not attract success while you are thinking of poverty and failure.

Every man is where he is, as the result of his own dominating thoughts, just as surely as night follows day. *Thought* is the only thing that you absolutely control, a statement of fact which we repeat because of its great significance. You do not control, entirely, the money you possess, or the love and friendship that you enjoy; you had nothing to do with your coming into the world and you will have but little to do with the time of your going; but you do have *everything* to do with the state of your own mind. You can make that mind *positive* or you can permit it to become *negative*, as the result of outside influences and suggestions. Divine Providence gave you supreme control of your own mind, and with this control the responsibility that is now yours to make the best use of it.

In your own mind you can fashion a great building, similar to the one which stands in front of the author's study, and then transform that mental picture into a reality, just as Adolph Zukor did, because the material out of which he constructed the Paramount Building is available to every human being; moreover, it is *free*. All you have to do is to appropriate it and put it to your use. This universal material, as we have said, is the *power of thought*.

The difference between success and failure is largely a matter of the difference between positive and negative thought. A negative mind will not attract a fortune. Like attracts like. Nothing attracts success as quickly as success. Poverty begets more poverty. Become successful and the whole world will lay its treasures at your feet and want to do something to help you become more successful. Show signs of poverty and the entire world will try to take away that which you have of value. You can borrow money at the bank when you are prosperous and do not need it, but try and arrange a loan when you are poverty-stricken, or when some great emergency faces you. You are the master of your own destiny because you control the one thing which can change and redirect the course of human destinies, the power of *thought*. Let this great truth sink into your consciousness and this book will have marked the most important turning point of your life.

HOW TO CONVERT THIS PHILOSOPHY INTO CASH

The author is engaged in the business of helping other people to find themselves. His work consists of two forms of procedure, as follows: First, the student is taught how to co-ordinate and apply the seventeen factors of the Law of Success philosophy in the solution of any problem. Second, the student is analyzed and a chart is made of his or her good qualities and poor ones. In other words the student's entire mental equipment is thoroughly diagnosed and the result plainly stated in a written chart, which shows what line of work should be followed and the best plan for carrying out that work. Whenever possible the author interviews the student in person. When this is not possible the student is served through class instruction, or by correspondence, if he lives at a great distance from New York City.

THE NATURE OF PERSONAL INTERVIEWS

Personal interviews between students of the Law of Success philosophy and the author are for the purpose of aiding the student in applying this philosophy to the end that his or her *definite chief aim* may be selected, and a practical working plan for its achievement adopted. The interview constitutes a very effective application of the Master Mind principle, through which two minds are co-ordinated for the purpose of attaining a given objective.

These interviews are productive of phenomena which often startle both the author and his students. For illustration, not long ago a lady called for an interview for the purpose of finding the life work for which she was best fitted. She had been a student of the Law of Success philosophy for several months, and had mastered the eight textbooks on the subject, and was familiar with the fundamentals of this philosophy. Within fifteen minutes after her arrival at the author's office she had "stepped up" the vibrations of her mind to where she was "tuning in" on the Master Mind principle. The creative faculty of her imagination began to work rapidly, with the result that the ideas described below began to "flash" into her mind.

The author made notes of these ideas, which came as fast as he could write in shorthand. The flow of ideas did not cease, but was voluntarily cut off because the time of her interview had expired and another client was waiting. The ideas are listed here, just as she received them:

FORTY UNIQUE IDEAS FOR MAKING MONEY

Interpreted by Miss M. C.
Through the Aid of
the Master Mind
Principle

1. Rewrite the Law of Success philosophy in a brief
   form which can be presented in one volume, at a
   very low cost, so it can be placed in the hands of
   hundreds of thousands of students who might
   otherwise never have the benefit of such a philosophy of success, and permit teachers of the
   philosophy, throughout the world, to use this
   book as a textbook, in private classes and success
   clubs to be organized by them. (Author's note:
   The book you hold in your hands is the concrete
   result of the foregoing idea.)
2. A chain of automatic gas filling stations at which

the motorist may serve himself, day or night, by
dropping coins in a slot machine.

3. A chain of automatic newsstands, dispensing
   magazines, newspapers and periodicals through
   slot machines.

4. A chain of automatic five and ten cent stores,
   dispensing merchandise through slot machines,
   thus saving labor and loss from steal-age over
   the counters.

5. An elastic support, to be made of flexible steel,
   which will cause one to hold the spine and
   shoulders erect, thereby permitting the nervous
   energy to pass freely to all parts of the body.

6. A vibrating machine, to be attached to the seats
   of chairs of office and factory workers who must
   work in a sitting position, which may be turned
   on at intervals during working hours, for the
   purpose of distributing the nervous energy and
   preventing fatigue, or "laziness."

7. New profession of Environment Artist, whose
   work will be that of creating a positive environment in home, office or workshop, store, etc., for
   the purpose of relieving the monotony of such
   places.

8. Combination locks for automobiles (keyless locks)
   for the prevention of theft, joy riding, etc.

9. A new profession to be known as "Personality
   Artist," whose members will assist men and
   women in the selection of clothes of appropriate
   lines and color harmony, to work in conjunction
   with high-grade clothing stores, and whose services will be free to the customer.

10. Research Secretary, whose business it will be to gather and classify data on any subject.

11. Country Club for people of small means, equipped with play-grounds for children, and competent nurses and play directors who will assume full responsibility for children during certain hours of the day or night, to be conducted in connection with suburban real estate developments, as an added inducement for people to locate there.

12. Idea Specialist for daily newspapers whose business it would be to create new and unique ideas for sales and advertising campaigns for small merchants who cannot afford to employ expensive people, and whose services would be free to all advertisers of the paper.

13. A Summer Camp Ground, near the city, where people may secure a plot of ground large enough for a tent, or small portable buildings, and sufficient ground for a garden, on a rental basis within the means of the man of small income.

14. Week-end outing information, supplying data on all near-by places of interest where the motorists may spend a day's or a week-end's outing, with road maps, descriptive literature etc., to be operated by chain of filling stations as a means of building up their business.

15. A moving picture service operated for the purpose of making short reels of children at play (to preserve the memory of their childhood days for parents), birthday parties, weddings, business gatherings, and banquets.

16. Typewriters for rent in hotels and on Pullman cars, through the aid of coin slot machines.

17. Box lunches for office and factory workers, made up of home-cooked foods, consisting of a properly balanced diet of pure food products. (Business can be conducted by a housewife, from her own kitchen.) Several clients of the author are now profitably employing this idea.

18. Home baking of pies, bread, and cakes, selling the output through regular arrangement with a number of local grocers and drug stores.

19. Book giving accurate information to beginners in the field of writing, as to subjects on which to write, and where and how to market their manuscripts.

20. Summer house boat that can be propelled by an automobile, for rent to motorists who wish to spend a part of their time on water and at the same time have their motor cars available for land use.

21. Window card advertising service for retail stores, carrying snappy, interesting epigrams instead of news pictures, that will cause the crowd to stop and read.

22. A set of fifty-two blotters, to be used for advertising purposes, each blotter carrying an epigram or motto appropriate to the business of the advertiser using the blotter, one blotter to be mailed out to a selected mailing list each week. (This is a plan to enable a printer to build up a business on printed blotters.)

23. Fountain drinks made of the juices of vegetables which have food value, and served fresh each

day, without preservatives or chemicals of any
sort.

24. Signs for office doors made of removable glass,
    which may be taken along when a tenant moves.

25. A Clearings House for the exchange of practical
    sales ideas among retailers.

26. A home nursery, to be conducted by married
    women who wish an independent source of in-
    come, to serve women who wish to leave their
    children in reliable hands.

27. Clothing Exchange, where used clothes may be
    exchanged for other used clothes.

28. New York City mailing address for out of the city
    small firms and individuals who wish their mail
    sent to New York and then forwarded, because
    of the prestige of the New York address, on a ser-
    vice fee basis of five dollars per month for each
    client. (Two hundred such clients would give one
    person a very substantial income.)

29. Moving pictures for children only, catering exclu-
    sively to the child mind, based upon plots which
    educate as well as entertain, to be distributed
    through the public schools.

30. Comic strip for newspapers, advertising some
    brand of merchandise, and at the same time en-
    tertaining, to be run in local newspapers by mer-
    chants selling the product advertised.

31. Success Editor for newspapers, to conduct a daily
    column based upon the material in the eight vol-
    umes of the Law of Success, through a working
    alliance with the author of the Law of Success.

32. Removable feet for hosiery, made of an absor-
    bent material which will keep the feet free from

perspiration, thus adding to the life of the hosiery and the health and comfort of the wearer.

33. Reversible neck ties, made of two sorts of material, thus giving the service of two different ties.

34. Special sets for men, consisting of shirt, tie, hose,
and handkerchief to match, to be packed in a
neat box, and sold at popular prices.

35. Elastic band fastened to top of trousers (on inside) thus eliminating the necessity of belt or
suspenders.

36. Daily menu made up of health foods, to be syndi-
cated in newspapers.

37. Physical Culture Club where exercise is given
through properly designed dances, thus making
physical exercise a pleasure instead of a torture.

38. A Sales Service Agency, to be conducted by telephone, providing real estate dealers, automobile
dealers, or any other business, with properly
qualified prospective purchasers. (This plan may
be conducted in any city, and it has unlimited
possibilities for the person who understands
how to present a telephone preliminary sales
talk.)

39. House organs for small business firms, to be
printed on the mimeograph, at a cost much less
than that of printing, in small quantities. (Note:
This idea has been put into use by two young
men in New York City, and they are prepared to
supply all the copy and other material necessary
for others who wish to carry on a similar business in other cities. They have copy suitable for
practically all sorts of business, such as banks,
life insurance, real estate, retail stores, etc. Their

names will be supplied to interested persons
upon application to the author of this book.)

40. Organize Success Classes in business houses for
the purpose of teaching the employees how to
apply the Law of Success philosophy in their
respective positions, to the end that both they
and their employers may profit. (Note: This idea
is now being carried out. It will provide employment for thousands of men and women who will
prepare themselves to teach the Law of Success
philosophy.)

> If you must slander someone do not
> speak it, but write it—write it in the sand,
> near the water's edge.

Think of the possibilities of stupendous achievement, financial and otherwise, with a mind that can create forty unique
money-making ideas in less than ten minutes. Such a mind has
no limitations. The Law of Success philosophy was organized for
the purpose of "stepping up" any mind and causing it to make
use of its potential powers. Reports from students of this philosophy from all over the world show that they are experiencing
results similar to those described in this book.

The foregoing are but a few of the many hundreds of useful ideas which develop from application of the Master Mind
principle, in the author's daily contact with his students who
come for personal interviews in connection with their sundry
problems of life. These interviews turn an interesting side light
on human nature, as they are connected with practically every
human problem, ranging all the way from the man who wishes

to improve the appearance and habits of his 1898 model wife without hurting her pride, to the man who wishes to find a way to increase his earning capacity by a few thousands of dollars per year. Such a great variety of discussion brings knowledge of the man animal which could be secured in no other way. When men and women come to the author and pay him a substantial sum to listen to their troubles and to offer plans for solving their problems, they do not make any attempt to deceive, nor do they try to set their best foot forward for the sake of making a favorable impression. They discuss their weaknesses as readily as they do their virtues.

In the solution of the problems of his clients, the author often finds it necessary to bring different clients together in business and professional alliances. One man will have a useful invention, or an idea for the expansion of some business enterprise, but lacks the capital to promote it. Perhaps the very next client will have ability to raise capital. The two are brought together and shown how to pool their resources through the aid of the Master Mind principle.

There is a practical solution for every human problem. When two or more people sit down and seriously concentrate their minds upon the solution of any problem, in a spirit of harmonious co-operation, ways and means leading to the desired end suggest themselves in a most miraculous fashion.

Not all students of the Law of Success philosophy have the opportunity to come to the author for personal interviews, as thousands of them live outside of the United States. These students receive help from the author through the aid of a Personal Analysis Questionnaire. This Questionnaire brings to the author a perfect mental picture of the one who fills it out, and thus provides the necessary data out of which the solution of practically any problem may be evolved without the author seeing the student.

The author is preparing to establish an authorized analyst and teacher in every city in the United States and eventually in many cities in other countries, who will personally teach the Law of Success philosophy and serve students of the philosophy through personal interviews, just as the author is doing here in New York City. Undoubtedly many of these teachers will be recruited from the rapidly declining profession of the clergy, as these splendid gentlemen have the personality and the education and the intelligence and the knowledge of pedagogy and the understanding of human problems which are so essential in the successful interpretation of the Law of Success philosophy.

Other teachers will be recruited from the business and professional fields. The philosophy will be taught in every language spoken in the civilized world, which calls for teachers and analysts of every nationality. The necessary steps to be taken by those who wish to become teachers and analysts will be thoroughly explained by the author of the Law of Success, upon application addressed to his New York City office.

A MESSAGE TO THOSE WHO HAVE TRIED AND FAILED!

The author would not be satisfied to send this book out on its mission of inspirational service without adding this short chapter as a personal message to those who have tried and "failed"!

Failure! What a misunderstood word! What chaos and distress and poverty and heartaches have come out of misinterpretation of this word.

Just a few days ago the author stood on a humble spot of ground in the mountains of Kentucky, not far from his own birthplace, where a well-known "failure" was born. When a very young man this "failure" went away to war, commissioned as a captain.

His record was so poor that he was demoted to corporal and finally returned home as a private.

He took up surveying, but he could not make a living at this work and very soon he was humiliated by having his instruments sold for his debts.

Next he took up law, but he got very few cases, and most of these he lost on account of incompetence.

He became engaged to a young lady, but changed his mind and failed to show up for the wedding.

He drifted into politics and by chance was elected to Congress, but his record was so drab that it caused no favorable comment. Everything he undertook brought him humiliation and failure.

Then a miracle happened! A great love experience came into his life, and despite the fact that the girl who aroused this love passed beyond the Great Divide, the lingering thoughts of that love caused this "Nobody" to fight his way out of his humble rôle as failure, and at the age of fifty-two he became the greatest and most beloved President who ever occupied the White House.

Men are made, or broken, according to the use they make of the *power* of thought. Failure may be transformed into success overnight, when one becomes inspired with a great impelling motive to succeed. The eight basic motives which move men to action have been described in a previous chapter. One of these eight is the motive of *love*.

Abraham Lincoln's love for Anne Rutledge turned mediocrity into greatness. He found himself through the sorrow that came to him through her death.

Elbert Hubbard left his impress for good upon the world, through the expression of genius that was inspired by Alice Hubbard, his second wife.

Henry Ford is the richest and most powerful man now living. He had to master poverty, illiteracy, and other handicaps which the average man never encounters. He became successful because of the love inspired by a truly great woman, his wife, and this despite the fact that his biographers have never mentioned her name.

Every Ford automobile, and the Ford millions, and every Ford factory, and all that Henry Ford has accomplished for the good of mankind, may be appropriately submitted as evidence of the soundness of the Law of Success philosophy, as he is the most practical student of this philosophy now living. From his life work, more than from any other source, has come the material that made this philosophy a reality.

The seed of all success lies sleeping in well-defined *motive!*

Without a *burning desire* to achieve, superinduced by one or more of the eight basic *motives*, no man ever becomes a genius.

Motivated by a highly developed urge of sex, Napoleon became the greatest leader of men of his time. His ignoble ending was the result of his lack of observance of two of the seventeen factors of success, namely, Self-Control and the Golden Rule.

Lester Park entered the moving picture business twenty-five years ago, at about the same time that the author began the organization of the Law of Success philosophy. The "miracle" which transformed Mr. Park from a self-styled "failure" into an outstanding success was described in a page editorial written by the author and published recently in a New York newspaper. This editorial is here reproduced as a fitting close for this chapter:

ANOTHER MIRACLE

"For twenty-five years I have been studying, measuring, and analyzing human beings. My research has brought me in contact with over twenty thousand men and women. Two people out of this vast army stand out in bold contrast with nearly all the others. These two are Henry Ford and Lester Park.

"Mr. Ford's general average, according to my last analysis, was ninety-five per cent. Lester Park's general average, according to an analysis which I have just completed for him, is ninety-four per cent. I first analyzed Henry Ford over twenty-three years ago. At that time his rating, on the seventeen factors of success, was sixty-seven per cent. His gradual rise from sixty-seven per cent to ninety-five per cent has been an outstanding achievement, but nothing to compare with the transformation

which took place in Lester Park's mental machinery, over a period of but a few weeks, as shown by the accompanying graphic chart of his analysis.

"When I first analyzed Mr. Park (as indicated by the dotted line, at the bottom of the chart), his general average was forty-five per cent. Less than a month later I made a second analysis and lo! he had jumped from 'zero' to one hundred per cent on two of the most important of the seventeen factors of success, and had made astounding advances on many of the other factors.

A SWEEPING ENDORSEMENT

"This analysis chart, showing Lester Park's two ratings on the factors which give men power and wealth, is a sweeping endorsement of the belief which many philosophers have held, that all success is merely a state of mind! That man is lifted to great heights of power, or dashed into oblivion, solely by the thoughts he releases on the wings of the ether.

SOLITARY CONFINEMENT

"Lester Park was formerly one of the most active moving picture executives in America. His name was linked with those of other men who have since made huge fortunes out of this business (which many believe to be still in its infancy). But something "snapped" in Lester Park's mental machinery. He lost his grip on himself. His self-confidence dropped to zero. He ceased to have a definite chief aim. He drew himself away from contact with others in his profession, thereby depriving himself of the greatest of all the Laws of Success, the Master Mind. (A mind that is a composite of two or more minds working in perfect harmony, for the attainment of some definite objective.)

"For years Lester Park committed himself, figuratively and literally, to solitary confinement, in a dark dungeon! That dungeon was his own mind and he, himself carried the key to the door.

THE WHEEL OF FATE

"*In September, 1928, I conducted a class on the Laws of Success, at the Waldorf-Astoria Hotel, in New York City. By a queer turn of the wheel of chance—or was it the "wheel of fate"?—Lester Park became a student in that class. The transformation which has taken place in Lester Park occurred in a fractional part of a minute, during the first half hour of my first lecture! In a single sentence I made a statement which served as a key that unlocked the door to the cell in which Lester Park had confined himself,* and* he stepped out, ready to pick up the reins where he had laid them down several years ago. *The transformation is no imaginary one. It has been both real and complete. Within two weeks' time after the light again shone into the brain of Lester Park he had completed all arrangements for the production of one of the greatest pictures of his career. When I say he had 'completed all arrangements' I mean just that! The money for the production was offered him from more than one source. Friends whom he had known in the heydey of his career as a producer suddenly appeared upon the scene as if by magic, and greeted him like long-lost brothers! 'Corianton,' the dream picture of his life, became a living, pulsating reality, and that picture is now in preparation for production.*

A MODERN MIRACLE HAD HAPPENED!

"*That miracle brings great joy to my heart, because it proves, once more, that the child of my heart and brain—the* Law of Success *philosophy—is destined to emancipate millions of Lester Parks from the dark dungeons of despair to which they have confined themselves. Over twenty years ago Andrew Carnegie gave me an idea which caused me to start a period of labor and research that has lasted almost a quarter of a century. That idea was the hub around which the Law of Success philosophy has been built. I have lived to see it bring freedom to no less than ten thousand people, and to how many more it has brought similar freedom I have no way of knowing, because the philosophy is now being studied by thousands of students in nearly every civilized country on earth, with whom I have not personally come in contact.*

A PROPHECY FULFILLED

"Years ago, when I predicted that Henry Ford would one day become the most powerful man on earth, my statement caused me great embarrassment, because Ford had not then shown any signs of becoming the world's richest man. I stood back of that prediction and lived to see it become more than justified.

ANOTHER PROPHECY

"I now publicly predict that Lester Park will become the most successful moving picture producer in the field. I have the best of reasons to believe—even to know—that this prophecy is well on the road toward fulfillment, and I shall be willing to assume full responsibility for it.

"The scientific world is on the border of the greatest of all discoveries, and when the nature of this discovery has been announced it will overshadow all else that mankind has learned about the physical laws of nature and things material. The nature of this discovery was discussed with this writer by the late Dr. Alexander Graham Bell and Dr. Elmer R. Gates, nineteen years ago, but the principle to which I refer was not then sufficiently understood to enable man to harness and use it. Nineteen years of experimentation have changed this, and the world is now practically in possession of knowledge of a law which will enable any man to change the course of his worldly destiny at will!

"Study the graphic chart analysis of Lester Park and you may gather a slight idea of what man may do for himself when he has learned how to harmonize himself with natural laws.

Napoleon Hill

EDITOR'S NOTE—

"The above statement is made under the personal signature of Napoleon Hill, author of the Law of Success philosophy. Those who do not know of Mr. Hill or his work are entitled to know that he has been engaged, for almost a quarter of a century, in experimenting with the human mind. In his research he has had valuable assistance from the best-known scientists of the world, such men as the late Dr. Alexander Graham Bell, Dr. Elmer R. Gates, Chas. P. Steinmetz, and Luther Burbank. In a recent series of articles which appeared in McClure's Magazine, *Henry Ford publicly admitted that the philosophy outlined in Mr. Hill's Seventeen Laws of Success had been the foundation of his own rise to power and wealth.*

"Mr. Hill is the Success Editor of the New York Evening Graphic, *and his 'Success Column' is appearing in other newspapers. Through this column he has kindled anew the fires of enthusiasm and ambition in the minds of thousands of men and women who had all but lost hope of achieving financial success.*

"The late Elbert H. Gary, former Chairman of the Board of the United States Steel Corporation, was preparing, at the time of his death, to present the Law of Success course to every employee of the steel corporation who could read English, at a total cost of something like one hundred and fifty thousand dollars.

"Cyrus H. K. Curtis, owner of the Saturday Evening Post, *and one of the most successful publishers of the world, openly endorsed Mr. Hill's discoveries and asked permission to*

reprint material from one of the lessons, in the Philadelphia Public Ledger.

"Wm. Howard Taft, *former President of the United States, endorsed the Law of Success philosophy in a most enthusiastic letter which Mr. Hill received from him.*

"Edwin C. Barnes, *a business associate of Thomas A. Edison, not only endorsed the Law of Success philosophy, and gave it credit for enabling him to retire from business, with all the wealth he wants, at the age of forty-five, but also gave a most sweeping endorsement of Mr. Hill personally, whom he has known for twenty years.*

"From this it may be said, without exaggeration, that Napoleon Hill is one of the great thinkers of the age—because no man could possibly command the respect and secure the endorsement of such men as those who have endorsed him, unless he were a sound thinker."

The man who sows a single beautiful thought in the mind of another renders the world, through that act, a greater service than that rendered by all the fault-finders combined.

THIS IS AN AGE OF ACTION!

Summarizing the seventeen factors of success described in this volume, the reader may better grasp the entire philosophy by keeping in mind the fact that success is based upon *power;* that power is knowledge expressed in *action.*

All of the major stimuli which arouse the mind and put it into action have been described in this volume. The main purpose of the seventeen factors of success is that of providing one with practical plans and methods of application for the use of these stimuli.

Careful analysis has disclosed the startling fact that a single incident, or experience, often results in such marked influence upon a mind of the most mediocre type that the owner of that mind surpasses, in achievement, others who have superior and better trained minds.

The Law of Success, as described through the seventeen factors outlined in this volume, provides all the known methods of mind stimulation which inspire the individual with high ambition and supply the courage essential for the attainment of the object of that ambition.

It is hardly sufficient to say that one may achieve more if one will undertake more. The author has aimed to offer the individual a practical mind stimulant, or source of inspiration, which may be used to build greater ambition and supply the motive for *action* in carrying out that ambition.

Ninety-five per cent of the energy of the human mind remains passive throughout life. The major purpose of this philosophy of success is to supply the stimuli which will arouse this sleeping ninety-five per cent of mind energy and put it to work. How? By planting in the mind some strong motive that will lead to action. By stepping up the mind, through contact with other minds, and causing it to vibrate on a higher plane.

This volume inadequately describes the majority of the seventeen factors of success. The more extensive outline of the philosophy, in eight volumes, devotes as much space to each of the other sixteen factors of success as is here devoted to the Master Mind.

In the more extensive volumes the subjects of Accurate Thought and Enthusiasm have been so thoroughly discussed that the exact method of mind stimulation has been made plain. The author regrets that the limitations of this volume made impossible a more thorough description of the exact procedure in applying the known sources of mind stimuli.

Readers who desire more detailed data concerning the Law of Success philosophy, or who wish to ask questions regarding methods of applying the philosophy in connection with their own problems, have the privilege of addressing the author for this purpose. If more personal service is desired than that which can be supplied through correspondence, the reader should make application to the nearest teacher of the Law of Success philosophy, names and addresses of whom will be supplied upon request.

To the extent that available time will permit, the author will gladly assist any reader of this book to properly interpret and make practical use of this philosophy.

ADVERSITY—
A BLESSING
IN DISGUISE

ADVERSITY—A BLESSING IN DISGUISE

Friend, do not become discouraged, disappointed and disheartened, if the seemingly cruel hand of fate knocks you off of your feet. Maybe the blow will prove to be the greatest blessing that ever came your way.

It has happened to many and doubtless it will happen to you, when the dark clouds of despair have darkened the pathway of life's progress, that behind each dark cloud is a silver lining, if we only learn how to see it.

There were two men who established and built up an enormously successful commercial institution. They owned the stock in the company about equally. One of the men, who had lots of initiative, began selling off some of his stock, thus enjoying for personal use a large amount of ready cash from the proceeds.

His associate in the business, who didn't possess quite so much initiative, wanted to sell some of his personal stock that he might also enjoy some ready cash from the proceeds. But not a dollar could he sell. He appealed to his associate who was finding a ready market for his stock, requesting the associate to help him dispose of his stock. But the associate refused, suggesting that "he do his own selling." This refusal resulted in a serious disagreement between the two men, which finally ended in a complete dissolution of their friendly business relations.

Now let us see what happens. The one who could not find a market for his stock was the fortunate one in the final crisis. The one with the ready initiative, who sold his stock, sold with it by so doing, his voice in the management of the business. When the climax was reached in their disagreement, the one who couldn't sell his stock naturally had, BY FORCE OF CIRCUMSTANCES, the control of the business, so he used his power to his own salvation and to the great detriment of his associate, by voting him out of the Presidency of the corporation and voting himself into that office.

The fact that he couldn't sell his stock was A BLESSING IN DISGUISE.

There was once a young man who was President of a corporation which was making lots of money. He owned automobiles, had servants and all the other luxuries which go with a successful business. He trusted his banker too far by borrowing money for expansion purposes. The banker wanted this young man's interest in the corporation, because he knew the young man was making lots of money and the banker happened to be dishonest. In the 1907 Roosevelt Panic he saw his chance and closed him out. It seemed like a dark day for the young man. All was lost. But watch the roulette wheel of destiny as it spins around by the force of the hand of fate. His loss forced him to go back to the practice of law. This brought him in touch with a million-dollar corporation which employed him at a salary of $5,000 a year, a salary which he wouldn't have thought of accepting from an outsider while he was in control of his own business. This brought him to the middle west, and likewise in touch with the "big opportunity" of his life.

So his loss proved a blessing in disguise, for it literally drove him into a greater success.

A young bank clerk was discharged on account of his habit of drawing pictures of automobiles and sketching mechanical parts of automobiles during business hours. The loss of his job was quite a shock to him, for he supported his mother and two sisters from his small earnings as a bank clerk.

The loss of his bank job was the greatest blessing that ever came to him, for six months later he invented an automobile part which made him a fortune. He is now president of the largest automobile accessories companies in America. His clerks are all supplied with desk pads and pencils, with instructions to do all the drawing of automobiles they wish, and to submit to him any new ideas for improvements of automobile parts. Any of their ideas which he uses are paid for extra, at one hundred dollars each.

John D. Rockefeller discharged one of his faithful employees who he thought went too far in the exercise of his authorized duties, in making a financial transaction for Mr. Rockefeller in his absence, even though the deal netted Mr. Rockefeller several thousand dollars in cash.

A blessing in disguise. This office clerk, who had been honest and faithful, but not overly well paid, was immediately employed by one of Mr. Rockefeller's rivals, at a handsome salary. He now holds a high official position with the rival company.

And, while I write, further evidence of the soundness of my theory that "Adversity is usually a blessing in disguise" reaches me. One of the men mentioned in the beginning of this narrative—the one who was successful in selling stock, but who thereby lost the presidency of his company—has been elected president of a ten-million-dollar corporation, with an excellent chance to make $50,000 a year from his salary and dividends on his bonus stock in the company.

The ten-million-dollar corporation never would have been organized in all probability, except for the fact that this man's business associate supplanted him in his original position.

A blessing in disguise, for the ten-million-dollar corporation has patents and secret processes for making fuel, heat and light which probably will make this man immensely wealthy.

Every change in one's environment is for a purpose. That which seems like disappointment and ill "luck" usually is a blessing in disguise. If we do not carefully study cause and effect in all that we do and all that comes our way, we may never discover when and where our apparent failures are, in reality, blessings instead.

Stop and take an inventory of your life's record and see if you cannot find evidence in your own case which will support the correctness of this. Take an inventory of the lives of those you know intimately and see if the same is not true.

Then, when you become discouraged; when the hand of fate seems to be against you; when your destiny seems doubtful and life's pathway fraught with many thorns of disappointment; when the rough and rugged hand of time spins the roulette wheel of fate so hard that the little pointer goes past your number just remember, friends, that there is a bigger stake awaiting you, if not in your present environment, then later on in some other "game" in the sphere of human accomplishments.

Hang on!

LET AMBITION BE
YOUR MASTER

LET AMBITION BE
YOUR MASTER

LUCKY is the man who is driven by that determined master called AMBITION! Those who have enjoyed the greatest success in life were literally driven to succeed by AMBITION! It made Harriman, Rockefeller, Carnegie, Hill, Roosevelt, and a good many thousands of other successful men of whom we never hear.

Ambition is the mainspring of life, but we must keep it wound up! Self-confidence is the balance wheel which keeps ambition moving at an even momentum. Enthusiasm is the oil with which we keep the human machine greased and in smooth running order. The well-organized, capable, and productive man is AMBITIOUS, ENTHUSIASTIC, and, possesses plenty of SELF-CONFIDENCE. Without these success is uncertain, if not impossible.

One of the greatest men America has ever known divorced his first wife because she was beneath his mental plane, and therefore had a tendency to keep down his ambition. This great man is not with us any more, but the world is testifying to his greatness by quoting his writings and reading his books more than ever before. It is a commonly known fact that his second wife was his chief source of inspiration—that she was responsible for keeping his AMBITION alive and constantly on the alert. That is why he married her. He foresaw the need for a constant attendant who would see to it that his AMBITION let him have no rest.

Lucky is the man who has formed a partnership with such a wife. We all get lazy at times. We need someone to keep our AMBITION alive and spur us on to bigger and better accomplishment. The chief reason that I consent to my wife going back to the farm every summer is that while she is away she constantly writes me letters which fire me with AMBITION. She understands me as few wives understand their husbands. She knows how necessary it is to constantly remind me of my *chief aims in life,* and she has a way of doing it which is pleasing and inspiring.

When I secured my first $5,000 a year position I thought I was fixed for life, and probably I would have been, had it not been for that little master for whom I was slaving—AMBITION! My wife and AMBITION collaborated against me and made me resign that position—FOR A BIGGER ONE! Five thousand a year would have satisfied me had it not been for my master, AMBITION. In my bigger and broader field I serve a hundred of my fellow men where I served one before, which means that I get a hundred times as much enjoyment out of life as well as financial returns which are adequate and in proportion to the service which I perform.

In addition to my regular work I lecture three times a week in one of the local colleges, on the subject of Advertising and Salesmanship. The course is a heavy one, covering a period of ten months. The students are taught everything about Advertising and Selling that I can teach them, both from my own experience and from that of a score or more of able advertising specialists. THE FIRST LECTURE IN THE COURSE IS ON THE SUBJECT OF THE VALUE OF AMBITION! I use every ounce of influence that I possess to fire these young men and young women with an everlasting knowledge of the value of AMBITION, SELF-CONFIDENCE, and ENTHUSIASM! If I succeed no further than to cause my students to cultivate that wonderful power, AMBITION, my time and theirs will have been well spent in the effort.

AMBITION is what freed America from over-the-sea rulership.

Once in my life, while I was working for a salary, I was discharged from my position—just ONCE! The head of the institution for which I worked told me that I was too "ambitious." That was the greatest compliment anyone ever paid me, even though it cut me off temporarily from my bread and meat.

I have always had my suspicions why this man "fired" me, although he claimed it was because his "help" were unanimously agreed that I ought to go! His "help" who objected to me was one of his brothers who had his eye on the General Managership of the institution. He knew what "AMBITION" might lead me to. I have never blamed the brother, for he has a wife and two babies to support, and "AMBITION" on my part seemed to him a dangerous barrier between him and his coveted goal.

That institution of which I write was organized nearly twenty years ago. It is doing a business of about $600,000 a year. Another institution, engaged in the same line of business, started in just six years ago, on a capital of less than $6,000. I was formerly Advertising Manager of this institution. It does not discourage "AMBITION." It is now doing a business of $1,500,000 a year, and clearing more net profits every month than the other firm is doing in gross business. The older institution, the one which was organized and has been doing business for nearly twenty years, is headed by men who are afraid of the "AMBITIOUS MAN." Those who are working for a salary are afraid he will get their jobs (which said fear is not without some foundation). The head of the firm is afraid of the "AMBITIOUS MAN" because he is afraid he will find in him a compeitor in business (which, also, is not without well-grounded foundation).

BUT—AND HERE IS THE CRUX OF MY WHOLE STORY OF THESE TWO FIRMS—THE MAJORITY OF BUSINESS FIRMS ARE LOOKING FOR MEN WHO HAVE PLENTY OF "AMBITION." Do not worry because one firm is afraid of the ambitious man. The very fact that such a firm is afraid of him is, in itself, strong evidence of weakness on the part of those who manage the firm.

While I was Advertising Manager of the younger firm of which I have written, I had three young men in my department. I put them on notice that some day one of them would get my position, and I commenced training them for my job. I told them that the man who "made good" first would get the place, if my recommendations would help any. My Secretary landed the prize. He is still with that firm, making more money than he ever made in his life, and more money than the average man of his age receives. I did not discourage "AMBITION" for fear of losing my job. I encouraged it so that someone would grow to be big enough to push me out of the rut and into a bigger position. That is what happened. I have no patience to speak of, with the man who is so narrow that he is afraid to inspire "AMBITION" in his fellow workers.

Show me a man who believes he has a corner on the details connected with his job and I will show you, in the same person, a man who will never develop beyond petty selfishness. I beseech you not to fall into the habit of neglecting to cultivate your "AMBITION." You will need something more than mere services with which to succeed. You will need that ever alert little master which is the subject of this chapter. But, I must here give you a word of warning—*do not let your ambition become a selfish one!* The greatest object over which to develop ambition is the desire to serve our fellow men. We cannot serve them if we are jealous of them. Remember, also, that AMBITION is a contagious thing. If you give it to the world, the world will give it back to you in increased measure. But keep it unto yourself and you will lose it. It will take wings and fly!

Ambition finds expression in a thousand different forms. It is the foundation which underlies all invention, art, music, industry, commerce—nay, the very foundation upon which the progress of the world has been built. Within the present generation we have seen it expressed in the most wonderful inventions the world has ever known; the automobile, the telephone, the wireless, the submarines, the X-ray, and the airplane. AMBITION was the very warp and woof out of which these things were constructed. Ambition leads us to think, and when we begin to think the nebulous problems in the world's evolution begin to become clarified and simplified. BE AMBITIOUS IF NOTHING MORE. OTHER THINGS WILL TAKE CARE OF THEMSELVES.

WHAT I HAVE LEARNED FROM ANALYZING TEN THOUSAND PEOPLE

WHAT I HAVE LEARNED FROM ANALYZING TEN THOUSAND PEOPLE

When I was requested to write this article, I was overjoyed at such an opportunity to pass on to thoughtful men and women, who are trying to "find themselves," the benefit of my experience as a personal analyst.

During the past eight years I have analyzed over ten thousand men and women who were earnestly seeking their proper niche in the world's work. Incidentally, through my research I have discovered some of the fundamental qualities without which no human being can hope for success. Five of these are mentioned in this article, in words which a school boy can easily understand.

I have also discovered some of the things which break men's hearts and send them to the scrap-heap of human failures. It is my sincere hope that every person who reads this article may profit by one or more of the points which it covers. I am placing the results of my discoveries in print for the first time, solely out of my deep desire to make life's pathway just a little smoother for my fellow man.

It is my purpose to pass on to you, in as few words as possible, that portion of my discoveries which I believe will aid you in planning and achieving your "chief aim" in life, whatever that may be. I shall not preach to you. Whatever suggestions I make are based upon discoveries which I have made in my work.

I believe it befitting to state that twenty years ago I was working as a laborer, at wages of $1 a day. I had no home and no friends. I had but little education. My future then looked very unpromising. I was downcast in spirit. I had no ambition. I had no definite purpose in life. All around me I saw men, some young and some old, who were whipped—just as I felt that I was. I absorbed my environment as a sponge absorbs water. I became a part of the daily routine in which I lived.

It had never occurred to me that I could ever amount to anything. I believed my lot in life was to be that of a laborer. I was just like a horse which has had the bit slipped into its mouth and the saddle buckled on its back.

Here is the turning point in my career. Note it well!

A chance remark, no doubt made in a half-jocular way, caused me to throw the bit out of my mouth, kick off the saddle, and "run away" as young horses sometimes do. That remark was made by a farmer with whom I lived. I shall never forget it if I live to be a hundred, because it has partly bridged the gap over that awful chasm which nearly all human beings want to cross, "failure"!

The remark was this: "You are a bright boy. What a pity you are not in school instead of at work as a laborer at a dollar a day."

"You are a bright boy!" These were the sweetest words I had ever heard.

That remark aroused in me the first ambition I had ever felt, and, incidentally, it is directly responsible for the personal analysis system which I have worked out. No one had ever hinted to me before that I was "bright." I had always imagined that I was exceedingly dull. In fact, I had been told that I was a dunce. As a boy I was defeated in everything I undertook, largely because those with whom I associated ridiculed me and discouraged me from engaging in the things which interested me most. My work was selected for me—my associates were selected for me—my studies were selected for me—and my play, well, I was taught that play was a waste of time.

With this first-hand knowledge of the great handicap under which the average person starts out in life, as a working basis, I began many years ago to work out a system for helping people "find themselves" as early in life as possible. My efforts have yielded splendid returns for I have helped many find the work for which they were most suited, and started them on the road to happiness and success. I have helped not a few to acquire the qualities for success which are mentioned in this article.

THE FIRST TWO SUCCESS REQUISITES

With this prelude I shall tell you first what I believe to be the two most important of the five chief requisites for success. These are SELF-CONFIDENCE and ENTHUSIASM. The other three I will mention later.

What is self-confidence?

I will tell you what it is: It is the little glass window through which you may look and see the real man-power within your body. Self-confidence is self-discovery—finding out who you are and what you can do. It is the banishment of fear. It is the acquirement of mental courage. It is the turning on of the light of human intelligence, through the use of common sense.

It was self-confidence, plus enthusiasm and concentration, that caused the birth of the world's greatest inventions, the incandescent electric light, the automobile, the talking machine, the airplane, the moving picture, and all the other great mechanical creations.

Self-confidence, then, is an essential quality for all worth-while accomplishments. Yet, it is the quality in which most of us are weakest. Not a weakness which many of us acknowledge, but it exists just the same. A man without self-confidence is like a ship without a rudder—he wastes his energy without moving in the right direction.

I wish I might be able to tell you exactly how to acquire full self-confidence. That would be a big undertaking. I will give you this suggestion, however—I made my first step in the direction of self-confidence the day I heard those words, "You are a bright boy." That was the first time I had ever felt ambition tugging at my coat sleeve, and with it, apparently, came self-confidence.

It is remarkable what clothes have to do with building self-confidence. A man came to me for analysis not long ago. He had been earning a good salary, but conditions for which he was in no way responsible caused him to be let out. I asked him how much money he had and he said, "Seventy-five dollars." I told him to invest one-third of it in a new suit of clothes. He demurred on the ground that he "couldn't afford it." But I insisted and went with him to buy the clothes. Then I insisted on his going to the cobbler's and having the heels of his shoes straightened up. Then I persuaded him to have his shoes shined and get a clean shave and a hair cut. I then sent him to see the president of a large cor-poration who employed him at $3,000 a year.

If I had sent him to interview the president of that corpo-ration without the new suit and the clean-up, he wouldn't have gotten the position, in all probability, because he would not have had the proper self-confidence. Good clothes, clean linen, polished shoes, and a clean shave are not luxuries—they are a necessity to the man who comes in contact with the business public.

THE SECOND SUCCESS REQUISITE

Then comes the second requisite for success, enthusiasm, that great dynamic force which puts self-confidence into action. Enthusiasm may be likened to the steam which runs the locomotive. The most powerful locomotive ever built might stand upon the sidetrack with coal in the bunker and the engineer in the cab, but if there is no steam, the wheels will not turn—there is no action.

It is exactly the same with the human machine. If there is no enthusiasm, there is little or no action. Lack of these qualities—self-confidence and enthusiasm—stands between the great majority of men and success. This statement is no mere conjecture upon my part. I have proved it in thousands of cases. I am proving it in more than a hundred cases a week right along. Enthusiasm is something which cannot be counterfeited. Only the real article will fill the bill. Enthusiasm usually comes automatically when you find the vocation into which you can pitch your whole heart and soul—the work you love best.

THE THIRD SUCCESS REQUISITE

The third requisite for success is a definite working plan—the habit of working with a "chief aim" in life. From my work as a vocational director, I have learned that most people have no such plan. Men who are working without a well-defined plan—without a pre-determined objective—are going no-where in particular and most of them are getting nowhere. In my personal Analysis Chart, which all whom I examine must fill out, is this question.

"What is your 'chief aim' in life?"

An actual tabulation of answers to this question shows that only one out of every fifty has any "chief aim." But few have any sort of a real aim, "chief" or otherwise. Yet, nearly all whom I have analyzed expect to succeed. Just when or how or in what work the majority of them do not undertake to say.

Nearly every man wants a "big position," yet not one out of a hundred, even though he may be competent, knows how to get it. A "big position" is not something that we find hanging on a bush ready to be plucked off by "pull" by the first person who comes along. It is the sum total of a number of smaller positions or tasks which we have efficiently filled; not necessarily with different firms, but, as often as otherwise, in the employment of one firm. A big position is built just as we build a big skyscraper—by first formulating a definite plan and then building according to that plan, step by step.

The possible exception to this rule is the man who gets into a "big position" through "pull." There are exceptions to most rules, but the question to ask yourself is this: "Am I willing to go through life and take a chance on getting ahead on 'pull'?" Look about you and I dare say you will find that for every man who is succeeding by "pull" you may find a hundred who are succeeding by "push"!

There are varying degrees of success, just as there are different ideas as to what success is, but whether your idea of success is the accumulation of wealth or the rendering of some great service to mankind, or both, you will not likely achieve it unless you have a "chief aim"—a definite goal with a definite plan mapped out for reaching it.

No architect ever started a building until he had first created a perfect picture of it in his mind, and then carefully transferred the detail of the picture to a blueprint. And no human being may hope to build a worthwhile success until he has planned the building and decided what it shall be.

SELECTING A VOCATION

A very large proportion of the people whom I have analyzed are in positions which they hold, not by selection, but by chance. Even those who are following vocations which they deliberately chose, in the majority of cases, have not observed even the most elementary rules of self-analysis. They have never stopped to find out whether or not the work in which they are engaged is the work for which they are best fitted by nature and education.

For example, a young man whom I recently analyzed, had prepared himself for the practice of law, but had made an utter failure of that profession. He failed, first, because he did not like the profession after he got into it; secondly, because he had absolutely no native ability for that profession. He was badly deformed physically and, as a consequence, made a very poor impression before courts and juries. He lacked enthusiasm and that dynamic force which we call "personality," without which he could not hope to succeed as a lawyer. Such a person might succeed to some extent as advisory counsel or "office lawyer," but not as a trial lawyer where a strong personality and the ability to speak with force and conviction count for so much.

The surprising part of this particular case was the fact that this man had never understood just why he did not succeed in the practice of law. It seemed simple enough to him after I had pointed out the negative qualities which I believed had stood between him and success. When I asked him how he came to take up law, he replied, "Well, I just had a hunch that I would like it!"

"I just had a hunch that I would like it!"

Selecting a life work on a "hunch" is a dangerous thing. You wouldn't purchase a race-horse on a "hunch"; you would want to see him perform on the track. You wouldn't purchase a bird-dog on a "hunch"; you would want to see him in action or know something of his pedigree. If you selected a bird-dog in this haphazard way, you might find yourself trying to set birds with a bull-pup!

A court reporter, whom I analyzed, said to me: "My fifteen years of experience have proved to me that a jury seldom tries the defendant, but instead, they try the lawyers in the case. The lawyer who makes the best impression generally wins." Everyone who is familiar with court actions knows that this is too often true. You can see, therefore, what an important part "personality" plays in the practice of law.

Mr. Carnegie says that his success is due largely to his ability to pick men. Mr. Frank A. Vanderlip and Mr. Rockefeller say the same. If you will stop and analyze all the successful men you know, you will probably find that they either possess all the requisites for success in the business in which they are engaged, or, they know how to select men who will supply what they lack—men who are their opposites in nearly every particular.

Probably 50% of those who call themselves salesmen are of poor personal appearance, have weak faces, and speak without force. A salesman conveys to his prospective buyer a positive or negative influence, according to his own personality and manner of approach in presenting his case. A man who is badly deformed, or the man who suffers from impediment of speech and otherwise makes a negative appearance had better not take up oral salesmanship. If he can hide behind the written page, he may succeed, but in person never!

THE FOURTH SUCCESS REQUISITE
The fourth success requisite is the habit of performing more service than you are actually paid for. It is the practice of the majority of men to perform no more service than they feel they are being paid to perform. Fully 80% of all whom I have analyzed were suffering on account of this great mistake.

You need have no fear of competition from the man who says, "I'm not paid to do that, therefore I'll not do it." He will never be a dangerous competitor for your job, but watch out for the fellow who does not let his pick hang in the air when the whistle blows, or the man who stays at his desk or work bench until his work is finished—watch out that such a fellow does not "Challenge you at the post and pass you at the grandstand," as Andrew Carnegie said.

Before mentioning the fifth and last requisite for success I shall ask your indulgence while I digress for just a few moments. After I had commenced work on this article I decided to have the five points which I have covered put to the acid test to see whether or not they would square up with the experience of other vocational directors. I took the manuscript to Dr. J. M. Fitzgerald, Chicago, who is, without doubt, the most able vocational director in the world.

Dr. Fitzgerald went over the manuscript with me word for word and I have his permission to quote him as saying that he fully endorses the five chief points covered by this article. He says that they square up with his own experience, exactly. But, before we went over the manuscript, I asked Dr. Fitzgerald to state the chief negative qualities which he had discovered to be standing as barriers between those whom he had analyzed and success. His reply was quick and concise, as follows:

1. Lack of self-discernment; the lack of ability upon part of most men to analyze themselves and find the work for which they are best prepared.
2. Lack of intensified concentration and the disposition not to put more into their work than they expect to get out of it.
3. Lack of moral self-control.

Dr. Fitzgerald has analyzed, in person, more than fifteen thousand men and women. Many of the largest corporations of the middle West will not employ a man for any important position until he has been analyzed by Dr. Fitzgerald. He has taken men from the bookkeeper's desk and enabled them to become successful executives. He has converted clerks into managers in much less time than is ordinarily required, merely by having started them in the right direction, through accurate personal analysis.

I mention these details concerning Dr. Fitzgerald's work because I want you to feel that my own experience, as stated in this article, is not mere conjecture on my part—that it is authentic and that it has the endorsement of the world's greatest personal analyst. Bear in mind that the five chief points covered by this article have been discovered, classified, and charted from the personal analysis of twenty-five thousand people, ten thousand of whom I have analyzed and fifteen thousand of whom were analyzed by Dr. Fitzgerald.

THE FIFTH SUCCESS REQUISITE

This article ought to be of benefit to those who are about to select a vocation and those who are in the wrong vocation but wish to make a change. However, there is another class to be taken into consideration. It is represented by those who have selected the right vocation but who, nevertheless, are not succeeding. I have found the Key to Success for this class. In this Great Magic Key you will find the fifth and last of the success rules which I have discovered in my vocational work.

In presenting to you this key let me first explain that it is no invention of mine.

This Great Magic Key is a most wonderful power, yet perfectly simple of operation. So simple that most people have failed to make use of it. We human beings are too prone to look askance at so simple a formula for success—a formula which will open the door to health and wealth; yet, such a formula is the Great Magic Key.

Through the Great Magic Key we have unlocked the secret doors to all of the world's great inventions. Through its magic powers all of our great geniuses have been produced. We will suppose that you desire a better position. The Great Magic Key will help you attain it! Through its use Carnegie, Rockefeller, Hill, Harriman, Morgan, and Guggenheim have accumulated millions of dollars in material wealth.

You ask—"What is this Great Magic Key?"

And I answer with one word: CONCENTRATION!

To stop here would be insufficient. You must know how to use this Great Magic Key! First, let me tell you that AMBITION and DESIRE are the great dynamic powers which you must summon to the aid of CONCENTRATION. They form the lock which this great key fits. Without ambition and desire the Great Magic Key is useless. The reason that so few people use the key is that most people lack ambition!

Desire whatever you may, and if your desire is strong enough the Great Magic Key of CONCENTRATION will help you attain it, if the object of your desire is something which it is humanly possible for you to attain.

There are learned men of science who tell us that the wonderful powers of prayer itself operate through the principle of CONCENTRATION, plus faith and strong DESIRE!

I am making no attempt to associate the Great Magic Key with occultism or religion. I am treating it from the ordinary layman's viewpoint. I am dealing with it from actual knowledge that I have gained in carefully analyzing and charting over ten thousand people.

We will assume that you are skeptical of the powers of CONCENTRATION and DESIRE. Let's put these powers to the test, through a concrete example, for unless we do this it would be just like telling you to be honest without telling you how to be honest.

HOW TO CONCENTRATE

First, you must do away with skepticism and doubt! No unbeliever ever enjoyed the benefits of these great powers. You must believe in the test which I am going to ask you to make. You must let no feeling of unbelief creep in.

Now we will suppose that you have thought of becoming a great writer, or a great public speaker, or a great business executive, or a great advertising manager. Suppose we take the latter as the subject of this test. But remember that if you expect results you must follow instructions to the letter.

Take a plain piece of paper, ordinary letter size, and write on it in large letters—the largest it will carry—these words:

I AM GOING TO BECOME A SUCCESSFUL ADVERTISING MANAGER BECAUSE THIS WILL ENABLE ME TO RENDER THE WORLD A USEFUL SERVICE—AND BECAUSE IT WILL PROVIDE ME WITH THE NECESSARY MATERIAL THINGS OF LIFE!

I WILL CONCENTRATE ON THIS DESIRE FOR TEN MINUTES DAILY, JUST BEFORE RETIRING AND JUST AFTER RISING.

(Sign your name.)

If you are not good at lettering just clip out the foregoing, sign it, and place where you will read it just before retiring and just after getting up each day. Do exactly as you have pledged yourself to do, for at least ten days.

Now when you come to do your "CONCENTRATING" this is the way to go about it: Look ahead three, five, ten, or even

fifteen years from now and see yourself in a position as advertising manager paying a big salary. See the happy faces of your
loved ones—maybe a wife and babies—maybe a mother with
silvery hair. Be a dreamer if you choose to call it that, but be also
a "doer"! The world needs this combination of "dreamer-doers."
They are the Lincolns, Grants, Edisons, Hills, Carnegies, Vander-
lips, and Schwabs.

See yourself laying aside a "nest-egg" for a rainy day. See
yourself in your motor car which you will be able to afford. See
yourself in your own cozy little home that you will own. See yourself a person of influence in the business world.

See yourself INCREASING IN VALUE AND EARNING
STILL MORE MONEY as you grow older. See yourself engaged
in a line of work where you will not fear the loss of a job when
the gray hairs begin to put in their appearance.

Paint this picture through the powers of your imagination,
and lo! it will turn into Desire. Use this Desire as the chief object
of your CONCENTRATION, and see what happens!

It may take longer than ten days for you to master this lesson
in CONCENTRATION. Again it may take only one day. That
will depend upon how well you perform the task.

You now have the secret of the Great Magic Key!

It will unlock the door to whatever position in life you want,
if that position is one that you are prepared by nature and education to fill. It will make of you a better citizen and show you the
road to true happiness if the object of your CONCENTRATION
is a worthy one.

Use this Great Key with intelligence! Use it only for the attainment of worthy purposes, and it will give you the things of
life for which your heart may crave. So simple, so easy of application, yet so MARVELOUS IN RESULTS! Try it! Begin right now.
Forget the mistakes you have made in the past. Start all over
again, and make the next five or ten years tell a story of human

accomplishment in whatever line of work your calling may have placed you, that you will not be ashamed of—that the future generations of your family will be PROUD OF!

MAKE A NAME FOR YOURSELF THROUGH AMBITION, DESIRE, AND CONCENTRATION!

Vocational guidance has not yet become a universally accepted science. It may never be accepted as a science by everyone, but this does not preclude a person from using common sense in selecting a vocation. The trouble is, too many people act on a "hunch." If you are engaged in work in which you are not succeeding, take inventory of yourself and see if you cannot locate the trouble. The chances are that you can. Just apply common sense in selecting a life work. You may not be able to analyze yourself as well as a man who has many years of experience could do, therefore, if you have any doubts place yourself in the hands of a man who is experienced in analyzing men. He will undoubtedly see your weak spots more quickly than you could. Few of us can be our own best critics because we are inclined to overlook our weaknesses or place too little importance on them.

There are but few, if any, ironclad rules to follow in the selection of a vocation that would apply in every case. Probably these come as near being applicable in all cases as is possible: Be sure you love the vocation you adopt. Be sure you are enthusiastic over it and that you intend to stick to it. Be sure you are prepared, educationally, for the work you select. Be sure the vocation is one in which you can render a service that is beneficial to humanity. Be sure the work is permanent. Be sure that it is work that will not impair your health.

Let me summarize the five chief requisites for success, so you will not forget them. They are—first, Self-confidence; second, Enthusiasm; third, Working with a "chief aim"; fourth, Performing more work than you are paid for; fifth, Concentration, backed by desire and unwavering faith. By a reasonably intelligent application of these qualities you can become master of your own career.

Finally, I wish to leave this thought with you. It has been my constant companion through life. It has supported my tired legs when they would otherwise have allowed me to fall by the wayside. It is this:

"EVERY ADVERSITY IS, IN REALITY, A BLESSING IN DISGUISE. THE UNIVERSITY OF HARD KNOCKS SENDS FORTH ITS GRADUATES TO FIGHT LIFE'S BATTLES, WITH PLENTY OF STRENGTH TO OVERCOME EVERY OBSTACLE THAT MAY CONFRONT THEM. FROM EVERY FAILURE WE MAY LEARN A GREAT LESSON IF WE WILL. SOMEWHERE IN THE WORLD YOUR PLACE IS WAITING FOR YOU. THROUGH PERSISTENCE AND INTELLIGENT EFFORT YOU WILL EVENTUALLY FIND IT. YOU WILL NEVER BE DEFEATED IN YOUR LIFE'S PURPOSE IF YOU KEEP FAITH IN THE ONLY PERSON IN THE WORLD WHO CONTROLS YOUR DESTINY—YOURSELF!"

ABOUT THE AUTHOR

Napoleon Hill was born in 1883 in a one-room cabin on the Pound River in Wise County, Virginia. He is the author of the motivational classics *The Law of Success* and *Think and Grow Rich*. Hill passed away in November 1970 after a long and successful career writing, teaching and lecturing about the principles of success. His life's work continues under the direction of the Napoleon Hill Foundation.

Napoleon Hill's anecdotes, stories and speeches on intention, self-discipline and how to achieve success.

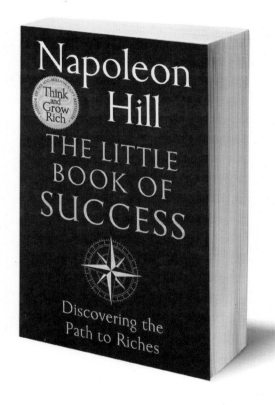